BYZANTIUM
AND THE DECLINE
OF ROME

Byzantium

AND THE DECLINE
OF ROME

BY WALTER EMIL KAEGI, JR.

PRINCETON, NEW JERSEY
PRINCETON UNIVERSITY PRESS
1968

TO THE MEMORY OF MY MOTHER

preface

I DISCOVERED THE SUBJECT of this book while reading Zosimus and Theodoret of Cyrus (= Cyrrhus) at Harvard University in January-March 1963. I noticed the absence of a real discussion of Byzantine political and intellectual reactions to the decline and disappearance of the Western Roman Empire. Yet fifth- and sixth-century sources offered rich materials on this topic. I therefore decided to make this the subject of my Harvard doctoral dissertation, which I wrote under the direction of Professor Robert Lee Wolff. This book is a revision of that dissertation. I have presented some of my ideas at the session on "Antiquité et Christianisme" at the 12th International Congress of the Historical Sciences at Vienna in September 1965 and at the annual meeting of the American Historical Association in December 1965. I have profited from the subsequent discussions.

Understandably I have imposed limits on the scope of this study. While I analyze some implications and repercussions of western Roman decline for Byzantium, this is primarily a study of Byzantine political and intellectual responses or reactions. Many questions are of course too broad and complicated to discuss here without expanding this work at great length—and at the risk of overlapping and repeating previous scholarship to a tedious degree. In Chapter VI I mention some topics which in my opinion deserve further research. The sixth century is discussed only insofar as necessary for an understanding of fifth-century intellectual developments. I do not pretend in Chapter I to offer a complete history of east-west diplomatic relations. I only present and discuss such data which indicate, to a greater degree than one usually has supposed, eastern interest and involvement in western affairs in the fifth century.

I wish to acknowledge with gratitude the assistance and encouragement of many people too numerous to mention here, but in particular the helpful suggestions of Professors Robert Lee Wolff, Glanville Downey, Alfred R. Bellinger, Stewart Oost, Arthur Vööbus (who generously gave me advice at the American Society of Church History meeting in December 1965), Mason Hammond, William Sinnigen, Reginald Brill, Frank M. Clover (who kindly spared time from his own thesis to read my first chapter), David Evans, Demetrios Constantelos, Klaus Baer, and William Thurman. Needless to say, I alone am responsible for all deficiencies in this work. In addition I wish to thank the Harvard University Press for permission to quote from the Loeb Classical Library translation of Polybius and from the *Harvard Theological Review*; Cambridge University Press for the right to quote from the Chadwick translation of Origen, *Contra Celsum*; and Oxford University Press for permission to quote from the Driver and Hodgson translation of Nestorius, *Bazaar of Heracleides*. I also wish to give grateful acknowledgment to the British Museum, the Harvard University Dumbarton Oaks Collection, and to the American Numismatic Society for the right to publish coins in their respective collections. In addition, I owe thanks to Roy A. Grisham, Jr., my editor, who patiently and carefully gave me assistance in the preparation of this book. Finally, I wish to thank the Division of the Social Sciences at The University of Chicago for research grants which have made possible the completion of this book.

19 January 1968
Institute for Research in the Humanities,
The University of Wisconsin, Madison, Wisconsin.

contents

ABBREVIATIONS

For guides to abbreviations used in this book, see:

"Notes for Contributors and Abbreviations," *American Journal of Archaeology* 69 (1965) 199-206
Oxford Classical Dictionary
Ernest Stein, *Histoire du Bas-Empire* I-1I

In addition:

DTC = *Dictionnaire de Théologie Catholique*
MGHa.a. = *Monumenta Germaniae Historica, auctores antiquissimi*

Full citations are given in the Annotated Bibliography at the end of this book.

KEY TO COINS

ΤΟΙΣ ΔΥΤΙΚΟΙΣ

Οὕτω δὴ καὶ αὐτοὶ πρὸς ἔσχατον ἥκοντες τῶν κακῶν τῆς εἰς Θεὸν ἐλπίδος οὐκ ἀφιέμεθα, ἀλλὰ πανταχόθεν αὐτοῦ περισκοπούμεθα τὴν βοήθειαν. Ὅθεν καὶ πρὸς ὑμᾶς ἀπεβλέψαμεν νῦν, τιμώτατοι ἡμῖν ἀδελφοί, οὓς πολλάκις μὲν ἐν καιρῷ τῶν θλίψεων ἐπιφανήσεσθαι ἡμῖν προσεδοκήσαμεν· ἀποπέσοντες δὲ τῆς ἐλπίδος εἴπομεν πρὸς ἑαυτοὺς καὶ ἡμεῖς ὅτι " Ὑπέμεινα συλλυπούμενον, καὶ οὐχ ὑπῆρχεν, καὶ παρακαλοῦντας, καὶ οὐχ εὗρον". Τοιαῦτα γὰρ ἡμῶν τὰ παθήματα ὡς καὶ τῶν περάτων ἐφικέσθαι τῆς καθ᾿ ἡμᾶς οἰκουμένης, καί, εἴπερ πάσχοντος μέλους ἑνὸς συμπάσχει πάντα τὰ μέλη, ἔπρεπε δήπου καὶ ἡμῖν ἐν πολλῷ χρόνῳ πεπονηκόσι συνδιατεθῆναι τὴν εὐσπλαγχνίαν ὑμῶν. Οὐ γὰρ ἡ τῶν τόπων ἐγγύτης, ἀλλ᾿ ἡ κατὰ πνεῦμα συνάφεια ἐμποιεῖν πέφυκε τὴν οἰκείωσιν ἣν ἡμῖν εἶναι πρὸς τὴν ἀγάπην ὑμῶν πεπιστεύκαμεν.

St. Basil, *Ep.* 242. 1 (Y. Courtonne, ed. tr.
Lettres, Paris 1966, III 65-66).

To The Westerners

Thus we ourselves, having reached the last extremity of misfortunes do not abandon hope in God, but look everywhere for His help. Hence we now look to you, most honored brothers, who we often have expected would show yourselves to us in our moment of afflictions. Disappointed in our hope we said to each other: "I awaited someone who would share my grief, and he did not come, and for comforters and I did not find any." So great are our sufferings that they have reached the ends of the world which we inhabit; and if indeed one part suffers all parts suffer along with it, it was surely appropriate that your compassion should show sympathy for that which we have suffered for a long time. For not the proximity of places, but spiritual union produces the affinity which we believe exists for us in proportion to your love.

chapter i

EASTERN EMPERORS AND WESTERN CRISES:
OFFICIAL EASTERN RESPONSES
TO THE DETERIORATION OF THE
WESTERN ROMAN EMPIRE

. . . and behold suddenly I was informed of the death
of Pammachius and Marcella, the siege of the city of
Rome and the falling asleep of many brothers and sisters.
I was so astonished and stunned that I thought day and
night of nothing else but the deliverance of all. I considered myself a captive in the captivity of the saints. I
was not able to open my mouth until I could speak with
more certainty. Anxious, I was suspended between hope
and desperation and I tormented myself with the misfortunes of others. After the most brilliant light of all lands
was extinguished, rather the head of the Roman Empire
was cut off, or more accurately I would say that in one
city the whole world perished, "I was mute and hum-
bled. I was silent respecting good words, my grief revived,
my heart glowed inside me and I kindled my fire in medi-
tation."[1]

In these moving words Saint Jerome records his initial personal reaction to the report of the sack of Rome on the
24th of August, 410 by Alaric, King of the Visigoths.[2] His

---

[1] Saint Jerome, *Commentar. in Ezechielem* 1. 1 (*PL* 25, 15-16).
Cf. Ps. *xxxviii*, 4. This commentary was completed in 414-15. M.
Schanz and C. Hosius, *Geschichte der römischen Literatur*, 2nd edn.,
(Munich 1959) IV 1,464.

[2] On the sack of Rome in 410: Prosper, *Epitoma chronicon* (1240),
T. Mommsen, ed. *MGHa.a.* IX (Berlin 1892) 466; Hydatius, *Con-*

response to that event may properly serve to introduce the problem of Byzantine reactions to Roman decline. Writing at Bethlehem, Saint Jerome demonstrates in this passage (from his commentary on the Book of Ezekiel) how emotional reactions in the eastern Roman provinces to distant western Roman events might be. Yet he was not necessarily a typical easterner. He had deep western roots. Born in the west, at Stridon, on the borders of Pannonia and Illyria, and using Latin as his most familiar tongue, his reactions to western misfortunes might be regarded as the natural response of a man with such strong western ties and unrepresentative of his eastern contemporaries.[3] Yet what was the reaction of his eastern contemporaries and their government to the sack of Rome? In the ensuing years of the fifth century reports of many other western political and military catastrophes were to reach the east. What eastern opinions were formed about these developments and what courses of action, if any, were resolved upon? A brief survey of some principal fifth-century events will explain how the question of Roman decline was thrust upon fifth-century Byzantium.

The Roman Empire had faced severe internal and external challenges in the third and fourth centuries, but it was during the fifth century that certain elements of its po-

---

tinuatio chronicorum Hieronymianorum, 43, T. Mommsen, ed. MGHa.a. XI (Berlin 1894) 17; Sozomen, Hist. Eccl. 9. 9. 4-9. 10. 1-4, 2nd edn., J. Bidez and G.C. Hansen, eds. (Berlin 1960) 401-402; Socrates Scholasticus, Hist. Eccl. 7. 10 (PG 67. 756-757); Olympiodorus of Thebes = Photius, Bibliotheca, c. 80, R. Henry, ed. tr. (Paris 1959) I 167-168; Philostorgius, Hist. Eccl. 12. 3, J. Bidez, ed. (Leipzig 1913) 142; Orosius, Historiae adversum paganos, 2. 19. 13-15, C. Zangemeister, ed. (Vienna 1882) 132-133. See also Stein, Histoire du Bas-Empire, 2nd edn. rev. J.R. Palanque (Paris 1959) I 255-258; É. Demougeot, De l'unité à la division de l'Empire romain (Paris 1951) 441-485; O. Seeck, Geschichte des Untergangs der antiken Welt (Stuttgart 1922) V 391-416.

[3] F. Bulic, "Stridone luogo natale di S. Girolamo," Miscellanea Geronimiana (Rome 1920) 253-300.

litical and military structure collapsed permanently.[4] Strains had appeared by the beginning of the century. In accord with the wishes of Emperor Theodosius I the empire had been divided at his death in 395 into two parts. The eastern half, comprising roughly Greece, Macedonia, Dacia, Libya, Egypt, Palestine, Syria, and Anatolia, was given to Theodosius' son, Arcadius, to rule. The western section of the empire, which included those European provinces stretching from northwest Illyria to Spain, as well as North Africa, was confided to the rule of Theodosius' other son, Honorius.[5] At the death of Arcadius in 408 the government of the eastern and western provinces was not reunited in the hands of Honorius. The de facto division of the empire was perpetuated: Arcadius' seven-year-old son, Theodosius II, became nominal ruler, but the Pretorian Prefect of the East, Anthemius, actually wielded effective power until 414. After this date effective power fell to Theodosius II's sister, Pulcheria, his wife, Eudocia, and ultimately toward the conclusion of Theodosius' reign in 450, to the Alan *magister militum* Aspar.[6]

During this century the western half of the empire faced such overwhelming crises that its political and military au-

[4] For general background: E. Stein, *Histoire du Bas-Empire* I 1-254; O. Seeck, *Geschichte des Untergangs der antiken Welt* (Stuttgart 1921-23) I-V; J.B. Bury, *History of the Later Roman Empire*, 2nd edn. (London 1923) I 1-173; R. Paribeni, *Da Diocleziano alla caduta dell'impero d'occidente* (Storia de Roma, VIII, Bologna 1941); A.H.M. Jones, *The Later Roman Empire, 284-602* (Oxford 1964) I 1-169.

[5] On the division of the empire: Marcellinus Comes, *Chronicon*, a. 395, T. Mommsen, ed. *MGHa.a.*, XI (Berlin 1894) 64; Prosper, *Epit. chron.*, 1,206-1,207 (463-464 Mommsen); Sozomen, *Hist. Eccl.* 8. 1. 1 (347 Bidez-Hansen); *Chronicon paschale*, L. Dindorf, ed. (Bonn 1832) 565; Bury, *Later Rom. Emp.*, I 26-28; Theodoret of Cyrus, *Hist. Eccl.* 5. 25. 1 (*Kirchengeschichte*, L. Parmentier and F. Scheidweiler, ed., 2nd edn. [Berlin 1954] 327).

[6] *Marcell., Chron.*, a. 408. 3 (69 Mommsen); Sozomen, *Hist. Eccl.* 9. 1. 1-13 (390-392 Bidez-Hansen); *Chron. pasch.* (570-571 Dindorf). Cf. Stein, *Hist. du Bas-Empire* I 246, 275, 283-285, 321.

thority disintegrated. In 405-406 Radagaisus and his Goths invaded Italy. Although he was defeated, other Alans, Vandals, and Suevi breached the Rhine frontier and poured into what is modern-day Belgium and France.[7] On 24 August 410 Alaric captured and sacked the city of Rome, the first foreign seizure of Rome since the Gauls had captured it in 390 B.C. This event, of course, laid bare western Roman weakness.[8] The island of Britain was permanently abandoned by the Roman military sometime between the first and fifth decades of the century.[9] After leaving Italy the Visigoths occupied southern Gaul and ultimately established their own kingdom in Spain.[10] The Burgundians set-

[7] *Consularia Italica*, a. 405-406, T. Mommsen, ed., *MGHa.a.* IX (Berlin 1892) 299; *Chronica Gallica*, 50, 52, T. Mommsen, ed. *MGHa.a.*, IX (Berlin 1892) 652; Prosper, *Epit. chron.*, 1,228, 1,230 (465 Mommsen); Orosius, *Hist. adv. pag.*, 7. 37-38 (536-544 Zangemeister); Zosimus, *Historia nova*, 5. 26. 3-5, L. Mendelssohn, ed. (Leipzig 1887) 249-250. Cf. Stein, *Hist. du Bas-Empire* I 249-51; E. Demougeot, *De l'unité*, 353-60, 376-96.

[8] Prosp., *Epit. chron.*, 1,240 (466 Mommsen); Hydat., *Cont. chron.*, 43 (17 Mommsen); Sozom. *Hist. Eccl.* 9. 9. 2-9. 10. 4 (401-402 Bidez-Hansen); Socrates, *Hist. Eccl.* 7. 10 (*PG* 67, 756-757); Olympiodorus = Photius, ed. Henry, *Bibliothèque* I 167-68; Philostorg., *Hist. Eccl.* 12.3 (142 Bidez); Augustine, *De civitate Dei*, 1. 36, E. Hoffmann, ed. (Vienna 1899) 58; *id. De excidio urbis Romae sermo*, Sis. M.V. O'Reilly, ed. tr., *Cath. Univ. Am. Patristic Studies*, 89 (Washington, D.C. 1955); Oros., *Hist. adv. pag.* 7. 39-40 (544-549 Zangemeister). Cf. V.A. Sirago, *Galla Placidia e la trasformazione politica dell' occidente* (Louvain 1961) 109-113. For a recent anthology of texts on the sack of Rome see A. Piganiol, *Le sac de Rome, vue d'ensemble* (Paris 1964) 67-114, 250-314.

[9] *Chronica Gallica*, 62 (654 Mommsen); Zosimus, *Hist. nov.*, 6. 5. 2-3, 6. 1, 6. 10. 2 (286-287, 292 Mendelssohn); Stein, *Hist.* I 251-252; Demougeot, *De l'unité* 501-503, 513, 528-529; Bury, *Lat. Rom. Emp.*, 2nd edn., I 200-202.

[10] Visigoths in Gaul: Prosp., *Epit. chron.*, 1,246, 1,271 (466, 469 Mommsen); *Chron. Gall.*, 67 (654 Mommsen); Jordanes, *Getica*, 160, T. Mommsen, ed., *MGHa.a.*, V, Pt. 1 (Berlin 1882) 99-100. In Spain: Jordanes, *Getica*, 229-231, 244 (116, 120-121 Mommsen). Cf. Bury, *Lat. Rom. Emp.* I 202-205; Stein, *Hist.* I 266-269, 381, 385-389, 393, 396.

tled in the Rhone valley.[11] Pannonia was abandoned.[12] The Vandals migrated across Gaul and Spain and invaded Roman Africa, where they succeeded in creating an independent kingdom by the fourth decade of the century.[13] Throughout the 440s and until the death of Attila in 453 Hunnic raids remained a constant danger.[14]

After the death of Valentinian III (425-55) a number of men in turn briefly assumed the western throne but were unable to achieve general acceptance of their rank from all sections of the empire; the German *magister militum*, Flavius Ricimer, held effective power from 456 to 472.[15] Between 2 and 16 June 455 the Vandal king, Geiseric, pillaged Rome.[16] Finally on 23 August 476, Odoacer (an Herulian

[11] *Cons. It.*, a. 457. 2 (305 Mommsen); Marii episcopi Aventicensis *Chronica*, a. 456, T. Mommsen, ed., *MGHa.a.*, XI (Berlin 1894) 232; Fredegarius Scholasticus, *Chronica*, 2.46, B. Krusch, ed., *MGH Script. rer. Merov.* II (Hannover 1888) 68; cf. Bury, *Lat. Rom. Emp.* I 200.

[12] The standard study of this complex subject is A. Alföldi, *Untergang der Römerherrschaft in Pannonien* (Berlin, Leipzig 1926) II esp. 70-97.

[13] On the Vandal conquest of Africa see: Jordanes, *Romana*, 330, T. Mommsen, ed., *MGHa.a.*, V, Pt. 1 (Berlin 1882) 42; *Chronicon paschale* (581 Dindorf); Jordanes, *Getica*, 167-169 (101-102 Mommsen); Prosp., *Epit. Chron.*, 1,321 (474 Mommsen); Cassiodorus, *Chronica*, 1,225, T. Mommsen, ed., *MGHa.a.*, XI (Berlin 1894) 156; Marcell., *Chron.*, a. 439 (80 Mommsen); C. Courtois, *Les Vandales et l'Afrique* (Paris 1955) 155-64.

[14] Examples of the influence of the Huns on Byzantine foreign policy: Priscus, frg. 1, C. Muller, ed., *FHG* (Paris 1868) IV 71-72; Prosp., *Epit. chron.*, 1,344, 1,346 (478-479 Mommsen); Theophanes, *Chronographia*, A.M. 5,941, C. de Boor, ed. (Leipzig 1883) 101-102. In general on the Hunnic threat to the Byzantine Empire: E.A. Thompson, *A History of Attila and the Huns* (Oxford 1948) 78-149, 188-203; F. Altheim, *Geschichte der Hunnen* (Berlin 1962) IV 289-304; in general for barbarian pressure on the Balkans: P. Lemerle, "Invasions et migrations dans les Balkans depuis la fin de l'époque romaine jusqu'au VIIIᵉ siècle," *Revue historique*, 211 (1954) esp. 265-281.

[15] Stein, *Hist.* I 372-95.

[16] *Cons. It.*, a. 455 (304 Mommsen); Prosp., *Epit. chron.* 1,375 (484 Mommsen); Hydat., *Cont. chron.*, 167 (28 Mommsen); Victor

or Hun) was proclaimed king by his soldiers. He immediately deposed the nominal emperor, the youth, Romulus Augustulus, and executed his father, Orestes. Odoacer regarded himself as King of Italy; his assumption of this authority marked the end of autonomous Roman government in the western provinces although he purported to rule in the name of that Roman authority which the eastern emperor, Zeno, delegated to him.[17] The last pretender to the western throne was Julius Nepos, who temporarily ruled Italy and parts of the western provinces in 474-75. Orestes had forced him to flee to Dalmatia, from whence he continued to announce his claims until he was assassinated in 480.[18]

The eastern half of the empire endured the rigors of the critical fifth century remarkably well. It suffered some damage from Hunnic and Ostrogothic invasions but ultimately managed to buy off the barbarians. It was plagued by Vandal piratic raids from North African bases and by nomadic attacks of the Blemyes and Nobades tribes in Upper Egypt, but these enemies inflicted no permanent damage. The Persian frontier remained stable. Essentially the eastern em-

---

Tonnennensis, *Chronica*, a. 455, T. Mommsen, ed., *MGHa.a.*, XI (Berlin 1894) 186; John Malalas, *Chronographia*, L. Dindorf, ed. (Bonn 1831) 365-366. Cf. Stein, *Hist.* I 366; and esp. O. Seeck, *Geschichte des Untergangs der antiken Welt* (Stuttgart 1920) VI 324-325 and notes.

[17] On Odoacer: *Cons. It.*, a. 476 (308 Mommsen); Marcell., *Chron.*, a. 476 (91 Mommsen); Cassiodorus, *Chron.*, 1,303 (158-159 Mommsen); Jordanes, *Romana* 344 (44 Mommsen); *id.*, *Getica*, 242 (120 Mommsen); Ennodius, *Vita Epifani*, F. Vogel, ed., *MGHa.a.*, VII (Berlin 1885) 96; Procop., *Goth.* 1. 1. 2-8, eds. J. Haury and G. Wirth (Leipzig 1963) 4-5; *Excerpta Valesiana*, 37, J. Moreau, ed. (Leipzig 1961), 11; cf. Stein, *Hist.* I 398-99.

[18] On Nepos: *Cons. It.*, a. 480 (311 Mommsen); Marcell., *Chron.*, a. 480.2 (92 Mommsen); Auctarium Prosperi Havniensis, 475. 1, T. Mommsen, ed., *MGHa.a.*, IX (Berlin 1892) 307-308; Malchus, frg. 10, C. Muller, ed., *FHG* (Paris 1868) IV 119; cf. W. Ensslin, "Nepos," *RE*, 16.2 (1935) 2,505-2,511; Stein, *Hist.* I 398.

perors managed to preserve the territorial integrity of their part of the empire and succeeded in holding together a reasonably effective military, financial, and political administration.[19] Thus the eastern half of the Roman, or Byzantine, Empire survived the test of the fifth century and continued to exist for another thousand years. But how did it react to the collapse of its western counterpart? Did it remain indifferent?[20] Did the momentous events occurring in the western provinces leave no impression upon the eastern empire and its inhabitants?

Modern historians have continued to examine the causes for Roman decline since Montesquieu wrote his *Considérations sur les causes de la grandeur des Romains et de leur décadence* (1734) and Edward Gibbon published his *The History of The Decline and Fall of the Roman Empire* (1776).[21] But as yet there is no account and analysis of the

[19] For the Vandal raids: Courtois, *Vandales*, 196-197, 200, 205-209; Stein, *Hist.*, I 359, 362. On the Huns: Stein, *Hist.*, I 332-335; Bury, *Lat. Rom. Emp.*, I 271-288. On the Ostrogoths: W. Ensslin, *Theoderich der Grosse*, 2nd edn. (Munich 1959) 1-79. On the general condition of the east see Demougeot, *De l'unité* 495-519.

[20] *Ibid.* 476, 483-485. Note esp. 485: "L'indifférence des Orientaux prouve nettement que la Rome d'Occident n'était plus la leur."

[21] Montesquieu, *Oeuvres complètes*, R. Callois, ed. (Paris 1958) II 69-224. The best edition of Gibbon is by J. B. Bury, *The Decline and Fall of the Roman Empire*, J.B. Bury, rev. ed., 7 v. (London 1887-1902). For a recent evaluation of Gibbon: *The Transformation of the Roman Empire: Gibbon's Problem after Two Centuries* (Contributions of the UCLA Center for Medieval and Renaissance Studies, III), L. White, Jr., ed. (Berkeley and Los Angeles 1966). See also S. Mazzarino, *La fine del mondo antico* (Milan 1959), a brief but competent discussion. In addition see J.J. Saunders, "The Debate on the Fall of Rome," *History* 48 (1963) 1-17. A short anthology of views has been compiled by D. Kagan, *Decline and Fall of the Roman Empire* (Boston 1962) and M. Chambers, *The Fall of Rome: Can It Be Explained?* (New York 1963). Also see: S. Katz, *The Decline of Rome and the Rise of Mediaeval Europe* (Ithaca 1955) 71-84; A.E.R. Boak, *Manpower Shortage and the Fall of the Roman Empire in the West* (Ann Arbor 1955); F. Altheim, *Niedergang der antiken Welt: eine Untersuchung der Ursachen* (Frankfurt 1952). A recent contribution is R. MacMullen, *Soldier and Civilian in the Later Ro-*

reactions of the government and population of the eastern half of the Roman Empire to the gradual collapse of Roman authority in the western provinces during the fifth century. There had been speculation on the possible fall of the Roman Empire by inhabitants of the eastern provinces previous to A.D. 400, but in the fifth century for the first time the threat of the actual disappearance of the Roman Empire not only in the west but also in the east became a reality.[22] It would have been natural for the intellectuals and ordinary citizens of the eastern provinces to have expressed their opinions on these important contemporary developments.

The fifth-century event that most stunned western Romans was Alaric's sack of Rome in 410. Reactions and opinions of contemporary Romans in the western provinces on the collapse of the empire have been analyzed repeatedly.

---

man Empire (Cambridge, Mass. 1963) 152-77. And a careful discussion of the problem is found in three works of A.H.M. Jones, "Decline and Fall of the Roman Empire," *History*, 40 (1955) 209-226; *The Later Roman Empire, 284-602* (Oxford 1964) II 1025-68; *The Decline of the Ancient World* (New York 1966); J. Vogt, *Der Niedergang Roms: Metamorphose der antiken Kultur* (Zurich 1965); and R. Rémondon, *La crise de l'Empire romain de Marc-Aurèle à Anastase* (Paris 1964).

[22] On the correctness of the term "Byzantine" for the eastern half of the Roman Empire in the fifth century, see the following discussions: E. Stein, "Introduction à l'histoire et aux institutions byzantines," *Traditio*, 7 (1949-1951) 95-101; G. Ostrogorsky, "Die Perioden der byzantinischen Geschichte," *HZ*, 163 (1941) 229-254; E. Balogh, "Die Datierung der byzantinischen Periode," *Studi in memoria di Aldo Albertoni* (Padova 1938) II 153-189; S. Salaville, "De l'hellénisme au byzantinisme. Essai de démarcation," *Échos d'Orient*, 30 (1931) 28-64; G. Bratianu, "Les divisions chronologiques de l'histoire byzantine," *Études byzantines* (Paris 1938) 23-40; G. Downey, "Review Article: Byzantium and the Classical Tradition," *The Phoenix*, 12 (1958) 125; E.K. Rand, *The Building of Eternal Rome* (Cambridge, Mass. 1943) 215-216; K. F. Stroheker, "Um die Grenze zwischen Antike und abendländischem Mittelalter," *Saeculum*, 1 (1950) esp. 439-456. The pagan rhetorician, Libanius of Antioch, had openly voiced his fears that the Roman Empire was to fall (when he learned of the death of Emperor Julian): Libanius, *Oratio*, 18. 298, R. Förster, ed., *Opera* (Leipzig 1904) II 366-367.

In particular, scholars have examined Saint Augustine of Hippo's views in his masterful *De civitate Dei* and *De excidio urbis Romae sermo,* and those opinions of his friend and disciple, Orosius, in his *Historiae adversum paganos,* and finally those expressed later in the century by Salvian of Marseilles in his *De gubernatione Dei.*[23] The only resident of the eastern provinces whose reaction to western catastrophes has been studied is Saint Jerome, a resident of Palestine but a native of the western provinces, who wrote in Latin.[24]

Despite intensive study of western responses, no special investigation of eastern reactions exists. Therefore scholars have limited themselves to general observations about this problem. Bury, in his *History of the Later Roman Empire,*

[23] Some significant modern works which discuss the views of Augustine are: T. Mommsen, "St. Augustine and the Christian Idea of Progress: the Background of *The City of God," Mediaeval and Renaissance Studies,* E.F. Rice, Jr., ed. (Ithaca 1959) 265-98; *ibid.,* "Orosius and Augustine," *Med. and Ren. Stud.,* 325-348; J. Straub, "Christliche Geschichtsapologetik in der Krisis des römischen Reiches," *Historia,* 1 (1950) 65-81; C. N. Cochrane, *Christianity and Classical Culture: A Study of Thought and Action from Augustus to Augustine,* rev. edn. (London, New York 1957), 477-516; H. Werner, *Der Untergang Roms: Studien zum Dekadenzproblem in der antiken Geistesgeschichte* (Stuttgart 1939), 141-48; W. Rehm, *Der Untergang Roms im abendländischen Denken. Ein Beitrag zur Geschichtsschreibung und zum Dekadenzproblem* (Leipzig 1930) 22-30; H. J. Diesner, "Orosius und Augustinus," *Acta Antiqua,* 11 (1963) 98-102; P. Courcelle, "Propos antichrétiens rapportés par Saint Augustin," *Recherches Augustiniennes,* 1 (1958) 149-86. On Salvian's views on Roman decline see: A. Schaefer, *Römer und Germanen bei Salvian* (Breslau 1930); R. Thouvenot, "Salvien et la ruine de l'Empire romain," *Mélanges d'archéologie et d'histoire de l'école française de Rome,* 38 (1920) 145-163. See the collection of sources in André Piganiol, *Le sac de Rome: vue d'ensemble* (Paris 1964) and, José Oroz Reta, "Imperium sine fine dedi: Christianismo y paganismo ante la caida del imperio," *Nuovo Didaskaleion,* 13 (1963) 83-95.

[24] Saint Jerome, *Commentar. in Ezech.,* 1. 3-4; 3 *praef.* (*PL* 25 15-16, 75); *id., Epistulae,* 123. 16; 127. 12-13; 128. 5, J. Labourt, ed. tr., *Lettres* (Paris 1961) VII 93, 146-147, 153-154. Cf. J. Forget, "Jérôme," *DTC,* 8 (1947) 894-983; J.-R. Palanque, "St. Jerome and the Barbarians," *A Monument to St. Jerome,* F.X. Murphy, ed. (New York 1952) 171-200.

merely comments in a single footnote that the sack of the city left only a "faint" impression on the Greek ecclesiastical historians of the fifth century.[25] É. Demougeot, in her thorough and detailed study of the period 395-410, speaks briefly of "the feeble repercussion of the events of 410 in the East," refers to the "indifference of the easterners," and concludes that "the Romans of the East therefore were not moved by the misfortunes of the Romans of the West . . . all of these successive catastrophes remained distant for them."[26] N. I. Golubtsova, whose study is specifically confined to contemporary reactions to Alaric's sack of Rome, only briefly mentions the comments of a few eastern historians of the fifth century.[27] A. Lippold argues, "If the eastern church historians (Theodoret, Socrates, and Sozomen) . . . paid only a little attention to the event, it seems to me a sign that in the east the fall of Rome was regarded as no special shock, because Rome's importance had already sharply sunk." R. A. Markus observes that "East and West, pagan and Christian, seem to unite in lamentation over the fall of Rome; the only voice conspicuous by its absence from the harmony is that of the imperial government of the East." Finally, the eminent historian, P. Petit, judges that "What caused the loss of the west was not only the great passage over the Rhine, on the frozen river, on 31 December 406, by the Vandals, the Alans, and the Suevi . . . but especially the fact that the east abstained from coming to her aid. . . ."[28]

In contrast to all of the above conclusions, Ernst Stein,

[25] Bury, *Lat. Rom. Emp.*, 2nd edn., I 302n2.

[26] Demougeot, *De l'unité* 483, 485, 493.

[27] N.I. Golubtsova, "Sobytia 410 goda v Rime v otsenke sovremennikov," *Doklady i soobshcheniia istoricheskogo fakultet, Mosk. Gosud. Univers.*, 8 (Moscow 1950) 51-55.

[28] Lippold, *Rom und die Barbaren in der Beurteilung des Orosius* (diss. Erlangen 1952) 17; Markus, "The Roman Empire in Early Christian Historiography," *The Downside Review* 81 (1963) 341; P. Petit, *Précis d'histoire ancienne*, 2nd edn. (Paris 1965) 344.

in his careful and comprehensive *Histoire du Bas-Empire*, remarks that the event of 410 did make a "profound impression" on the inhabitants of the eastern provinces, but he does not elaborate on this conclusion. Furthermore, R. Rémondon briefly observes, "If it is sure that there was opposition between east and west, this opposition is less an hostility than a growing differentiation. The examples are too numerous, in the course of the fifth century, of the maintenance of the Concord of the Augusti."[29] All of these above conclusions rest on no detailed probing of the available sources. Other neglected problems remain, such as the extent of any eastern reaction to the successive disasters which befell the western provinces in the years after 410. If no eastern saint composed a *De civitate Dei* during the fifth century, can any explanation for the absence of such a composition be adduced? To endeavor to probe these questions is not easy—our relative ignorance of the Byzantine Empire in the fifth century remains a fundamental hurdle. The sources are sketchy and fragmentary compared with the relatively rich documentation of fourth- and sixth-century developments. Particularly significant is the lack of scholarly studies on fifth-century eastern paganism. Thus the precise situation of eastern pagans in that century remains uncertain. The noted historian of late paganism, Johannes Geffcken, concluded that fifth-century pagans were no longer interested in political activity, but he did not make a detailed examination of this question.[30] Schultze's old study on the disappearance of paganism is still a useful collection of some sources but his data is ill digested.[31] Did the eastern pagans join their coreligionists in the west-

[29] Stein, *Hist.*, I 259. R. Rémondon, *La crise de l'Empire romain de Marc-Aurèle à Anastase*, "Nouvelle Clio" L'Histoire et ses problèmes, No. 11, R. Boutruche and P. Lemerle, eds. (Paris 1964) 259.

[30] J. Geffcken, *Der Ausgang des griechisch-römischen Heidentums*, 2nd edn. (Heidelberg 1929) 178.

[31] M.V. Schultze, *Geschichte des Untergangs des griechischrömischen Heidentums*, 2 v. (Jena 1887).

ern provinces in blaming catastrophic political and military events on the Christians? The lack of an adequate study of eastern reactions to the fall of Rome is only one instance of a general scholarly neglect of the fifth century. Indeed the entire fifth century deserves to be as carefully reexamined, as the fourth century has been in the last fifty years. Possibly the fifth century has been neglected because it is too late for the historians of antiquity and too early for the concern of most Byzantinists.[32]

A number of other questions deserve consideration. To what extent did eastern views and concern for the west shift as western conditions worsened during the course of the century? To what degree were fifth-century and sixth-century Byzantine opinions on the collapse of the Roman Empire in the west (and the possibility of its disappearance in the east as well) related to earlier Roman speculation on the future prospects and ultimate end of their empire?[33] In what ways did the fifth- and sixth-century Byzantines believe that western catastrophes affected them and to what extent did they believe themselves involved in this process of decline? Did they believe that they could or should assist their beleaguered western fellow Romans? Furthermore, what was the relative significance of discussions of Roman

[32] Several important studies, however, have been written on the fifth century in recent years: E. A. Thompson, *A History of Attila and the Huns* (Oxford 1948); É. Demougeot, *De l'unité à la division de l'Empire romain (395-410)* (Paris 1951); W. Ensslin, *Theoderich der Grosse*, 2nd edn. (Munich 1959); C. Courtois, *Les Vandales et l'Afrique* (Paris 1955); V.A. Sirago, *Galla Placidia e la trasformazione politica dell' occidente* (Louvain 1961). Prof. S. I. Oost of The University of Chicago is preparing another study on Galla Placidia, and his former student and my good friend, Prof. Frank M. Clover of The University of Wisconsin, is examining Vandal-Byzantine relations.

[33] Cf. C. Koch, "Roma aeterna," *Religio: Studien zu Kult und Glauben der Römer*, ed. O. Seel (Nürnberg 1960) 142-175; E.M. Sanford, "Contrasting Views of the Roman Empire," *AJP* 58 (1937) 437-56; E. von Ivanká, "Zur Selbstdeutung des römischen Imperiums," *Saeculum*, 8 (1957) 17-31.

decline in fifth-century and sixth-century Byzantine literature? How much attention did the leading intellects of the century devote to this problem in comparison with other subjects of interest?

The basic position of this study is that the eastern half of the Roman Empire not only reacted to the disasters that plagued the west during the fifth century, but that it also reacted in a distinctly eastern manner, and reflected quite naturally the special conditions prevailing in the eastern provinces. Such a conclusion has further implications for the study of regionalism within the fifth-century Roman Empire and for the growth of a distinctive "Byzantine" society in the east. An assessment of the significance of these eastern reactions for Byzantine history, it is hoped, will lead to a better understanding of the importance of the fifth century in Byzantine and Roman history. In this way, the present ignorance of this period, which separated the very different worlds of the fourth and sixth centuries, may be at least partially bridged.

II

The official views and opinions of the Byzantine government were a fundamental component of the eastern reaction to western Roman difficulties. Beyond their intrinsic importance Byzantine governmental policies shaped the context in which individual easterners developed their own opinions about the condition of the empire, and in particular, their views about the critical western Roman situation. Were the eastern emperors officially inactive throughout the fifth century or did they offer more than token assistance to their beleaguered colleagues in the west? Under what conditions and for what reasons did they proffer aid to the west? The diplomatic relations of the eastern half of the Roman Empire with its western partner have not yet been studied for the fifth century as a whole. Though it is not possible here to embark on a full-scale survey of east-west relations,[34] it is possible to trace briefly the record of eastern official attempts to intervene in the west during its prolonged death struggle. These expeditions deserve more attention than they have hitherto received. It is valuable to assess the results of these expeditions and try to determine if they prolonged at all the life of the western Roman Empire.

Eastern Roman emperors dispatched military expeditions of comparatively large size to the western Mediterranean at various times during the fifth century. A chronological survey of those expeditions will be followed by an assessment of their purposes and relative importance. Unlike the political and military situation of the first years of the century, when the western empire waxed strong under the leadership of Stilicho, *magister utriusque militiae*, the balance of power during the remainder of the century unquestionably tilted in favor of the eastern emperors.[35] So it was only from the east that the hard-pressed western emperors might expect large-scale assistance to meet their difficult internal and external problems.

Theodosius II first sent military assistance to his uncle, Honorius, against Alaric's invasion of Italy (410). The historian Sozomen's description of the circumstances surrounding the arrival in Italy of Byzantine relief forces indicates

[34] Professor R. L. Wolff is working on a general study of east-west relations from the reign of Justinian through the Crusades. At present, cf. W. Ohnsorge, *Abendland und Byzanz* (Darmstadt 1958), a collection of essays. Also see his outline of problems: *Das Zweikaiserproblem im früheren Mittelalter* (Hildesheim 1947).

[35] For the authority given by Theodosius I to Stilicho: Orosius, *Hist. adv. pag.* 7. 37 (536-537 Zangemeister); Claudian, *In Rufinum* 2. 4-6, T. Birt, ed., *MGHa.a.*, X (Berlin 1892) 34; *Panegyricus de tertio consulatu Honorii*, 157-58 (147 Birt); *Panegyricus de quarto consulatu Honorii*, 430-487 (166-168 Birt); *De consulatu Stiliconis*, 2. 53-55, 2. 59-60 (205 Birt); Zosim., *Hist. nov.*, 4. 51, 5. 1, 5. 4, 5. 34; Cf. S. Mazzarino, *Stilicone, La crisi imperiale dopo Teodosio* (Rome 1942) 99-113; Demougeot, *De l'unité* 119-438.

how close Honorius' ties were with the eastern empire:
"Affairs were in such condition that ships were ready, if
necessary, to convey Honorius to his nephew [Theodosius
II] when unexpectedly six *arithmoi*—about 4000 men—arrived at Ravenna during the night from the east."[36] Procopius also stresses the importance of their unanticipated
appearance. These troops arrived before Alaric took Rome,
but they were not employed in the city's defense. Instead,
Sozomen reports, Honorius assigned them to guard the
walls of Ravenna itself, ". . . since he feared that the local
troops were preparing for treachery."[37] Although these soldiers did not succeed in thwarting Alaric they helped
Honorius preserve his throne at a critical juncture. This was
a relatively substantial commitment of troops on the part
of Theodosius II, and their transport by sea involved a substantial sacrifice of eastern resources.[38] Moreover, the presence of these troops may have had some effect on Alaric's
plans. Socrates Scholasticus even reports that "Having done
these things [Alaric] turned to flight, being terrified by a
rumor that the Emperor Theodosius was sending a force
to fight him." The previous appearance of the above mentioned 4,000 eastern soldiers at Ravenna probably lent some

[36] Sozom., *Hist. Eccl.*, 9. 8. 6 (400 Bidez-Hansen). In general, for
arguments in favor of Theodosius II's active interest in the west:
Johan Willem van Rooijen, *De Theodosii II moribus ac rebus politicis*
. . . (diss. Leiden 1912) 54-71. Thomas Hodgkin, *Italy and Her
Invaders*, 2nd edn. (Oxford 1892) I. 2. 788n2, argues for reading
40,000, not 4,000, in the text of Zosim., *Hist. nov.*, 6. 8. 2 (289-290
Mendelssohn). Zosimus states that 4,000 Eastern Roman troops arrived.

[37] Quotation: Sozom., *Hist. Eccl.*, 9. 8. 6 (400 Bidez-Hansen). See
also Procop., *Vand.*, 1. 2. 36, J. Haury and G. Wirth, eds. (Leipzig
1962) 316-17.

[38] Demougeot appears to be unnecessarily critical of the aid sent
by Theodosius II ("tardifs et insuffisants") *De l'unité* 493. But Beli-
sarius required only 18,000 men to conquer Africa and smash the
Vandal kingdom, Procop., *Vand.* 1. 11. 2-16 (360-363 Haury-Wirth);
cf. Stein, *Hist. du Bas-Empire*, J.-R. Palanque, ed. (Paris 1949) II
312-13.

credence to such rumors. The Pseudo-Dionysius *Chronicle* (late eighth century, which may not represent contemporary views) erroneously states: "Theodosius killed Alaric the barbarian and his entire army perished in battle."[39] Obviously, easterners believed that Theodosius had attempted to aid Honorius!

Theodosius II also cooperated with Honorius against Alaric by closing all ports and checkpoints in the east to western travelers on 24 April 410, a measure designed to prevent the infiltration of agents favorable to Alaric and his puppet emperor, Attalus.[40] In justifying this policy Theodosius II officially reiterated the program of cooperation between eastern and western emperors: "For an occasion of tyrannical madness and barbarous savagery persuades Us to this measure, which has been agreed upon between Me and My Lord and uncle, Honorius, in memoranda that We have exchanged with each other."[41] It is evident, therefore, that in 410 Theodosius II and his Pretorian Prefect, Anthemius, did not remain indifferent to the critical Italian situation. They did resolve to undertake major actions within their power to assist Honorius, although they apparently were not willing to risk all of their resources on his behalf.

There is numismatic evidence for continued east-west cooperation. Recently Mrs. Aline Abaecherli Boyce argued plausibly that in 411 Theodosius II at Constantinople struck solidi for the simultaneous celebrations of his own decen-

---

[39] Socrates, *Hist. Eccl.*, 7. 10 (*PG* 67. 756-757); *Chronicon Pseudo-Dionysianum*, J.-B. Chabot, tr., *CSCO*, 121, Scriptores Syri, Ser. III, Vol. I, Versio (Louvain 1949) 143. Of course this chronicle is of a late date and represents the garbled views of another time: I. Ortiz de Urbina, *Patrologia Syriaca*, 2nd edn. (Rome 1965) 211-212.

[40] On Attalus: Stein, *Hist.*, I 256-259; Demougeot, *De l'unité*, 448-462; Seeck, "Priscus Attalus," *RE*, 2 (1896) 2,177-2,179.

[41] *Codex Theodosianus*, 7. 16. 2, T. Mommsen and P. Krueger, eds. (Berlin 1954) 342; quot. from trans. of C. Pharr, *The Theodosian Code* (Princeton 1952) 174.

nial and the impending vicennial of Honorius. The obverse of one Constantinopolitan issue shows a facing bust of Honorius, while the reverse displays a helmeted Constantinopolis goddess seated on a throne, holding a scepter in the right hand and in the left a shield bearing the inscription XX VOT XXX (vicennalian vows for Honorius).[42] Mrs. Boyce contends that Theodosius II struck this issue, together with his own vota solidi (1) to demonstrate east-west cordiality, and (2) possibly to aid western morale in the wake of Alaric's sack of Rome. She notes that Theodosius subsequently minted another solidus whose reverse shows the seated goddess Constantinopolis and Roma with the inscription VOT XV MVL XX; again the motive was proclamation of east-west cordiality.[43] She furthermore describes a Constantinopolitan solidus later struck by Theodosius II in the name of Honorius.[44] The obverse shows a facing bust of Honorius; the reverse contains a goddess Victory holding a long cross in her hand. The reverse inscription reads VOT XX MVL XXX / CONOB [*CONstantinopoli OBryziacus* = "fine gold from the mint of Constantinople"]. However, Mrs. Boyce believes that another reverse struck by Honorius at Ravenna may proclaim the senior position of Honorius and Rome against the pretensions of Constantinople.[45] Her interpretation of this coin, which shows two seated goddesses (possibly Roma and Constantinopolis, or maybe even Roma and Ravenna), is somewhat strained and unpersuasive.

The next important Byzantine intervention in western Roman affairs occurred as the response to the western succession problem that arose in the wake of the death

---

[42] A. A. Boyce, "A New Solidus of Theodosius II and Other Vota Solidi of the Period," *Festal and Dated Coins of the Roman Empire: Four Papers, Numismatic Notes and Monographs* No. 153 (New York 1965) 43-45.

[43] *Ibid.*, 46-47.   [44] *Ibid.*, 50-53.   [45] *Ibid.*, 51, 54-57.

of Honorius in 423. (The east had refused to recognize Constantius III.) The *primicerius notariorum*, John, immediately usurped the imperial throne in the west.[46] Honorius' half-sister, Galla Placidia, and her son, Valentinian III, had taken refuge in Constantinople because of court intrigues in early 423 even before Honorius' death on 15 August 423. They claimed the western empire. Valentinian became engaged to Licinia Eudoxia, the daughter of Theodosius II and Empress Eudocia.[47] Accordingly, Theodosius had Valentinian proclaimed Caesar at Thessalonica 23 October 424. Theodosius commemorated this occasion by striking a solidus (FIG. 1) which not only proclaimed the elevation of Valentinian to the rank of Caesar, but also celebrated the consulships of Valentinian and Theodosius in 425. The obverse, with the inscription DNTHEODO-SIVSPFAVG [*Dominus Noster Theodosius Pius Felix Augustus*] shows a facing bust of Theodosius II in military dress, holding spear and shield. The reverse shows Theodosius II (left) and Valentinian. Both are wearing consular dress and each holds a *mappa* in his raised right hand and a cross in his left hand. Theodosius, who is seated, wears a diadem and a more elaborate (bejeweled or embroidered) robe. These features mark him as Augustus and distinguish him from Valentinian, who is shorter, stands instead of being seated, and wears no diadem and absolutely plain robes. The reverse inscription is SALVS REI - *PVBLICAE / CONOB [*Constantinopoli obryziacus*]. This coin should

---

[46] Cf. Stein, *Hist.*, I 282-284. Theophanes, *Chronographia*, A.M. 5,915 (84 De Boor).

[47] On the flight to Constantinople: Prosper, *Epit. chron.*, a. 423, 1,280 (470 Mommsen); *Chron. Gall.*, 90, 95 (658 Mommsen); Cassiodorus, *Chron.*, 1,205 (155 Mommsen). On Galla Placidia: W. Ensslin, "Placidia," *RE* 20 Pt. 2 (1950) 1,910-1,931; V.A. Sirago, *Galla Placidia*; Prof. S.I. Oost of The University of Chicago is preparing a detailed, major study of Galla Placidia; for the date of the flight: Stein, *Hist.*, I 275.

be dated to 425, a consular year for both Theodosius II and Valentinian, yet it must have been struck before 23 October 425, for on that date Valentinian became Augustus and would have been represented with a diadem. A similar type, with the mint mark $\dfrac{A \mid Q}{\text{COMOB}}$ [*Aquileiae/ Comitis obryziacus*, or "fine gold struck at Aquileia by the *Comes auri*"] was issued at Aquileia immediately preceding and following the siege and capture of John at Ravenna (FIG. 2). These were only the first of a series of solidi struck by Theodosius II to announce his solidarity with Valentinian, his cousin.[48]

The eastern emperor had refused to receive the envoys of the usurper John and cast them into prison.[49] Instead,

[48] Valentinian is proclaimed Caesar: Olympiodorus = Photius, *Bibliotheca*, c. 80, R. Henry, ed., *Bibliothèque* I 186-187; Philostorgius, *Hist. Eccl.*, 12. 13 (149 Bidez); Prosper., *Epit. chron.*, a. 424 (470 Mommsen). In general on Valentinian: W. Ensslin, "Valentinianus III," *RE²*, 7 (1948) 2,232-2,259. On the solidus struck at Constantinople (FIG. 1), J. Sabatier, *Description générale des monnaies byzantines* (Paris 1862) I 115 No. 8, from American Numismatic Society Collection; and solidus of Aquileia (FIG. 2), Sabatier, I, 115, No. 9, taken from O. Ulrich-Bansa, *Moneta Mediolanensis* (Venice 1949) 231 and PL. L/a. See: J.P.C. Kent, "Auream Monetam . . . Cum Signo Crucis," *Numismatic Chronicle*, Ser. VI, Vol. 20 (1960) 130; also see on the date and significance of this solidus: A. Voirol, "Münzdokumente der Galla Placidia und ihres Sohnes Valentinian und Versuch einer Chronologie der Münzprägung unter Theodosius II (408-450)," *Verhandlungen der Naturforschenden Gesellschaft in Basel*, 56. 2 (1945) 434-435, 442. On the significance of consular dress: A. Alföldi, "Insignien und Tracht der römischen Kaiser," *Mitteilungen des deutschen archaeologischen Instituts, Römische Abteilung*, 50 (1935) 33-34; G. Galavaris, "The Symbolism of the Imperial Costume as Displayed on Byzantine Coins," *Museum Notes* [Am. Numis. Soc.], 8 (1958) 103-104. O. Ulrich-Bansa, *Moneta Mediolanensis* (Venice 1949) 231, makes an untenable argument in asserting that this solidus was struck after the death of Honorius but before Valentinian was made Caesar; this is impossible given the progression of the coin types, for then we would have a coin for Valentinian before he became Caesar, and coins struck for him by Theodosius after he became western emperor, but none for the year in which he was Caesar.

[49] Theophanes, *Chronographia*, A.M. 5,915 (84 De Boor); Socrates, *Hist. Eccl.*, 7. 23 (*PG*, 18. 789); John of Antioch, frg. 195 (Muller, *FHG*, IV 612-613).

Theodosius dispatched Ardaburius, his *magister militum,*
and the general's son, Aspar, to lead a large eastern army
to overthrow John and restore the western throne to Valentinian. During his passage of the Adriatic, Ardaburius was
shipwrecked and captured by John's forces. Nevertheless
Aspar resolutely proceeded to capture Ravenna—with the
important assistance of some disloyal elements of John's
army—and liberated his father Ardaburius and beheaded
John (May-June 425).[50] Theodosius II and the entire populace of Constantinople warmly received the news of John's
downfall. Socrates Scholasticus gives a contemporary account of the arrival of the news at the eastern capital:

> While the emperor was at the Hippodrome, it was an-
> nounced that the tyrant had been killed. Then the em-
> peror addressed the people: "Come if you wish, to the
> church, leaving the amusements. Let us offer up thanks-
> giving prayers to God, because His hand has overthrown
> the tyrant." After he said this the performances were
> halted and abandoned. The people proceeded with him
> through the middle of the Hippodrome singing thanks
> to God in unison and walked on to the Church of God.
> And the whole city became one church. When they
> reached the place for prayer, they spent the day there.[51]

50 On the defeat of John: Philostorgius, *Hist. Eccl.,* 12. 13 (149
Bidez); Hydat., *Cont. chron.,* 84 (20-21 Mommsen); John of Nikiu,
Chronicle, 84. 46 R. H. Charles, tr. (London, Oxford 1916) 96:
". . . the emperor Theodosius [II] did not forget nor forsake the city
of Rome." Also, Jordanes, *Romana* 327-328 (42 Mommsen); Malalas,
Chronographia (356 Dindorf); Theophanes, *Chronographia,* A.M.
5,915 (84-85 De Boor); Socrates, *Hist. Eccl.,* 7. 23 (*PG,* 67. 789);
John of Antioch, frg. 195 (Muller (*FHG,* IV 612-613; Olympiodorus =
Photius, *Bibliotheca,* c. 80 (Henry, *Bibliothèque,* I 186-187); Marcell.,
Chron., a. 425 (76 Mommsen); *Chron. Gallica,* 99, T. Mommsen, ed.,
MGHa.a., IX (Berlin 1892) 658. On Ardaburius: Seeck, "Ardabur,"
RE, 2 (1896) 606-607; on Aspar, his son: Seeck, "Fl. Ardabur As-
par," *RE,* 2 (1896) 607-610.
51 Socrates, *Hist. Eccl.,* 7. 23 (*PG* 67. 792).

This incident again demonstrates the very deep interest of the leaders and ordinary people of the east in western affairs. The victory of Aspar secured the restoration of Galla Placidia and Valentinian III. Theodosius II then proclaimed Valentinian III as Augustus. Socrates Scholasticus asserts that Theodosius had even planned to travel to Italy to be present at the formal accession of Valentinian on 23 October 425: "He hurried eagerly to reach Italy in order to proclaim his cousin emperor, and while present to instruct the Italians by his wisdom not easily to incline to tyrants. But when he had come as far as Thessalonica, he was deterred by illness."[52] Although unable to be present personally, Theodosius II sent as his representative the Patrician Helion, together with the imperial crown.[53] It seems almost certain that the Byzantines continued to exercise considerable influence over the government of Valentinian and his mother Galla Placidia as evidenced by the appointment of Ardaburius as western consul for 427.[54] Byzantine influence was also probably exercised through the person of the *magister utriusque militiae* and consul in 428, Flavius Constantinus Felix.[55]

The gold coinage of Valentinian and Theodosius reflects their collaboration. Valentinian III, probably immediately after his proclamation as Augustus (23 October 425) struck a solidus to commemorate this event (FIG. 3). The obverse, with the inscription DNPLVALENTI - NIANVSPFAVG [*Dominus Noster Placidus Valentinianus Pius Felix Augustus*] shows a profile bust of Valentinian facing left. The reverse inscription is VICTORI - AAVGGG / COMOB [*Vic-*

---

[52] *Ibid.*, 7. 24 (*PG* 67. 792).

[53] *Ibid.*, and Olympiodorus = Photius (Henry, *Bibliothèque*, I 187); Prosp., *Epit. chron.*, 1,289 (471 Mommsen); Hydat., *Cont. chron.*, 85 (21 Mommsen); *Chronica Gallica*, 101 (658 Mommsen).

[54] Concerning Byzantine influence on Valentinian, see the affirmative conclusions of V. A. Sirago, *Galla Placidia* 264-266.

[55] On Flavius Constantius Felix: *ibid.*, 265-86.

toria Augustorum / Romae / Comitis obryziacus]. It shows two facing Augusti standing in military dress, each holding a cross scepter in his right hand and an ordinary globus in his left. The left figure is Theodosius II who is taller and wears a diadem. Valentinian, on the right, is being crowned by a hand reaching down from heaven. The cross scepter of Valentinian, unlike that of Theodosius, rests on a human head. Mrs. Boyce describes this serpent with a facing head as one "that now seems human, now beast" (p. 79). Commenting that this human-headed serpent was "doubtless representing the barbarian world" (p. 85), she further observes (p. 86) that Honorius had previously struck solidi which depicted himself treading on a lion which represented a captive. She regards this new solidus reverse as a modified continuation of the "lion" series which Honorius had initiated. This is indeed one explanation for the appearance of this human-headed serpent. Babelon erroneously supposed that the head was of Attila, over whom Valentinian majestically celebrated his victory and coronation; yet this is unacceptable because Attila was not yet ruler of the Huns when this coin was minted. But O. Ulrich-Bansa argues that the human-headed serpent simply is a generalized representation of evil. Indeed, Eusebius remarks that Constantine had himself and his children depicted trampling on a serpent who represented the devil, consigned to perdition. Constantine placed a cross above his own head, in this painting. There may be a still more plausible, specific historical explanation. Since this human-headed serpent first appears on the coronation solidus of Valentinian III, it may very well be a bitter reference to the hated regime of the usurper John. After the capture of John at Ravenna he was paraded on an ass in the Hippodrome of Aquileia (after his hands were severed), was exposed to even more of this unprecedented public abuse and humiliation and then decapitated. Given these circumstances and the circumstances of the minting of this coin for the coronation, the human head with the serpentine body may be John himself, on whom Valentinian triumphantly rests his cross scepter, symbolizing his recent victory with the assistance of Theodosius II, as well as his coronation. By issuing this coin Valentinian affirmed his intimate ties with Theodosius II and recognized his senior status. The representation of an emperor in military dress trampling a human head with serpentine body became a common reverse type for the coins of Valentinian (FIG. 4) and his western successors.[56]

In an additional display of imperial unity Theodosius II used the Constantinople mint to strike solidi which proclaimed his cousin Valentinian as Augustus, and commemorated the consulship together of Theodosius and Valentinian. These coins were minted at Constantinople in late 425 (after 23 October) or in 426; Theodosius and Valentinian were consuls in both years. The obverse is Theodosius (FIG. 5) or Valentinian (FIG. 6). The reverse inscription is SALVS REI *PVBLICAE / CONOB [Constantinopoli obryziacus], with additional mint marks. The reverse shows

[56] On FIG. 3: H. Cohen, Description historique des monnaies frappées sous l'Empire romain, 2nd edn. (Paris 1892) VIII 213 (no. 25); taken from Ulrich-Bansa, Moneta Mediolanensis, PL. I/g. On FIG. 4: Cohen, VIII, 212, no. 19; from Am. Num. Soc. Collection. Display and abuse of John in the Hippodrome: Procop., Vand., 1. 3. 9 (320 Haury-Wirth); decapitation of John: Philostorgius, Hist. Eccl., 12. 13 (149 Bidez). The discussion of Mrs. A. A. Boyce, "A New Solidus of Theodosius II and other Vota Solidi of the Period," Festal and Dated Coins of the Roman Empire: Four Papers, Numismatic Notes and Monographs, No. 153 (New York 1965), is on pp. 79-86. Cf. my review, CJ, 62 (1967) 182. Cf. on Attila: E. Babelon, "Attila dans la numismatique," Revue numismatique, Ser. IV Vol. 18 (1914) 297-314. For the refutation of Babelon and the significance of this accession coin: O. Ulrich-Bansa, Moneta Mediolanensis (Venice 1949) 227-229. Military dress: Alföldi, "Insignien und Tracht," Mitt. deutsch. archeol. Inst., Röm. Abt., 50 (1935) 43-68; Galavaris, "Imperial Costume . . . ," Mus. Notes, 8 (1958) 101-103. See also Eusebius, Vita Constantini, 3. 3.

two seated facing figures in consular robes, each wearing a diadem and holding a *mappa* in his raised right hand and a cross in his left. The figure on the right, who is distinctly shorter, is Valentinian. By striking this issue Theodosius confirmed his solidarity with his western colleague.[57]

Theodosius again announced his collaboration with Valentinian on an issue struck in 430 (FIG. 7), which commemorated the renewal of vows to Theodosius and his and Valentinian's consulship in 430. The obverse shows a profile bust of Theodosius in consular dress holding a *mappa* in his right hand and a cross in his left. The inscription reads DNTHEODO - SIVSPFAVG [*Dominus Noster Theodosius Pius Felix Augustus*]. The reverse shows Theodosius and Valentinian seated nimbate, facing, in consular robes, each holding a *mappa* in his right hand and a cross in his left. Valentinian, on the right, is distinctly shorter. The reverse inscription is VOT XXX - *MVLT XXXX / CONOB [*Vota XXX *Multa XXXX / Constantinopoli obryziacus*].[58]

[57] FIG. 5: I. I. Tolstoi, *Monnaies byzantines* (St. Petersburg 1912) I 70 no. 28; no Sabatier no.; taken from Am. Num. Soc. Collection. Cf. Ulrich-Bansa, *Moneta Mediolanensis* 231; A. Voirol, "Münzdokumente der Galla Placidia . . . ," *Verhandlungen der Naturforschenden Gesellschaft in Basel*, 56. 2 (1945) 435, 444; he dates the coin at 426. Also, J.P.C. Kent, "Apearm Monetam . . . Cum Signo Crucis," *Numismatic Chronicle*, Ser. VI, Vol. 20 (1960) 130-131. For FIG. 6: Cohen, *Description historique*, VIII, 211, no. 9; from Am. Num. Soc. Collection. Cf. Ulrich-Bansa, *Moneta Mediolanensis* 231, 235-238. For these consulships: A. Degrassi, *I Fasti consolari dell' Impero romano*, nos. 1,178-1,179 (Rome 1952) 89; O. Seeck, *Regesten der Kaiser und Päpste für die Jahre 311 bis 476 N. Chr.* (Stuttgart 1919) 351-53.

[58] FIG. 7: H.G. Goodacre, *A Handbook of the Coinage of the Byzantine Empire* (London 1928) I 31, no. 14; Sabatier, *Description générale des monnaies byzantines*, I 116, 15. Taken from FIGS. 5-6, L. Laffranchi, "Appunti di critica numismatica, II," *Numismatica*, 8 (1942) 42. On the consulship for this year: Degrassi, *Fasti consolari*, 1,183, p. 89; Seeck, *Regesten*, 356-357. Cf. also: Ulrich-Bansa, *Moneta Mediolanensis* 231; A. Voirol, "Münzdokumente der Galla Placidia . . . ," *Verhandl. d. Naturfor. Gesell. i. Basel*, 56. 2 (1945) 435 (no. 8). In general on "Vota" issues: H. Mattingly, "The Imperial 'Vota,' "

There are other indications of Theodosius II's continuing interest in western affairs. In 431-34 he sent his general, Aspar, with a "large army" comprising troops from Rome and Constantinople to assist Valentinian in the defense of Africa against the invading Vandals. Ultimately the Vandal King Geiseric defeated the Byzantine expeditionary force and managed to capture the future Byzantine emperor, Marcian (450-57). Geiseric released Marcian only after he solemnly swore never again to fight the Vandals.[59] It was possible at that time for Theodosius II to release troops for western service because he had just purchased (in 430) peace from the troublesome Huns for 700 pounds of gold annually.[60] The failure of the expedition against the Vandals left them in occupation of most of Mauretania and Numidia. This state of affairs was confirmed by a treaty the western Romans signed with Geiseric in February 435.[61] Although this Byzantine expedition did not succeed in relieving the west it did represent a major effort on the part of Theodosius II.

The ties between the two emperors were more intimately knotted on 29 October 437 when Valentinian III married Licinia Eudoxia, daughter of Theodosius II, at Constantinople. Before returning to Rome he ceded Sirmium in Illyricum to Theodosius II, thus removing an old point

---

Proceedings of the British Academy, XXXVI-XXXVII (1950-51). Vota decennalia: M. Hammond, *The Antonine Monarchy* (Rome 1959) 31-33.

[59] Theophanes, *Chronographia*, A.M. 5,931 (95 De Boor); Procop., *Vand.*, 1. 4. 1-11 (324-326 Haury-Wirth); *Nov. Valent.*, 9 (524 Pharr). For the date: J.L.M. De Lepper, *De rebus gestis Bonifacii comitis Africae et magistri militum* (Tilburg-Breda 1941) 96-97. On Geiseric: Seeck, "Geisericus," *RE*, 7 (1912) 935-945; Sirago, *Galla Placidia* 287-88.

[60] Priscus, frg. 1, L. Dindorf, ed., *Historici Graeci Minores* (Leipzig 1870) I 277.

[61] A. Gitti, *Ricerche sui rapporti tra i Vandali e l'Impero romano* (Bari 1953) 16-17, 38.

of friction between the two halves of the empire.[62] Theodosius commemorated this marriage, which more tightly
knit east and west, by striking a special solidus (FIG. 8).
The reverse inscription is FELICITER - NVBTIIS /
CONOB [Constantinopoli obryziacus]. Three nimbate figures are shown in imperial dress. The center figure, who is
taller, is Theodosius II. He is diademed, as is Valentinian
III, the figure on the left. Together he and Valentinian hold
a globus, symbolizing once more the marriage of east and
west, as well as the union of Valentinian III and Licinia
Eudoxia.[63] This was the last coin issued by an eastern emperor which depicted himself together with a western colleague.

Doubtless it is due to the marriage union and the settlement of the Sirmium question that Theodosius II again
agreed to intervene militarily in the western Mediterranean
against the Vandals. In 441 he dispatched by sea a large
contingent of troops under the leadership of Areobindus,
Ansila, Inobindus, Arintheus, and Germanus to attempt to
destroy the Vandal kingdom. This force reached Sicily but
never saw action against the Vandals, for a devastating
Hunnic invasion of Thrace and Illyricum compelled the
eastern emperor to recall his troops to defend home terri-

[62] Jordanes, Romana, 329 (42 Mommsen); Cassiodorus, Chron., a.
437 (156 Mommsen); Theophanes, Chronographia, A.M. 5,926 (92
De Boor). Cf. Stein, Hist. I 285; Sirago, Galla Placidia 248, 264-266.
[63] FIG. 8: Goodacre, Handbook of the Coinage of the Byzantine Empire, I 31, 5 (no Sabatier or Tolstoi listing); from British Museum;
cf. Ulrich-Bansa, Moneta Mediolanensis, 224; Voirol, "Münzdokumente der Galla Placidia . . . ," Verhandlungen der Naturforschenden
Gesellschaft in Basel, 56. 2 (1945) 435-436, 444. Mrs. Boyce, "A
New Solidus of Theodosius II" 62-67, makes a sensible case for the
eastern origin of those western Roman solidi whose reverse shows
the goddess Victory holding a long cross on the ground. She believes
that this series began with Theodosius II and spread to the west with
the return of Galla Placidia from the east. Here then is other numismatic evidence for official eastern influence on the western Roman
Empire.

tories. The expedition was very large, possibly comprising 1,100 ships. Geiseric may have been so overawed by the magnitude of the expedition that he began to negotiate before the recall of the troops. The ninth-century chronicler Theophanes, representing an eastern tradition, explains: "Because this force had anchored near Sicily, Geiseric became terrified and sent ambassadors for a truce." On the other hand, the withdrawal of the Byzantine fleet in early 442 may have left the west no choice but to negotiate peace with Geiseric.[64]

During the decade of the 440s the eastern empire was so preoccupied with the Hunnic menace of Attila, from both a military and fiscal standpoint, that it seems unlikely it could have spared many troops or provided much financial aid to the west.[65] The Hunnic threat remained great throughout the last years of Theodosius II's reign.

Theodosius II's successor, Marcian (450-57), showed some interest in the west. He struck a solidus at Constantinople for Valentinian III and even sent troops to the Hunnic homelands, which may have induced Attila to halt his approach on Rome; yet the connection between the arrival of these eastern troops and Attila's withdrawal is uncertain. However, much of his western policy was passive. Initially, Valentinian did not wish to recognize Marcian. Marcian had

[64] The quotation is from Theophanes, *Chronographia*, A.M. 5,941 (101 De Boor). The Huns force a Byzantine withdrawal: *ibid.*, A.M. 5,942. Other sources: Prosper, *Epit. chron.*, 1,344, 1,346 (478-479 Mommsen). Valentinian was therefore compelled to make peace with Geiseric (having no other source of aid): *ibid.*, 1,347 (479 Mommsen). Cf. Courtois, *Vandales*, 173; Gitti, *Ricerche sui rapporti tra i Vandali e l'Impero romano*, 39-40; Sirago, *Galla Placidia* 296-300; F. Giunta, *Genserico e la Sicilia* (Palermo 1958) 52-55.

[65] In general on the Hunnic threat to the eastern Roman Empire: Stein, *Hist.*, I 291-293; Thompson, *A History of Attila and the Huns* 78-149, 188-203; Altheim, *Geschichte der Hunnen*, IV 289-304.

pledged to avoid conflict of arms with the Vandals—a vow he managed to keep. There is one possibly garbled report in the *Excerpta de insidiis* that Valentinian was plotting to overthrow him. After Valentinian's death Marcian did not endeavor to prevent the Vandals from capturing Rome (2-16 June 455). In addition to his own unpleasant military experience in Africa and his vow to Geiseric, Marcian may have been under strong domestic pressure not to engage in any western ventures. Aspar, who had played an influential role in the selection of Marcian as emperor, attempted later in 468 to sabotage Leo I's expedition against the Vandals, fearing that any such success might weaken his own position. It would have been equally embarrassing to him if someone else should succeed against the Vandals while he had failed (in 431). He may well have discouraged Marcian from any active intervention in the west.[66] Marcian did not attempt to retaliate against the Vandals for the capture and kidnapping of Valentinian III's widow, Eudoxia, daughter of Theodosius II, together with her children Eudocia and Placidia, but only sent an embassy to ask for

[66] Prosper, *Epit. chron.*, 1,375 (484 Mommsen). On Aspar's action: Procop., *Vand.*, 1. 6. 3-4 (335-336 Haury-Wirth). On the sack of Rome in 455: *Cons. It.*, a. 455 (304 Mommsen); Hydatius, *Cont. chron.*, 167 (28 Mommsen); Vict. Tonn., *Chron.*, a. 455 (186 Mommsen); Malalas, *Chronographia* (365-366 Dindorf). Cf. Gitti, *Ricerche sui rapporti tra i Vandali e l'Impero romano*, 85-98; on the date (he argues for 14-28 June): *ibid.*, 102-105. On Marcian: W. Ensslin, "Marcianus" *RE*, 14 (1930) 1,514-1,529. On the solidus which Marcian struck for Valentinian: Boyce, "A New Solidus of Theodosius II . . ." 66 no. 101. Valentinian's plans against Marcian: *Excerpta de insidiis ex Joanne Antiocheno*, 85; C. De Boor (*Excerpta Historica iussu Imp. Constantini Porphyrogeneti* (Berlin 1905) III 125. Marcian opportunely sends troops against the Huns: Hydatii Lemici *Continuatio Chronicorum Hieronymianorum*, 154, T. Mommsen, ed., *MGHa.a.*, XI, *Chronica Minora*, II (Berlin 1894) 26-27. For east-west relations, see also: E.A. Thompson, "The Foreign Policies of Theodosius II and Marcian," *Hermathena*, 76 (1950) 66-70.

their return.[67] Geiseric compelled Eudocia to marry his son, Huneric, in late 456, and she was not able to escape to Constantinople until 472.[68] The Vandal attack on Rome had been triggered by the death of Valentinian III and the resulting western succession crisis. Legally Marcian became sole sovereign for the Roman Empire. Apparently he prepared for war with Geiseric when diplomacy failed to secure the release of Eudoxia. Death, however, terminated his plans in early 457. Otherwise he asserted his western sovereignty by granting part of Pannonia to the Ostrogoths and the Tisza region to the Gepids.[69]

IV

Marcian's successor, Leo I (457-74) immediately reversed his predecessor's policy of nonintervention in the west. He promoted Ricimer, of Suevian and Gothic origin and *magister militum* in the west, to *Patricius* and appointed Majorian *magister militum* in his place. Leo apparently first considered assuming the direct government of both east and west. He altered his decision, however, and allowed Majorian to become *magister militum* and then Caesar in the west, but refused to recognize him as Augustus when Majorian assumed that title 28 December 457. Majorian, in turn re-

[67] Hydat., *Cont. chron.*, 167, 216 (28, 32 Mommsen); Procop., *Vand.*, 1. 5. 3-7 (331-332 Haury-Wirth); cf. Priscus, frg. 29-30 (I 338-346 Dindorf); John of Antioch, frg. 204 (*FHG*, IV 616). On Geiseric's motives: Courtois, *Vandales*, 196; Gitti, *Ricerche*, 99-100.

[68] Procop., *Vand.*, 1. 5. 6; 1. 6. 5-6 (332, 336 Haury-Wirth); Priscus, frg. 29-30 (*FHG*, IV 103-104); John of Antioch, frg. 204 (*FHG*, IV 616). Cf. Courtois, *Vandales* 396-397.

[69] Procop., *Vand.*, 1. 4. 36-39 (330-331 Haury-Wirth); Hydat., *Cont. chron.*, 167 (28 Mommsen); Marcell. *Chron.*, a. 455 (86 Mommsen); Theophanes, *Chronographia*, A.M. 5,947 (108 De Boor). On the Ostrogoth occupation of Pannonia and the Gepid settlement in the Tisza region: Jordanes, *Getica*, 263-266, 268 (126-127 Mommsen). Marcian prepares against Geiseric: Theodore Lector, *Hist. Eccl.*, 1. 7 (*PG*, 86. 1. 169).

fused to recognize Leo as eastern emperor and consul in his novels (new laws) of 11 January and 10 March 458. His first known mention of Leo as Augustus and consul is found in his third novel, *De defensoribus civitatum,* of 8 May 458. He probably began to recognize Leo in the hope that the eastern emperor would agree to assist him against the Vandal threat.

I have here summarized the views of Otto Seeck, Ernst Stein, Wilhelm Ensslin, Lucio Vassili, and Jean-Remy Palanque; I agree with them that the preponderance of evidence indicates there was an estrangement between Leo and Majorian and that Leo never recognized Majorian. Although Norman Baynes denied that there was any estrangement I must concur in the majority opinion that the omission of Leo's name from the early legislation of Majorian, and the complete absence of Majorian's name from Leo's legislation is decisive in the absence of evidence to the contrary.[70]

[70] Majorian as *magister militum: Cons. It.,* 582, T. Mommsen, ed., *MGHa.a.* IX (Berlin 1892) 305; Sidonius Apollinaris, *Carmen,* 5. 378, 384 (*Poèmes,* A. Loyen, ed. tr. [Paris 1960] I 42, 43). Majorian as Caesar: Marcell., *Chron.,* a. 457 (87 Mommsen); Majorian did not mention Leo I either as emperor or as consul in his earliest known novels: *Nov.* 1, *De ortu imperii D(omi)ni Maioriani* [11 Jan. 458], and *Nov.* 2, *De indulgentiis reliquorum* [10 Mar. 458], *Theodosiani Libri xvi cum constitutionibus Sirmondianis et leges novellae ad Theodosianum pertinentes,* 2nd edn., T. Mommsen and P.M. Meyer, eds. (Berlin 1954) II 156-159. But Majorian does mention Leo in *Nov.* 3, *De defensoribus civitatum* [8 May 458] *Theodosiani Libri xvi . . .* (Mommsen-Meyer, eds., 159-160), and he continued to recognize Leo in all of his other (eight) known novels. Apparently there was a brief period before 8 May 458 in which he did not recognize Leo as Augustus or consul. Cf. Seeck, *Geschichte des Untergangs* (Stuttgart 1920) VI 478-479; Stein, *Hist.,* I 374-375. Baynes contends that Seeck and Stein erred in asserting that there was any schism between Majorian and Leo and argues that the absence of Leo's name from two of Majorian's six novels proves nothing: N.H. Baynes, "A Note on Professor Bury's 'History of the Later Roman Empire,'" *JRS,* 12 (1922) 223; *id.,* "[Review of] E. Stein, *Geschichte des spätrömischen Reiches,* I," *JRS,* 18 (1928) 225. But W. Ensslin

Apparently none of these historians was aware of a rare solidus struck by Majorian. The obverse shows a facing bust of Majorian in consular dress, holding a *mappa* in his right hand and a cross in his left; he wears a diadem. The obverse inscription is DNIVLIVS - MAIORIANVS PF AVG [*Dominus Noster Iulius Maiorianus Pius Felix Augustus*]. The reverse inscription VOTIS - MVLTIS is rare. The mint mark is Ravenna: $\dfrac{\text{R} \mid \text{V}}{\text{COMOB}}$ [*Ravennae / Comitis obryziacus*] (FIG. 9) or Rome: simply COMOB (FIG. 10). The reverse shows two Augusti of equal height and similar appearance seated nimbate in consular robes. Each Augustus wears a diadem and holds a *mappa* in his raised right hand and a cross in his left hand. Oscar Ulrich-Bansa dated the coin 458, the consular year of both Leo and Majorian, due to the consular dress of the emperors on the reverse. But Harold Mattingly subsequently dated it 457 (erroneously believing the acces-

---

restudied the problem and agreed with Stein and Seeck. He argues that Majorian had temporarily not recognized Leo and that Leo never recognized Majorian: Ensslin, "Maiorianus," *RE*, 14 (1930) 585-586; *id.*, "Leo I, Kaiser," *RE*, 12 (1925) 1950-1951. Palanque and Vassili accept Stein's interpretation: J.-R. Palanque, "Collégialité et partages dans l'Empire romain au IVᵉ et Vᵉ siècles," *REA*, 46 (1944) 294-295; L. Vassili, "Nota cronologica intorno all' elezione di Maggioriano," *Rivista di filologia e d'istruzione classica*, N.S., 14 (1936) 163-169. Cf. A. Solari, *Il rinnovamento dell' Impero romano* (Milan, Genoa, *et al.* 1938) I 405-407. C.D. Gordon apparently believes that Majorian received eastern recognition in 457, although he is somewhat ambiguous: "For five months the Eastern emperor was sole ruler of the empire, but in April 457 Majorian was recognized as the Western ruler. . . ." *The Age of Attila* (Ann Arbor 1960) 116. L. Bréhier, "La crise de l'Empire romain en 457," *Šišićev Zbornik* = *Mélanges Šišić* (Zagreb 1929) 94-96, presumes some understanding with the east.

On the accession of Majorian as emperor: *Cons. It.*, 583 (305 Mommsen); Hydat., *Cont. chron.*, 185 (30 Mommsen); Cassiod., *Chronica*, 1268 (157 Mommsen); Jordanes, *Romana*, 335-336 (43 Mommsen); Jordanes, *Getica*, 236 (118 Mommsen); Vict. Tonnenn., *Chron.*, a. 458 (186 Mommsen); Marcell., *Chron.*, a. 457 (87 Mommsen). Ricimer's background: Sidonius Apollinaris, *Carmen*, 2. 361-362, A. Loyen, ed., *Poèmes* (Paris 1960) 17-18.

sion of Majorian was early 457) and thinking the coin commemorated that occasion and the great east-west expedition against the Vandals. Mattingly's date is chronologically
unsound, for Majorian and Leo are shown as consuls and
were consuls together only in 458; furthermore, the expedition against the Vandals occurred in 468, not 457, and under
Leo and Anthemius, not Leo and Majorian. One can date
this solidus more accurately than has been previously
achieved. It must have been struck during Majorian's only
consulate—458—but only after 10 March, for at least until
that date he was not mentioning or recognizing Leo as
consul and Augustus in his legislation. Ulrich-Bansa is the
only scholar to connect the coin with the relations of Majorian and Leo, claiming it proved Leo recognized Majorian.[71] This solidus is no proof; Majorian, not Leo, struck
the coin. The solidus does show that Majorian publicly
claimed equal status with Leo and attempted to enhance
his own claim to legitimacy in the west by showing himself
equal in height and seated next to Leo. This coin would
have assisted Majorian in winning general public acceptance. On the other hand, the coin did show Leo and it may
have been an effort to woo favor and recognition in turn
from Leo. Or it may have been struck after Majorian had
lost hope of receiving such recognition. In such a case the
coin would be an arrogant, unauthorized representation of
Leo on a coin which proclaimed to the world the imperial
status of Majorian. Thus, no simple, unequivocal interpretation can be given to the coin.

[71] FIGURES 9 and 10 have kindly been supplied to me by the Keeper
of the Coins, British Museum. For a description: H. Cohen, *Description historique des monnaies frappées sous l'Empire romain*, 2nd edn.
(Paris 1892) VIII 225 (no. 12). For the arguments, dating, and explanation of O. Ulrich-Bansa, *Moneta Mediolanensis* (Venice 1949)
264. For Harold Mattingly's interpretation: "The Imperial 'Vota' II,"
Proceedings of the British Academy, 37 (1951) 249 and 265n139.
For the date of the consulate of Leo and Majorian: A. Degrassi, *I
fasti consolari dell'Impero romano* (Rome 1952) 92, no. 1,211.

Libius Severus (461-65) was chosen emperor on 19 November 461 by Ricimer after the murder of Majorian (7 August 461). Leo I regarded him as an illegitimate usurper. He initially allowed Count Marcellinus of Dalmatia, who had also refused to accept Libius Severus, to wage war on the western pretender. Because of the desperate condition of the west, Libius Severus was compelled to request from Leo the Byzantine fleet for use against the destructive Vandal raids on Italy. Leo, however, refused, using as a pretext his peace treaty with Geiseric (462). Priscus comments: "The affairs of the Romans in the west were greatly damaged because the empire was divided." Although Leo had not turned his back against the problems of the west, he was unwilling to provide blanket assistance for any western ruler. He would agree to aid the west only on his own terms and would only assist an emperor who met his personal approval. Severus died on 14 November 465, and Ricimer then discovered the necessity for eastern assistance in meeting western problems. He and the western Roman senate resolved to meet Leo's terms. In 467 they dispatched an embassy which requested that Leo select and send them a western emperor.[72]

V

Leo's western policy was aimed primarily at halting the damaging incursions of Vandal pirates against the eastern empire and Italy. Partly in response to western requests,

[72] On the accession of Libius Severus: *Cons. It.*, a. 461 (305 Mommsen); Theophanes, *Chronographia*, A.M. 5,955 (112 De Boor); Hydat., *Cont. chron.*, 211 (32 Mommsen); Cassiod., *Chron.*, 1,274 (157 Mommsen). On nonrecognition of Severus by Leo I: Jordanes, *Romana*, 335-336 (43 Mommsen) and Seeck, *Geschichte des Untergangs*, VI 483n on p. 352. 5. Leo's unwillingness to assist Libius Severus against Geiseric: Priscus, frg. 30-31, L. Dindorf, ed., *Historici Graeci Minores* (Leipzig 1870) I 340-342; Leo restrained Marcellinus and sent him against Vandals, *ibid.*, frg. 30 (I 340 Dindorf); Giunta, *Genserico e la Sicilia* (Palermo 1958) 65-67. Death of Severus: Seeck, *Geschichte des Untergangs*, VI 352, 483-484.

Leo in early 467 ambitiously dispatched the Patrician Anthemius (of eastern origin), who had married a daughter
of the late Emperor Marcian, to conquer Italy. Hydatius
explains: ". . . Anthemius, emperor of the west and brother
of Procopius, proceeded to Italy with Marcellinus, other
counts and selected men and a numerous and well-supplied
army."[73] The historian, Procopius of Caesarea, provides important additional details: "Previously Leo had created emperor Anthemius, a senator of great wealth and lineage.
Leo sent him in order that he [Anthemius] might participate with him in the Vandalic War."[74] Thus, according to
Procopius, Leo's principal motive in sending Anthemius
was the prosecution of the projected Byzantine campaign
against the Vandals. This appears reasonable, for immediately after Anthemius had been established in power, Leo
sent an ultimatum to Geiseric, warning him to cease raid-
ing the territories of Anthemius—particularly Italy. His
demand was rejected.[75] Significantly, the pagan, Damascius (late fifth and early sixth century), reports that Anthemius "awakened hopes that he might revive fallen (πε-
σοῦσα) Rome."[76] The expedition of Anthemius therefore
made a strong impression on inhabitants of the east, espe-

[73] Hydat., *Cont. chron.*, 234, 247 (34, 35 Mommsen); cf. also,
Cassiod., *Chron.*, a. 467 (158 Mommsen); Jordanes, *Romana*, 336
(43 Mommsen); Marcellin., *Chron.*, a. 467 (89 Mommsen). The request from the west: Evagrius, *Hist. Eccl.*, 2. 16, J. Bidez and L.
Parmentier, eds. (London 1898) 66; Theoph., *Chron.*, A.M. 5,957
(114 De Boor). In general on Anthemius: Seeck, "Anthemius," *RE*,
1 (1894) 2,365-68; A. Solari, *Il rinnovamento dell' Impero romano*
(Milan, Genoa *et al.* 1938) I 433-449; Sid. Apoll. *Carm.*, 2. 348-86,
A. Loyen, ed. *Poèmes* (Paris 1960) 17-18.
[74] Procop., *Vand.*, 1. 6. 5 (336 Haury-Wirth).
[75] Rejection of Leo's ultimatum: Priscus, frg. 32, 40, 42 (I 343,
349, 350-351 Dindorf).
[76] Damascius, *Vita Isidori* = Photius, *Bibliotheca*, c. 242 (*PG*, 103.
1265) = *Das Leben des Philosophen Isidoros*, R. Asmus, ed. tr.
(Leipzig 1911) 65-66. On Damascius: Kroll, "Damaskios," *RE*, 4
(1901) 2,039-2,042.

cially the pagans, who felt that it might arrest and reverse the decline of the Roman west.

Leo not only officially recognized and supported Anthemius as his western colleague but also undertook to inform his subjects of their close association and of the unity of the eastern and western empires. He took seriously his cooperation with Anthemius. Fortunately, the official Byzantine record of the reception of the imperial laurel-leaved letters (*laureata*) of Anthemius and his recognition by Leo I was described by Emperor Constantine VII Porphyrogenitus (913-59) in the *De cerimoniis*:

> . . . the emperor [Leo] commanded that the *laureata* be sent into the whole empire and that images be raised to both emperors in common. This is his command:
> "Emperor Caesar Fortunate Leo Victorious Ever Augustus, said: We were made very glad that the picture (*charaktēra*), long awaited, of the most gentle emperor Anthemius has now been delivered. Therefore, with divine approval, we order that this picture be joined with our images (*hēmeterais eikosin*), so that all cities will know in joy that the governments of each region have joined and that by his clemency we are united."[77]

This statement was made in the summer of 467; it shows that Leo placed great importance on union with the western emperor, and illuminates and confirms the themes Anthemius stressed on his coins.

A solidus which was struck by Anthemius probably commemorated his accession and also acknowledged his gratitude to Leo I (FIG. 11). The obverse shows the inscription DNANTHEMI - V - SPF AVG [*Dominus Noster Anthemius Pius Felix Augustus*], and a facing bust of Anthemius in

---

[77] Constantine Porphyrogenitus, *De cerimoniis aulae byzantinae*, 1. 87, Io. Iac. Reiske, ed. (Bonn 1829), I 395-396. For the date: *Chron. Pasch.*, L. Dindorf, ed. (Bonn 1832) I 597.

military dress with a spear and shield. The interesting reverse contains the inscription SALVS REI - P - V - BLICAE / R | V [*Ravennae* / *Comitis obryziacus*]. Two standing figures are shown in military dress and wearing diadems. The figures are of equal height. The figure on the left holds with his left hand the right hand of the figure on the right. The figure on the right holds in his left hand a globus surmounted with a victory. Above and between the two figures is a rounded tablet surmounted with a cross. On the tablet is the word PAX. A somewhat cruder reverse, cut by an illiterate die-cutter in this troubled time at Rome, shows PAS inside the tablet (FIG. 12). An even rougher copy, which was minted at Milan, has no tablet and reads BAS (FIG. 13).[78]

The PAX must refer to some special event; although a common inscription in the early empire, at no other time in the fifth century does it appear with SALVS REIPVBLICAE nor does it appear on other A.D. fifth-century Roman coins. Numismatists have puzzled over the explanation for this coin. J. Friedländer asserted in 1849 that the most convenient identification of the two figures would be Leo I and Anthemius, but he rejected this hypothesis because he could not understand why PAX would appear on a coin showing them together, since they were always on excellent terms and never fought each other. In addition, he could not understand why the figure on the left, who would be the senior Augustus, Leo, was holding no victory globus. Friedländer instead argued that the figures were really Ricimer, *magister militum* (on the left without globus), and Anthemius on the right with a globus. He believed the

[78] FIG. 11: Cohen, *Description historique*, VIII, 231 no. 11; from Dumbarton Oaks Collection; FIG. 12: Cohen 12 var.; from Dumbarton Oaks Collection; FIG. 13: Cohen no. 12; from British Museum. Cf. Ulrich-Bansa, *Moneta Mediolanensis* 281-283.

PAX referred to the brief reconciliation of the two in 471 after Ricimer's rebellion.[79] C. Brambilla in 1870 concurred, although H. Cohen identified the figures as Leo and Anthemius.[80] In 1949 O. Ulrich-Bansa persuasively argued that the left figure on this reverse could not be Ricimer, because he is wearing an imperial diadem and is wearing normal imperial military dress. In addition, he pointed out that the conclusion of a domestic quarrel would be an unlikely subject for commemoration on a coin; one would not wish to advertise the quarrel.[81] (It would be extremely unlikely, too, for a *magister militum*, especially a barbarian, to be depicted on imperial coinage.) Ulrich-Bansa then asserted that the figures on the reverse must be Leo and Anthemius, with Anthemius, the junior Augustus, on the left of Leo. But why is only Anthemius holding a victory globus and why the inscription PAX? He concluded that PAX referred to some military event of Anthemius' reign, and that this event must have been the Vandalic expedition of Leo and Anthemius against Geiseric, King of the Vandals in Africa. He believed PAX referred to the peace made at the end of this expedition in 468, and therefore dated the coin to 468. Ulrich-Bansa realized such an explanation raised problems: the joint expedition against Geiseric failed miserably; the fleet was destroyed. But he explained that the peace made by Leo was presented to the distant and ill-informed Roman world as a victory, perhaps exaggerating some formal concessions wrested from Geiseric, while the dimensions of the disaster were "completely hidden." Therefore the coin depicts Leo graciously conceding the pretended victory to Anthemius, who alone holds the victory globus.[82]

[79] J. Friedländer, *Die Münzen der Vandalen* (Leipzig 1849) 56-57.
[80] C. Brambilla, *Altre annotazioni numismatiche* (Pavia 1870) 32-33; Cohen, *Description historique*, VIII, 231 no. 11.
[81] O. Ulrich-Bansa, *Moneta Mediolanensis* 284-285.
[82] *Ibid.*, 286.

Ulrich-Bansa's complicated explanation is unsatisfactory. Leo concluded no known peace with the Vandals at the end of the expedition of 468; only in 470 did another Byzantine expeditionary force compel Geiseric to make peace so that Leo could use all his troops to destroy Aspar, his Alan *magister militum*. There is no evidence that Anthemius participated in this expedition or in the peace of 470 that followed. It is also extremely unlikely that Anthemius would have risked offending Leo by striking a coin which excluded Leo from any honors in creating the peace, for Leo had spent large sums and sacrificed many ships and soldiers.[83] This peace, moreover, was only a temporary truce—apparently Leo was planning yet another war against the Vandals. Furthermore, there is no reason for the victory globus to refer necessarily to a military victory; it was merely a normal attribute of imperial sovereignty; one need not seek to relate it to any particular war. The only other war in which Anthemius engaged was against Euric, King of the Visigoths, in Gaul, a war that resulted in the annihilation in 471 of a Roman army and the death of Anthemiolus, son of the emperor himself. Such a war would not have been mentioned on this coin.[84]

[83] The peace of 470: Theophanes, *Chronographia*, A.M. 5,963 (117 De Boor); cf. Procop., *Vand.*, 1. 7. 26 (344 Haury-Wirth); Malchus, frg. 13, C. Muller, ed., *FHG* (Paris 1868) IV 120-121. The expedition and peace is carefully discussed by C. Courtois, *Vandales et l'Afrique* (Paris 1955) 204.

[84] The profound negative impression in the Byzantine sources on the expedition of 468 against the Vandals: Procop., *Vand.*, 1. 6. 10-23 (337-339 Haury-Wirth); Priscus, frg. 42 (I 350-351 Dindorf); Lydus, *Mag.*, 3. 43, R. Wuensch, ed. (Leipzig 1903) 132-133. On the globus see: Alois Schlachter, *Der Globus, Seine Entstehung und Verwendung in der Antike nach den literarischen Quellen und den Darstellungen in der Kunst*. F. Gisinger, ed. (Leipzig, Berlin 1927) 81-82; cf. *ibid.*, 66, 76. Also A. Alföldi, "Insignien und Tracht der römischen Kaiser," *Mitteilungen des Deutschen Archaeologischen Instituts, Römische Abteilung* 50 (1935) 119-122; P. E. Schramm, *Sphaira-Globus-Reichsapfel. Wanderung und Wandlung eines Herrschafts-*

Literary sources provide another, simpler explanation for this PAX coin. On 1 January 468 Sidonius Apollinaris (who was in Rome as the leader of a delegation from Gaul) delivered a panegyric in verse before the Roman senate on the occasion of Anthemius' assumption of the consulate for that year. The official circumstances of this verse speech make it a source for contemporary ideology. In it, Sidonius traced some of the circumstances by which Leo had agreed to send Anthemius to be western emperor. Sidonius stressed eastern collaboration with old Rome and addressed Constantinople:

> You were fortunate enough to share the
> triumphs of Rome / and we do not regret it
> any longer. Farewell, division of empire! /
> The parts of the scale agree; when you took
> our weights / you equalized them.[85]

It is significant that Sidonius mentioned here the empire had been divided and now was united. The division was the alienation of Libius Severus and Ricimer from Leo. Now, with the accession of an emperor approved and sent by Leo, there is no longer disunity. In another passage he stressed the agreement of the two parts of the empire: ". . . Concordia united the two parts, / for Rome was finally possessed by a ruler of her choice."[86] Sidonius developed explicitly the theme of unity of the two parts of the empire in this passage of the panegyric:

> You too, Castalides [Muses], disclose in
> a few words the god through whom / Anthemius

---

zeichens von Caesar bis zu Elisabeth II (Stuttgart 1958) 12-13, 16, 17-19; and J. Deér, "Der Globus des spätrömischen und byzantinischen Kaisers. Symbol oder Insigne?" *BZ*, 54 (1961) esp. 79-85.

[85] Sid. Apoll. *Carm.*, 2. 64-66 (*Poèmes*, A. Loyen, ed. tr. [Paris 1960] I 6); cf. Loyen, *Recherches historiques sur les panégyriques de Sidoine Apollinaire* (Paris 1942) 86-95.

[86] *Ibid., Carm.*, 2. 522-523 (23 Loyen).

comes to us with the alliance of both empires /
[*gemini cum foedere regni*]: the peace of the
world sent the man who will direct [our] wars
[*pax rerum misit qui bella gubernet*].[87]

The PAX on the solidus of Anthemius most probably should
be identified with the *pax rerum*, that is, the new alliance
of east and west which ended the period of eastern hostility
to and nonrecognition of Libius Severus. But why does only
the emperor on the right, the junior Augustus, Anthemius,
hold a victory globus? The globus in his hand simply proclaims that Anthemius is now emperor, and the person who
made him emperor stands beside him, clasping his right
hand as a visible sign of unity. Leo had himself stressed the
importance of displaying the portraits of the emperors together, ". . . so that all cities will know in joy that the governments of each region have joined. . . ."[88]

This interpretation of the PAX solidus of Anthemius is
reinforced by examining the other two basic reverse types
of solidi he coined. A rare solidus struck at Ravenna (FIG.
14) shows on the reverse two nimbate emperors of equal
height wearing helmets and the *paludamentum*. They face
each other and together support a cross with one hand and
hold a globus with the other. The reverse inscription is

SALVSREI – P – V – BLICAE / $\dfrac{\text{R} \mid \text{V}}{\text{COMOB}}$. Another reverse

type shows Leo and Anthemius in military dress, each
standing and facing frontwards. And each holds a spear in
his outside hand while together they hold a globus cruciger
(FIG. 15). The inscription is SALVSR – EIP – VBLICAE /

$\dfrac{\text{M}}{\text{COMOB}}$ [*Romae / Comitis obryziacus*]. Another solidus

[87] *Ibid.*, *Carm.*, 2. 314-316 (16 Loyen); cf. *Carm.*, 2. 478-488 (22 Loyen).
[88] Leo refused to recognize Libius Severus: Jordanes, *Romana*, 335-336 (43 Mommsen); Seeck, *Geschichte des Untergangs*, VI 483n on p. 352. 5.

(FIG. 16) of the same basic reverse type has the mint mark
CORMOB [*Comitis Romae obryziacus*] in the exergue and
a Christogram (a technical numismatic term meaning a
combination of an "X" for the Greek letter Chi and "P" for
the letter Rho—standing for "Christ") in place of the RM
on FIG. 15. Every solidus issued by Anthemius depicts his
collaboration with Leo. It is logical to regard the PAX solidus as simply one, probably the first, of this series of solidi
issued by Anthemius to announce his solidarity with his
eastern colleague. His coinage affords visible evidence of
the high official, western Roman dependence on and unity
with the imperial sovereign in the east. Leo himself, despite
his words recorded in the *De cerimoniis*, never used his
own coins to show his association with Anthemius.[89]

V I

Once Anthemius had secured his position in Italy major
conflict with Geiseric was only a matter of time. Geiseric
had claimed the Roman west on behalf of Olybrius (who
had married Placidia, the sister of that Eudocia who had
married Huneric, son of Geiseric).[90] Leo in 466-68 ordered
Count Marcellinus to clear the Vandals from Sardinia. He
successfully achieved this goal.[91] Thus the groundwork had

[89] FIG. 14: Cohen, *Description historique*, VIII 230 no. 3; taken
from Dumbarton Oaks Collection. Cf. Ulrich-Bansa, *Moneta Mediolanensis* 280-281. FIG. 15; Cohen 6; VIII 231; from Am. Num. Soc.
Collection. FIG. 16: Cohen 7 var.; from Am. Num. Soc. Collection; cf.
Ulrich-Bansa, *Moneta Mediolanensis*, 280-281.

[90] The claims of Geiseric on behalf of Olybrius: Theophanes,
Chronographia, A.M. 5,947, 5,949 (109, 110 De Boor); Priscus, frg.
29-30 (I 339-340 Dindorf). Cf. Hydat., *Cont. chron.*, 216 (32 Mommsen); Marcell., *Chron.*, a. 455. 3 (86 Mommsen); Vict. Tonnenn.,
Chron., a. 464 (187 Mommsen); Evagrius, *Hist. Eccl.*, 2. 7 (54 Bidez-
Parmentier); Gitti, *Ricerche sui rapporti fra i Vandali e l'Impero
romano* (Bari 1953) 56-59.

[91] Procop., *Vand.*, 1. 6. 8 (336-337 Haury-Wirth); Hydat., *Cont.
chron.*, 227 (33 Mommsen); Priscus, frg. 30 (I 339-340 Dindorf);
cf. Courtois, *Vandales*, 187. On Marcellinus: Ensslin, "Marcellinus,"
RE, 14 (1930) 1,446-1,448.

been laid for the great Byzantine expedition of 468 against the Vandals in Africa.

If Procopius can be trusted, Leo's ambitious plans were conceived basically as a defensive measure. The emperor hoped to end the destructive Vandal raids against his empire and Italy. Acting in accord with Leo, Anthemius also sent units for the invasion force. Procopius states that Leo spent 130,000 pounds of gold, and employed 100,000 troops and Cedrenus calculates 1,113 ships for this expeditionary force, commanded by the emperor's brother-in-law, Basiliscus.[92] Cedrenus' figure is probably accurate. Procopius also reports that the campaign was strongly opposed by the *magister militum*, Aspar, who feared the success of the expedition would weaken his own position of power: "They say that Aspar feared that if the Vandals were defeated, Leo would consolidate his rule. He repeatedly urged Basiliscus to trust the Vandals and Geiseric."[93] After a safe voyage across the Mediterranean the expedition reached Africa, while another force under the command of the general, Heracleius of Edessa, left Constantinople, marched overland to the city of Tripoli, which it captured, and occupied the surrounding countryside. Despite this initial Byzantine success Geiseric managed to defeat the major Byzantine force led by Basiliscus. Allegedly, Geiseric bribed Basiliscus to accept a short truce. He then broke the truce and succeeded in trapping and destroying most of the Byzantine fleet.[94] The catastrophe left a lasting impression on Byzantine memories. Priscus and Candidus in the fifth century,

[92] The number of ships: Cedrenus, *Historiarum compendium* I. Bekker, ed. (Bonn 1839) I 613. The number of troops and cost: Procop., *Vand.*, 1. 6. 1 (335 Haury-Wirth); on Basiliscus as leader: *ibid.*, 1. 6. 2 (335 Haury-Wirth). The cost and western participation in the expedition: Priscus, frg. 42 (I 350-351 Dindorf).

[93] Procop., *Vand.*, 1. 6. 3-4 (335-336 Haury-Wirth).

[94] *Ibid.*, 1. 6. 10-23 (337-339 Haury-Wirth); cf. Courtois, *Vandales*, 201-203.

and Procopius and John Lydus in the sixth century, all emphasize the magnitude of the undertaking.[95] But Lydus greatly inflates statistics when he complains:

> Therefore by placing an army which time has not yet ceased to marvel at, on many tens of thousands of ships which they call "Liburnians," Leo reduced the empire to the last extremity, straining it and forcing it to the expenditure of 400,000 men for overseas war and the rigors of a land fortified with inhospitable frontiers, and enriching barbarians beyond counting to bring the army to sufficient strength. For in that ill-starred war led by Basiliscus, there was expended 65,000 pounds of gold and 700,000 pounds of silver, and so many horses and weapons and men that one would fail in the whole of time to determine it satisfactorily.[96]

Despite this severe setback Leo attempted to conquer the Vandals via another naval expedition in 470 under the command of Heracleius of Edessa and Marsus the Isaurian, employing troops from Egypt and the nearby desert areas. The expedition successfully disembarked and managed to capture Tripoli and other Libyan cities before Leo, from fear of Aspar, recalled this force. Nevertheless, Geiseric had been forced to make peace.[97] A year later, by means of the emperor's intrigue, Aspar and his son, Ardaburius, were assassinated, thus removing a stumbling block to Leo's ambitions.[98] At any rate, the eastern empire was not so crippled by the failure of the 468 expedition that it could not

[95] Procop., *Vand.*, 1. 6. 1-23 (335-339 Haury); Priscus, frg. 42 (I 350-351 Dindorf); Lydus, *Mag.*, 3. 43 (132-133 Wuensch); Candidus, frg. C. Muller, ed., *FHG* (Paris 1868) IV 135.

[96] Lydus, *Mag.*, 3. 43 (132-133 Wuensch).

[97] Theophanes, *Chronographia*, A.M. 5,963 (117 De Boor); cf. Courtois, *Vandales* 204; Marcell., *Chron.*, a. 471 (90 Mommsen).

[98] Theophanes, *Chronographia*, A.M. 5,964 (117 De Boor); Procop., *Vand.*, 1. 6. 27 (340 Haury-Wirth).

gather and dispatch other naval forces to the western Mediterranean for major campaigns. Events, however, repeatedly showed that during the fifth century it was difficult for the Byzantine empire to spare sufficient troops for prolonged periods in the western Mediterranean fronts, because these troops were required to contain internal threats and external frontier pressures.

Leo wished to protect the Mediterranean coasts of his empire from raids, but his expedition against Africa was also meant to save Italy. His efforts to secure a western emperor of his own choice did not cease until his death in 474. It was of course during Leo's reign that the western empire's governmental structure underwent its final death struggle, which gave rise to frequent eastern intervention. According to the chronicler, Malalas—and it is impossible to confirm or reject his account—Leo wished to destroy the barbarian, western *magister militum*, Ricimer; his letter addressed to Emperor Anthemius urged such action: "I killed Aspar and Ardaburius in order that no one would oppose my commands. Kill your father-in-law Ricimer, so that he may not give you orders. Behold, I sent the Patrician Olybrius to you. Also kill him and rule, commanding and not being commanded."[99] This letter, intercepted by Ricimer, caused the *magister militum* to overthrow Anthemius and replace him in 472 with Olybrius. In 469 Arvandus, *Praefectus praetorio Galliarum*, was arrested by Anthemius for urging Euric, King of the Visigoths, not to make peace with Anthemius "*Graeco imperatore*," but instead to attack Gaul. Anthemius therefore was regarded by some westerners as an alien intruder.[100] Clearly eastern attempts at intervention

[99] The quotation is from Malalas, *Chronographia* (374 Dindorf). J.B. Bury favorably appraises the validity of this account in "A Note on the Emperor Olybrius," *EHR*, 1 (1886) 507-509.

[100] Anthemius as "Greek emperor": Sidonius Apollinaris, *ep.*, 1. 7. 5, C. Luetjohann, ed., *MGHa.a.*, VIII (Berlin 1887) 10-11. Cf. Stein,

in the west did make important contributions to the course of western events in the 470s. But the deaths of both Ricimer (19 August 472) and Olybrius (2 November 472) led to the elevation of Glycerius, who was chosen emperor through the influence of Gundobales, a nephew of Ricimer.[101]

Unhappy with this situation Leo once again chose a western emperor 19-24 June 474. He selected Julius Nepos, *magister militum Dalmatiae*, whom he sent with troops to Italy in the same year. Nepos succeeded in deposing Glycerius and established himself as western emperor in Italy, but in turn was compelled to flee from Rome by a revolt of Orestes, *magister militum et patricius*, on 28 August 475 at Ravenna. Nepos fled to Dalmatia where he continued to claim the western throne until his death in 480.[102] This was Leo's last attempt to interfere in the west's affairs, for he died by the time of Nepos' expulsion from Italy.[103] Although Leo devoted much of the resources of his realm to western affairs he achieved no permanent, positive results. Because

---

Hist., I 391. Succession of Olybrius after death of Anthemius: Malalas, *Chron.* (374-375 Dindorf); Theophanes, *Chronographia*, A.M. 5,964 (118 De Boor); John of Antioch, frg. 209 (*FHG*, IV 617-618): Marcell., *Chron.*, a. 472. 2 (90 Mommsen); Vict. Tonnenn., *Chron.*, a. 473. 6 (188 Mommsen); *Chronicon paschale* (I 594 Dindorf); Jordanes, *Getica*, 239 (119 Mommsen); *Cons. It.*, 606 (306 Mommsen); *Chronica Gallica*, 650 (664 Mommsen); Cassiod., *Chron.*, 1,293 (158 Mommsen).

[101] On Glycerius: Jordanes, *Romana*, 338 (43 Mommsen); *id.*, *Getica*, 239 (119 Mommsen); Marcell., *Chron.*, a. 473 (90 Mommsen); Cassiod., *Chron.*, 1,295 (158 Mommsen); Theophanes, *Chronographia*, A.M. 5,965 (119 De Boor); cf. Seeck, "Glykerios," *RE*, 7 (1912) 1,467-1,468.

[102] Accession of Nepos: John of Antioch, frg. 209 (*FHG*, IV 618); Marcell., *Chron.*, a. 474-475, 480 (91, 92 Mommsen); *Cons. It.*, 475 (307-308 Mommsen); Jordanes, *Romana*, 338, 344 (43, 44 Mommsen); Vict. Tonnenn., *Chron.*, a. 473. 7 (188 Mommsen); cf. Ensslin, "Nepos," *RE*, 16 (1935) 2,505-2,511.

[103] Death of Leo: Malalas, *Chronographia* (376 Dindorf); cf. P. Grierson, "The Tombs and Obits of the Byzantine Emperors," *DO Papers*, 16 (1962) 44, who argues for the date of 30 Jan. 474.

of his Vandal policy Leo appears to have become ever more entangled in the affairs of Italy, but he at least attempted to save the western part of the empire in the period of its final tottering collapse. Moreover, had Leo not died in 474, it is entirely plausible, given his active western policy, that he might have acted energetically when the *magister militum* Odoacer usurped power in 476 and deposed Romulus Augustulus and his father, Orestes.

VII

Leo's successor, Zeno (474-91), did not find himself free (as his predecessor had been) to intervene in the west. On his accession Zeno immediately faced a revolt led by Basiliscus, brother of the Emperor Leo's wife, Verina, and was compelled to flee from Constantinople to his native Isauria on 9 January 475. He did not succeed in defeating Basiliscus and returning to Constantinople until late in August 476.[104] It was just at this time that Odoacer deposed Romulus (23 August) Augustulus and was himself proclaimed King of Italy, thus ending the long succession of Roman emperors in the former western provinces.[105] Zeno decided to reverse

[104] Still useful on Zeno is E.W. Brooks, "The Emperor Zenon and the Isaurians," *EHR*, 8 (1893) 209-38. The revolt of Basiliscus: Stein, *Hist.*, I 362-363; Zeno's western policy: A. Solari, *Il rinnovamento dell'Impero romano* (Milan, Genoa *et al.* 1943) II 3-5, 12-15. Civil war with Basiliscus: Malchus, frg. 8-9 (*FHG*, IV 117-118); Malalas, *Chronographia* (377-380 Dindorf); *Chronicon paschale* (I 600-602 Dindorf); Vict. Tonnenn., *Chronica*, a. 475-476, T. Mommsen, ed., *MGHa.a.*, XI (Berlin 1894) 188-189. Accession of Romulus Augustulus: *Excerta Valesiana*, 36-37, J. Moreau, ed. (Leipzig 1961) 10-11; *Cons. It.*, a. 475 (308-309 Mommsen); Jordanes, *Getica*, 242 (120 Mommsen); Cassiod., *Chron.*, 1,301 (158 Mommsen); Theophanes, *Chronographia*, A.M. 5,965 (119 De Boor). Cf. on Romulus: Seeck, "Augustulus," *RE*, 2 (1896) 2,369; T. Hodgkin, *Italy and Her Invaders*, 2nd edn. (Oxford 1892) II 495-531.

[105] Odoacer displaced Romulus and became king: *Excerpta Valesiana*, 38, 45-47 (11, 12-13 Moreau); Theophanes, *Chronographia*, A.M. 5,965 (119 De Boor); Evagrius, *Hist. Eccl.* 2. 16 (67 Bidez-Parmentier); Cassiod., *Chron.*, 1,303 (158-159 Mommsen); *Cons. It.*,

Leo's policy of active intervention to save the western half of the Roman Empire, much as Marcian had chosen to avoid activity in the western Mediterranean in contrast to his predecessor Theodosius II's policy. On Zeno's return to Constantinople, according to Malchus, envoys from Odoacer and from Julius Nepos, both seeking recognition, and the latter seeking money and troops, awaited the emperor. Zeno reminded the envoys that the western Romans had mishandled two emperors that Byzantium had sent them—killing Anthemius and expelling Julius Nepos. He requested that they take back Nepos as their emperor.[106] Clearly Zeno saw little advantage in undertaking more costly ventures in the west; he was at the same time disillusioned with the meager results achieved by recent eastern undertakings in the west. Nepos' hopes of Zeno's aid for a restoration were destroyed by eastern internal crises following the death of Leo I. Nepos was related by marriage to Zeno's wife, Ariadne, and to his mother-in-law, Verina, and thus to Basiliscus (commander of the disastrous expedition against the Vandals in 468). Yet Basiliscus rebelled unsuccessfully against Zeno, attempting to seize the imperial throne through bitter civil war. Obviously Zeno needed to act cautiously to avoid inflating the prestige and power of a possible male claimant to the imperial throne in the east while helping a relative to the throne in the west. Yet to placate Ariadne and Verina he probably felt compelled to make a token gesture of public support for the legitimacy of Nepos. Thus dynastic problems affected the question of imperial restoration in the west during the crucial years 476-80.

---

a. 476 (309-310 Mommsen); Jordanes, *Getica*, 243 (120 Mommsen); cf. Nagl, "Odoacer," *RE*, 17 (1937) 1888-1896; Jordanes, *Romana*, 344 (44 Mommsen); Ennodius, *Vita Epifani*, F. Vogel, ed., *MGHa.a.*, VII (Berlin 1885) 96; Marcellin. *Chron.*, a. 476 (91 Mommsen).

[106] Malchus, frg. 10 Muller, *FHG*, IV 119; cf. Ensslin, "Nepos," *RE*, 16 (1935) 2,505-2,506.

On the other hand, had it not been for Nepos' marriage to the niece of Verina he might well have never been chosen by Leo I to be western emperor. The death of Leo I and the ensuing eastern events had a great effect on the question of the western succession. Zeno was not unwilling to confer the title of Patrician on Odoacer and supported him in his struggle against the rebellious Gauls after Nepos died. Zeno apparently made no further effort to compel Odoacer to recognize Nepos as western emperor. Illus, in his rebellion against Zeno (484-88), even attempted to secure western assistance from Odoacer, who answered that he was unable to offer an alliance.[107] In accordance with his policy of non-intervention in the west, Zeno successfully negotiated a treaty with the Vandals in 474 for a peaceful settlement of differences. Zeno did not cease to show interest in the west, however, but the history of his subsequent relations with Theodoric, and those of Anastasius I with Clovis, are beyond the scope of this study.[108]

Military reactions to Zeno's policy of disengagement are uncertain. A possible indication of military unrest and an unquestionable demonstration of the troops' awareness of the precarious situation of the empire is their riot in 479 against the alleged lethargy or softness of Zeno. In the words of Malchus: "Becoming rebellious they reproached each other for their cowardice. For they possessed hands and bore arms and still tolerated the mention of the very softness through which all cities and the entire power of the Romans had perished, since everyone in authority hacked away whatever they might wish." Zeno quelled this threat by dismissing these troops to their homes. Such unrest

---

[107] Candidus, frg. = Photius, *Bibliotheca* (*Bibliothèque*), R. Henry, ed. (Paris 1959) I 165. On Illus, see John of Antioch, frg. 214, 2, C. Muller, ed., *FHG*, IV 620.

[108] Malchus, frg. 3 (Muller, *FHG*, IV 114-115); Procop., *Vand.*, 1. 7. 26 (344 Haury-Wirth).

doubtless embarrassed Zeno and pressured him to rescue the state from its unstable situation, yet this very insecurity created by military restiveness would have discouraged him from making any major military expeditions to the west.[109]

The westerners had not entirely abandoned the idea of further eastern intervention. While in Africa in mid-484 Victor of Vita wrote his *Historia persecutionis africanae provinciae*, which, according to the latest, thorough study, appears to have been conceived as an African appeal for Byzantine assistance against the Vandal persecutors of African Christians. Victor, however, admits that up to this point the African Church had been unsuccessful in receiving compassion from the east: "The African Church sought from the east someone who would feel sorry and there was none, and at the same time, she sought a comforter and found no one."[110] African refugees from the Vandals, particularly the wealthy, dispossessed landowners, continued to agitate at Constantinople for imperial reconquest. There were no more Byzantine military expeditions to Italy or any other part of the former western empire until Justinian's expedition of 533. And yet by the last quarter of the century it had become quite clear that only through eastern aid would it be possible to maintain any Roman governmental authority in the western Mediterranean.

VIII

The total, permanent results of the eastern intervention may seem slight. The western half of the Roman Empire underwent barbarian occupation and the Vandal kingdom re-

---

[109] Malchus, frg. 16, ed. Muller, *FHG*, IV 124.

[110] Victor Vitensis, *Historia persecutionis Africanae provinciae sub Geiserico et Hunirico regibus Wandalorum* 3. 68, C. Halm, ed., *MGHa.a.*, III Pt. 1 (Berlin 1879) 57; cf. *ibid.*, 3. 65 (56 Halm). On the purpose of Victor in writing this tract, see the important remarks (which are persuasive to me) of C. Courtois, *Victor de Vita et son oeuvre: étude critique* (Algiers 1954) 18-22.

mained strong in Africa. On the other hand, the eastern empire suffered a heavy loss of ships, other military accoutrements—men, money, and of course prestige. Each successive eastern-supported candidate for the western imperial throne, except Valentinian III, soon lost power. It may be argued, in fact, that these considerable eastern efforts did not prolong the life of the western empire at all. But it would be inaccurate to claim that they had no influence at all on events. Without Byzantine intervention, at least three of the western emperors would never have achieved power. During the fifth century the eastern emperors succeeded in establishing themselves as a force to be reckoned with in the western Mediterranean. The term, western, or better still, central Mediterranean should be emphasized, for it is noteworthy that in the fifth century the Byzantines did not attempt to dispatch any forces beyond Italy and Africa and thus never made their presence felt in such sections of the Roman Empire as those located in northwestern Europe.

Although the reasons for eastern intervention in the western empire during the fifth century varied, territorial expansion does not ever appear to have been a motive. Nearly every eastern intervention occurred in response to a specific western request for assistance.[111] When such was not the case, the eastern emperors intervened because certain western developments threatened the security of their empire—for example, Vandal pirate raids.[112] The east was always prodded into western action. Dynastic ties played a major role in Theodosius II's decision to intervene in the west in

[111] Nov. Valent. 9, *The Theodosian Code*, C. Pharr, tr. (Princeton 1952) 524; Stein, *Hist.* I 325; Seeck, *Geschichte des Untergangs*, VI 119-120; and esp. Evagrius, *Hist. Eccl.*, J. Bidez and L. Parmentier, eds., *The Ecclesiastical History* (London 1898) 66.

[112] Procop., *Vand.*, 1. 5. 22-23, 1. 6. 5-6 (334, 336 Haury-Wirth). Cf. E.A. Thompson, "The Foreign Policies of Theodosius II and Marcian," *Hermathena*, 76 (1950) esp. 59-65.

425, 431, and 441,[113] but under ordinary circumstances eastern emperors were content to leave the west to its own devices. They were not eager to assume responsibility for the entire Roman Empire, although they had opportunities to do so at the deaths of Honorius, Valentinian III, and Anthemius.[114] It does not appear, then, that eastern help to the west was ever directed primarily toward the prevention of the "fall" of the western half of the empire, although at least some eastern pagans believed this to be the motive.[115]

It is not improbable that an additional motive for intervention by some emperors was their hope that they might increase their own prestige and power in the east through successes in the west. This was the fear of the *magister militum*, Aspar, when Leo I sent his expedition against the Vandals in Africa.[116] It also seems that Leo intervened in favor of Nepos because his prestige was at stake when his favored Anthemius was overthrown and murdered.[117] Overall, eastern action in the west occurred as an ad hoc reaction to specific problems in the west and not as part of any general eastern plan of expansion in that region. Eastern emperors consistently and pragmatically considered their own interests when they did intervene. Their aid was offered conditionally. For example, Theodosius II seemingly gained influence within Valentinian III's government for assisting in the overthrow of the usurper, John; likewise, Theodosius II received Sirmium in exchange for marrying his daughter Eudoxia to the young western emperor.[118] And Leo I at-

[113] Cf. note 111.

[114] Succession to Honorius: Sirago, *Galla Placidia*, 243-248; Stein, *Hist.* I 353.

[115] Damascius, *Vita Isidori* = Photius, *Bibliotheca*, c. 242 PG, 103, 1,265 = *Das Leben des Philosophen Isidoros* (40 Asmus).

[116] Procop., *Vand.*, 1. 6. 4 (336 Haury-Wirth).

[117] John of Antioch, frg. 209. 2 (*FHG*, IV 618).

[118] Sirago, *Galla Placidia*, 248, 264-266.

tempted to persuade his western nominee, Anthemius, to murder the *magister utriusque militiae* Ricimer and Olybrius—which resulted in the death of Anthemius himself.[119] Nor did Byzantium invariably intervene in the west when aid was requested. Aid was withdrawn in 441 against the Vandals and was refused in 462 to Libius Severus and in 476 to Nepos.[120]

I X

There were a number of reasons for the lack of greater success of the Byzantine expeditions and a number of factors that hampered the emperors' efforts to control the situation in the west. Geographically, given the distance between Constantinople and the western Mediterranean, the time required for troop movements from east to west was great. Also, the eastern empire could little afford to spare great numbers of troops. Adequate contingents for its own defensive requirements were not available. To embark on a major western expedition required the hiring of expensive barbarian mercenaries since there was an insufficient supply of able recruits within the borders of the Byzantine Empire.[121] Throughout the century the internal political situation in the east was unstable because the emperors found power concentrated in the hands of a succession of military leaders. Anthemius, as pretorian prefect, wielded power

[119] Malalas, *Chronographia* (374-375 Dindorf).

[120] Malchus, frg. 10 (*FHG*, IV 119); Theophanes, *Chronographia*, A.M. 5,942 (102 De Boor); Prosper, *Epit. chron.*, 1,344, 1,346 (478-479 Mommsen); refused aid to Libius Severus: Priscus, frg. 30 (I 340 Dindorf).

[121] Leo was compelled to hire expensive barbarian mercenaries to bring his 468 expedition up to full strength: Lydus, *Mag.* 3. 43 (132-133 Wuensch). Cf. also: E. Stein, *Studien zur Geschichte des byzantinischen Reiches* (Stuttgart 1919) 118-119; Benjamin, "Foederati," *RE*, 6 (1909) 2,817-2,818; R. Grosse, *Römische Militärgeschichte* (Berlin 1920) 260-264, 279-280.

from 408 to 414; by the end of the reign of Theodosius II *magister militum* Aspar was the most influential political leader, and continued to enjoy supreme authority until his assassination in 471. These men were always fearful that western success might strengthen the emperor's prestige and make them vulnerable, for Ardaburius and Aspar themselves had gained much prestige and power from their successful overthrow of the usurper, John, in 425. Since they had failed in 431-33 and 441 to defeat the Vandals they doubtless were unwilling to see someone else achieve this goal and thus prove to be a better commander. For this reason Aspar attempted to discourage Basiliscus from defeating the Vandals in 468.[122]

It must be emphasized that the full strength of the eastern empire was never really committed to these expeditions. Unlike the earlier period when Constantine I, Julian, and Theodosius I led their armies in person, no fifth-century Byzantine emperor appeared personally on the expeditions to the west. The emperors may well have feared to leave the capital because of the continual threat of a coup. Large contingents of troops had to remain in the capital to maintain domestic security. Another reason for the reluctance to spare troops for expeditionary purposes was an external threat. Until the Hunnic empire disintegrated on Attila's death in 453, the Byzantine empire was never free of this danger from the north. And thereafter the Ostrogoths posed a threat in the Balkans.

There was also the fallibility of such commanders as Basiliscus, who allegedly accepted a bribe to grant Geiseric a truce, which led to the debacle of the expedition of 468.[123] Furthermore, the eastern expeditions were not unanimously

---

[122] Procop., *Vand.*, 1. 6. 4 (336 Haury-Wirth).
[123] *Ibid.*, 1. 6. 13-24 (337-339 Haury-Wirth).

welcomed in the west. Anthemius was regarded as a "Greek emperor" by Arvand, a high official in Gaul.[124] The overthrow of both Anthemius and Nepos in the 470s was evidence of the lack of enthusiasm for eastern nominees, which doubtless dampened eastern readiness to continue intervening.[125] Much of the eastern emperors' attention was necessarily fixed on the vexing Christological disputes within the church that were causing so much internal unrest.[126] Basically, the eastern emperors were never prepared to sacrifice the welfare of their part of the old Roman Empire for the sake of saving the other part. Another limiting factor was the great cost of such expeditions. The 468 expedition against the Vandals in Africa required the expenditure of 130,000 pounds of gold, gravely straining the finances of the government. It is not necessarily true that the east was much wealthier than the west at this time.[127]

The record of the eastern interventions—and absence of them—indicates the nature of Roman imperial unity in the fifth century. There was a sufficient residue of loyalty to the concept of a unified empire that the Byzantines would still answer, at considerable cost to themselves, to some western appeals for aid. On the other hand, the empire had by then clearly split into two halves. This had become evident by the time of Zeno's accession (if not before). An-

[124] Sidonius, *Epist.*, 1. 7, C. Luetjohann, ed., *MGHa.a.*, VIII (Berlin 1887) 10-11; Ennodius, *Vita Epifani*, 54, F. Vogel, ed., *MGHa.a.*, VII (Berlin 1885) 91.

[125] Malchus, frg. 10 (*FHG*, IV 119).

[126] General studies on the Christological controversies: C.F. Braaten, "Modern Interpretations of Nestorius," *Church History*, 32 (1963) 251-267; M.V. Anastos, "Nestorius Was Orthodox," *DO Papers*, 16 (1962) 117-140; L. Duchesne, *Histoire ancienne de l'église*, 4th edn. (Paris 1911) III 313-518; A. Fliche and V. Martin, *Histoire de l'église* (Paris 1937) IV 163-240, 271-298.

[127] On the cost of the expedition: Priscus, frg. 42 (I 350-351 Dindorf). On the absence of any eastern financial superiority over the west: F. Lot, *Nouvelles recherches sur l'impôt foncier et la capitation personnelle sous le Bas-Empire* (Paris 1955) 159-179.

other factor, which doubtless caused hesitation before intervening in the west, was the fear of lost prestige in case of failure, which in turn might draw them to greater commitments. Ultimately since no expedition after 425 was truly successful, the emperors became discouraged, despaired of success, and ceased to commit themselves so deeply.

One other reason for eastern reluctance in aiding the west was the frequent division of actual power between the emperor and the *magister militum*, which hampered the determination and maintenance of effective policies. The emperors did not always possess the necessary authority to organize and decree command of a military undertaking. There was also the risk that a successful commander of such an expedition might utilize this force as a revolutionary element for seizing the existing government, a province, or even for attacking the capital. All this made the selection of a trustworthy and competent commander difficult. It must be noted that the emperors themselves were always much more eager to intervene in the west than were their military commanders, and it was their imperial decision which was most influential in determining policy.[128] The army leaders in the eastern empire during the fifth century showed scant interest in militaristic expansion. In sum, it would be difficult to argue that the eastern half of the Roman Empire could have done much more to aid the west than it actually did—especially without risking its own destruction in the process. Intervention came to a halt during the reign of Zeno, when it was apparent the western situation had deteriorated beyond any reasonable hope of improvement.

It is uncertain whether the east could have preserved the

[128] Fall of Aspar: Theophanes, *Chronographia*, A.M. 5,964 (117 De Boor); Candidus, frg. 1 (*FHG*, IV 135); Marcell., *Chron.*, a. 471 (90 Mommsen); Procop., *Vand.*, 1. 6. 27 (340 Haury-Wirth); cf. Seeck, "Flavius Ardabur Aspar," *RE*, 2 (1896) 607-610.

western empire by offering more military, diplomatic, and financial assistance. The Byzantine emperors *were* sufficiently involved in western affairs during the fifth century that their subjects could not remain ignorant of the critical state of the western provinces. Consciousness of the situation spread beyond official circles to the general populace. The fifth century eastern emperors' active intervention in the western crisis stimulated the public—especially the educated elite—to be concerned about western catastrophes and to reflect on their causes and significance.

cɧapter ii

POLITICAL AND
RELIGIOUS PAGAN PROTESTS:
CRITICISM AND OPPOSITION
IN THE EAST, 400-475

The strongest Roman reaction to the sack of Rome in 410 and to other Roman reverses of the fifth century came from the pagans in the western provinces. Did eastern pagans show any interest in the deterioration of the state? Indeed, who were the eastern pagans in the fifth century and what was their status and geographical distribution?

Every major area of the Byzantine Empire during the fifth century, with the possible exception of the Balkans, where sources are rare, contained at least a few pagans. The fragmentary state of the evidence and total lack of statistics makes it impossible to ascertain either the total number of pagans in the empire or their approximate proportion of the general population. It seems very doubtful, although impossible to prove, that the pagans commanded a majority of the population at any time during the century.[1]

[1] Ferdinand Lot, *La fin du monde antique et le début du moyen âge*, rev. edn. (Paris 1951) states on p. 47: "Au cours du Vᵉ siècle, les païens de majorité passent minorité; ils achèvent de disparaître au VIᵉ siècle." He probably overestimated the number of pagans who existed at the beginning of the century. On the other hand, Jacques Zeiller likely underestimated the number of pagans when he agreed with the optimistic declaration of Theodosius II that no pagans remained—or that at best only a very small minority existed. (See *L'Empire romain et l'église* [Paris 1928] 85.) Note that Stein, *Hist. du Bas-Emp.*, I 480n194, estimates that the pagan and Jewish popu-

Especially important for understanding the status and reactions of eastern pagans are the anti-pagan laws preserved in the *Codex Theodosianus* and *Codex Justinianus*. Legislation gradually accumulated during the fourth century, which: imposed penalties varying from fines of twenty-five pounds of gold to death and confiscation of property; imposed fines on public officials for failure to enforce such regulations; repealed previous privileges of pagan priests; ordered the suppression of pagan temples; and deprived pagans of the right to make a will.

Theodosius II expanded anti-pagan legislation. On 7 December 416 (or 415) he ordered that pagans "shall not be admitted to the imperial service, and they shall not be honored with the rank of administrator or judge."[2] And on 9 April 423 he optimistically announced: "The regulations of constitutions formerly promulgated shall suppress any pagans who survive, although We now believe that there are none."[3] A few months later, on 8 June 423, he decreed: "Proscription of their goods and exile shall restrain the pagans who survive, if ever they should be apprehended in the performance of accursed sacrifices to demons. . . ."[4] But

---

lation of Constantinople together did not amount to more than 20 percent of the total populace—20,000 out of an estimated 120,000 in A.D. 400. For a prosopographical analysis of fourth-century pagans and Christians see P. Petit, *Les étudiants de Libanius* (Paris 1957). For a broader study of Byzantine paganism, see: W.E. Kaegi, Jr., "The Fifth-Century Twilight of Byzantine Paganism," *Classica et Mediaevalia*, 27 (1968).

[2] *Codex Theodosianus*, 16. 10. 21; quotation from *The Theodosian Code*, C. Pharr, ed. (Princeton 1952) 475-76; *Theodosiani libri xvi cum constitutionibus Sirmondianis et leges novellae ad Theodosianum pertinentes*, T. Mommsen and P. Krueger, eds., rev. edn. (Berlin 1954) I Pt. 2, 904. For superficial studies see W.K. Boyd, *The Ecclesiastical Edicts of the Theodosian Code* (New York 1905) 15-32; and M.A. Huttmann, *The Establishment of Christianity and the Proscription of Paganism* (New York 1914) 77-249.

[3] *Cod. Theod.*, 16. 10. 22 (476 Pharr); 904 Mommsen-Krueger.

[4] *Cod. Theod.*, 16. 10. 23 (476 Pharr); 904 Mommsen-Krueger.

his measures failed to eradicate paganism and Theodosius II found it necessary in 435 to reiterate his prohibition against sacrificing, ordering that "all their fanes [*fannum*, temple, church], temples, and shrines, if even now any remain entire, shall be destroyed. . . ." He increased the penalty: ". . . if . . . any person has mocked this law, he shall be punished with death."[5]

Still paganism endured. In 451 Marcian repeated earlier prohibitions against sacrificing and performing various pagan ritual acts, while decreeing death and confiscation of property for violations. To encourage strict enforcement a fine of fifty pounds of gold was levied on any governor or judge who did not punish such crimes.[6] Subsequently, the Emperors Leo I and Anthemius, in about 472, decreed stern penalties for the owner of any property who was aware that acts of pagan worship were performed on his property— "if someone distinguished by a rank or office, he shall be punished by loss of his office or rank and also by proscription of his property. However, persons of private status or of the humble order after physical torture shall be condemned to perpetual exile at labor in the mines."[7]

By the end of the fifth century pagans were probably only a small religious minority within the Byzantine Empire, yet throughout the century they were an influential minority. Pagans were found in many occupations. Many lived in remote rural areas, such as the "high rugged mountains of Asia," where John of Ephesus converted them, and in villages such as Menouthis, and Smin in Egypt.[8] Probably

---

[5] *Cod. Theod.*, 16. 10. 25 (476 Pharr); 905 Mommsen-Krueger.

[6] *Codex Iustinianus*, 1. 11. 7; P. Krueger, ed., *Corpus Juris Civilis* (Berlin 1959) II, 63.

[7] *Cod. Iust.*, 1. 11. 8 (63 Krueger).

[8] John of Ephesus, *Lives of the Eastern Saints* (*PO*, 18. 659, E. W. Brooks, ed. tr.); Zachariah of Mitylene, *Vie de Sévère* (II 27-31 Kugener); *Sinuthii Archimandritae vita a Besa* . . . . c. 81, 83, 85, 88 (22-24 Wiesmann).

these pagans were farmers. They were comparable to the western Roman *pagani*, whose religion perhaps (although this is still controversial) received its designation "pagan" from the rural dwelling-places of its adherents.[9]

Not all eastern pagans were rustics, however. In the Greek-speaking section of the empire pagans were called "*Hellēnes*," that is, adherents of the ancient Greek culture, values, and religious beliefs and practices.[10] "*Hellēn*" does not suggest that only rural dwellers were pagans. Fifth-century eastern pagans included such members of the highly educated urban elite as the neo-Platonic philosophers, Plutarch, Syrianus, Proclus, Marinus, Isidore, and Hypatia; and grammarians such as Horapollon of Alexandria, Pamprepius, sophists Apollodorus and Proclus of Aphrodisias,

[9] J. Zeiller, *Paganus. Étude de terminologie historique* (Freiburg, Switzerland and Paris 1917) 29-34, 45, reaffirms the opinion that *paganus* acquired its religious meaning from the persistence of paganism in rural areas. For additional documentation see Zeiller, "*Paganus*. Sur l'origine de l'acception religieuse du mot," *Académie des inscriptions et belles-lettres, Comptes rendus* (1940) 526-543; E. Kornemann, "*paganus*," *RE*, 18 (1942) 2,295-2,297; and N. Turchi, "Paganesimo," *Enciclopedia Cattolica*, 9 (1952) 553-54. These articles decisively disprove the complicated and artificial argument that *paganus* received its religious meaning from the opposition of the *milites Christi* to the "civilians" (also termed *pagani*). This erroneous view is summarized by B. Altaner "*Paganus*: eine bedeutungsgeschichtliche Untersuchung," *Zeitschrift für Kirchengeschichte*, 58 (1939) 130-141. C. Mohrmann, "Encore une fois: Paganus," *VigChr*, 6 (1952) 109-121, points to difficulties in all of these conflicting theories, suggesting the origin of the use of the term in the concept of the "profane" or "individual" nature of pagans, since they did not belong to the Christian community. There is a detailed discussion, suggesting its origin as the Latin counterpart for the Greek term *ethnoi* for "Gentiles," in H. Grégoire, P. Orgels, *et al.*, *Les persécutions dans l'Empire romain*, 2nd edn., Mémoires de l'Académie royale de Belgique, Classe des lettres et des sciences morales et politiques, 56 fasc. 5 [1964] 117-119 and esp. 188-220. Cf. É. Demougeot, "'Paganus,' Mithra et Tertullien," *Studia Patristica 3 = Texte und Untersuchungen*, 78 (Berlin 1961) 354-365.

[10] For the significance of *Hellēn* (῞Ελλην) as "pagan": K. Lechner, *Hellenen und Barbaren im Weltbild der Byzantiner* (Munich 1954) 16-37.

and the epic poet Nonnus of Panopolis. Pagans such as these would have had considerable influence on other persons in their localities, especially younger students.

Further testimony to the strength of paganism in the east is the impressive number of anti-pagan tracts which such eastern Christians as Theodoret of Cyrus (= Cyrrhus), Cyril of Alexandria, Marcarius Magnes, Aeneas of Gaza, Zachariah of Mitylene, John Philoponus, and even the Empress Eudocia herself wrote. The anti-pagan activities of Saint Nilus of Ancyra, Saint Isidore of Pelusium, Shanudah of Atripe, Saint Domnica, Saint Symeon the Stylite, Thaleleus, and John of Ephesus also offer additional evidence for the persistence of significant pockets of paganism.[11]

[11] The bibliography of apologetical materials from the fifth century is enormous:

(1) By Theodoret: *Quaestiones et responsiones ad orthodoxos*, A. Papadopoulos-Kerameus, ed., *Zapiski, istoriko-filologicheski fakultet, St. Petersburg University*, 36 (1895); *De providentia* (*PG*, 83. 555-774); *Thérapeutique des maladies helléniques*, 2 v., P. Canivet, ed. and tr. (Paris 1958); Quasten, *Patrology*, III 536-554; G. Florovsky, *Vizantiiskie Ottsy V-VIII* (Paris 1933) 74-94; B. Altaner, *Patrology*, H.C. Graef, tr. (New York 1958) 396-399.

(2) By Cyril of Alexandria: *Adversus Julianum imperatorem libri X* (*PG*, 76.505-1,064); cf. P. Regazzoni, "Il *Contra Galilaeos* dell' Imperatore Giuliano e il *Contra Julianum* di S. Cirillo Alessandrino," *Didaskaleion*, N.S., 6 (1928) 1-114.

(3) By Macarius Magnes: *Apocriticus = Quae supersunt*, C. Blondel, ed. (Paris 1876). Cf. Quasten, *Patrology*, III 486-488; F. Corsaro, "L' 'Apocritico' di Macario di Magnesia e le Sacre Scritture," *Nuovo Didaskaleion*, 7 (1957) 1-24.

(4) By Aeneas of Gaza: *Teofrasto*, M.E. Colonna, ed. tr. (Naples 1958); cf. Altaner, *Patrology* 624; V. Valdenberg "La philosophie byzantine au IVᵉ-Vᵉ siècles," *Byzantion*, 4 (1927-1928) 262-268.

(5) By Zachariah of Mitylene: *De immortalitate animae et mundi consummatione*, J.F. Boissonade, ed. (Paris 1836); Altaner, *Patrology*, Graef, tr., 276; E. Honigmann, "Zacharias of Mitylene," *Patristic Studies, Studi e Testi*, 173 (Vatican City 1953) 194-204.

(6) By John Philoponus: *De aeternitate mundi contra Proclum*, H. Rabe, ed. (Leipzig 1899); cf. G. Bardy, "Jean Philopon,"

Yet pagans did not confine themselves to intellectual pursuits. They did not withdraw completely from participation in politics after they had lost the throne to the Christians. During Theodosius II's reign the pagan philosopher,

---

DTC, 8 (1924) 836-837. On Proclus: A.R. Noë, *Die Proklosbiographie des Marinos* (Heidelberg 1938).

(7) By Eudocia Augusta: *De martyrio S. Cypriani*, A. Ludwich, ed., in *Eudociae Augustae Procli Lycii Claudiani carminum graecorum reliquiae* (Leipzig 1897) 16-79.

(8) Refutations of paganism are found in S. Nilus of Ancyra, *Epistulae* I. 75, 1. 112, 1. 198, 1. 278, 1. 282, 2. 145, 2. 170, 2. 280, 3. 8, 3. 71, (*PG*, 79. 116, 131, 158, 184, 185, 268, 285, 340, 369, 421). Nilus also wrote an antipagan tract no longer extant: Nicephorus Callistus, *Hist. Eccl.*, 14. 54 (*PG*, 46. 1,256). On Nilus in general: Quasten, *Patrology*, III 502; on his struggle against paganism: K. Heussi, *Untersuchungen zu Nilus dem Asketen* (Texte und Untersuchungen, III. Reihe, Bd. XII, heft 2 [Leipzig 1917] 98); cf. also F. Degenhart, *Der Heilige Nilus Sinaita* (Munster 1915) 46-49.

(9) Refutations of paganism in the correspondence of Shanudah of Atripe: Sinuthii, *Epistulae*, 17, 18, 19, 23, 24, 25, 26 (*CSCO*, 96, H. Wiesmann, tr. [Paris 1931], 20-21, 22-34, 34-37, 42-43, 43-47, 47-48, 48-50); cf. Quasten, *Patrology*, III 185-187; J. Leipoldt, *Schenute von Atripe und die Entstehung des national ägyptischen Christentums* (Texte und Untersuchungen, N.F., 10 = Vol. 35 [Leipzig 1903] 175-182). On Shanudah's struggle against the pagans: *Sinuthii Archimandritae Vita a Besa discipulo eius scripta Bohairice* c. 81-83, 85, 88, H. Wiesmann, tr., *CSCO*, 129 (Louvain 1951) 22-24.

(10) Refutations of paganism by S. Isidore of Pelusium, *Epistulae*, 1. 21, 1. 54, 1. 63, 1. 139, 1. 270, 1. 379, 2. 46, 2. 137, 2. 228, 2. 272, 3. 61, 3. 388, 4. 27-4. 31, 4. 58, 4. 61, 4. 205, 4. 207, 4. 225, 5. 441. Cf. Quasten, *Patrology*, III 180-185. On the lost tract of Isidore *Against the Pagans*: Isidore of Pelusium, *Ep.*, 2. 137, 2. 228 (*PG*, 78. 580, 664-665). Cf. Quasten, *Patrology*, III 184.

(11) On St. Domnica: "Βίος καὶ Θαύματα τῆς ὀσίας μητρὸς ἡμῶν Δομνίκης," Μνημεῖα ἁγιολογικὰ νῦν πρῶτον ἐνδιδόμενα ὑπὸ Ἱεροδιακόνου Θεοφίλου Ἰωάννου (Venice 1884) 268-284, esp. c. 4-7, pp. 270-273.

(12) On Saint Symeon: Theodoret of Cyrus, *Religiosa historia*, c. 26 (*PG*, 82. 1,476). Cf. G. Downey, *A History of Antioch in Syria* (Princeton 1961) 459-460.

Cyrus, occupied several important posts. Suidas declares:

> [Cyrus] lived during the reign of Emperor Theodosius the Younger, by whom he was appointed Pretorian Prefect and Prefect of the City. He also became *consularius* and *patricius*. For Eudocia, the wife of Theodosius, being Empress and a lover of poetry, exceedingly admired Cyrus. But after she removed herself from the palace and passed time at Jerusalem in the east, Cyrus fell victim to a conspiracy, became bishop of Kotuaeia in Phrygia, and lived until the reign of Leo.[12]

Malalas and Theophanes report that a Christian mob forced Cyrus to convert to Christianity after he was dismissed because of his paganism.[13]

The connection of Cyrus's career with the fortunes of Empress Eudocia is interesting. Eudocia had once been pagan (formerly named Athenaïs, she was the daughter of a pagan professor at Athens, Leontius). Though a convert, she favored the pagan, Cyrus, and was responsible for his appointment and promotion. When she lost influence

---

(13) On Thaleleus: Theodoret, *Religiosa historia* c. 28 (*PG*, 82. 1,488-1,489). A. Vööbus, *History of Asceticism in the Syrian Orient. CSCO*, 197, Subsidia, XVII (Louvain 1960) 208-223.

(14) On John of Ephesus, *Hist. Eccl.*, 3. 36, E. W. Brooks, tr., *CSCO* (Louvain 1936) 106, Scriptores Syri, Ser. III, v. 3, Versio, 125-126; also John of Ephesus, *Lives of the Eastern Saints*, E. W. Brooks, ed. tr., *PO*, 18. 646, 650, 658-659, 681. In general on John: A. Diakonov, *Ioann' Efesskii i ego tserkovno-istoricheskie trudy* (St. Petersburg 1908).

[12] Suidas, "Kyros," *Lexicon*, A. Adler, ed. (Leipzig 1933) III 220.
[13] John Malalas, *Chronographia* (361-362 Dindorf); Theophanes, *Chronographia*, A.M. 5,937, C. De Boor, ed., I 96-97. A. Frantz, in an otherwise very excellent article, is not convincing when she argues that the dedication by two Neoplatonistic philosophers of a statue to Herculius, Prefect of Illyricum, meant he held "pagan sympathies" (perhaps—perhaps not—the evidence seems inconclusive to me): "From Paganism to Christianity in the Temples of Athens," *DO Papers*, 19 (1965) 192.

at court and was exiled to Jerusalem in 443 Cyrus's political eclipse soon followed.[14] Eudocia's presence at court may have made it possible for the pagan historian, Olympiodorus of Thebes, to dedicate his *History* (partly tinged with pagan themes) to Theodosius II.[15] Olympiodorus's work, as will be shown, was an important example of eastern pagan interest in contemporary political affairs.

II

In the second half of the fifth century some pagans continued to show an interest in politics. Severianus was born in Damascus. His father wished him to study law. After his father's death he went to Athens to study under Proclus. Having mastered philosophy Severianus turned to a more active life and, according to Suidas, "thrust himself away from philosophy and the love of ease, and as a fortunate person took himself to political life and government."[16] Zachariah of Mitylene states that during the reign of Zeno the Alexandrian clergy protested the paganism of the *assessor* who was a subordinate of Entrichius, the Pretorian Prefect of Egypt:[17] " 'It is not proper for someone who is of the pagan religion to be a government *assessor* and to participate in affairs of government, for the laws and edicts of the emperors forbid it.' The prefect had difficulty in saving his *assessor* when they demanded him. He ordered us to remain quiet. Then the entire people rose up against the

[14] Cf. Cohn, "Eudokia," *RE*, 6 (1909) 906-908; also Seeck, "Kyros (Flavius Cyrus)," *RE*, 12 (1925) 188-190; and C. Diehl, "Athénaïs," *Figures byzantines*, 2nd edn. (Paris 1939) I 25-49; F. Gregorovius, *Athenaïs. Geschichte einer byzantinischen Kaiserin* (Leipzig 1892) 144-193.

[15] On the dedication of Olympiodorus' *History*: Photius, *Bibliotheca*, c. 80, R. Henry, ed. tr., *Bibliothèque* (Paris 1959) I 167.

[16] Suidas, "Severianos," *Lexicon* (IV 333 Adler).

[17] Zachariah of Mitylene, *Vie de Sévère*, M.-A. Kugener, ed. tr., *Patrologia Orientalis*, II 25.

pagans. Those who had been accused, took flight. . . ."[18] The Christian clergy were sometimes more effective in enforcing imperial anti-pagan legislation than were the imperial officials themselves.

Other pagan officials late in the fifth century included Demochares, the *scholasticus*, or jurist, of the district of Aphrodisias in Caria.[19] The embittered pagan, Zosimus of Constantinople, was *advocatus fisci* in addition to holding the important title of *comes*.[20] The pagan philosopher, Pamprepius was consul, senator, and *patricius* about 480-81 and became in 479 *quaestor*. In 484 he was an important participant in the rebellion of Illus and his candidate for the emperorship, Leontius, in opposition to Zeno. Pamprepius was not only an adviser but also *magister officiorum* of Leontius.[21] It was hardly surprising that pagans held official positions in the fifth century when law students, who were preparing for official careers, were delving into pagan magic and astrology.[22] The pagan Severus left Alexandria to return to Rome to become consul under Emperor Anthemius.[23] These cases are sufficiently numerous to indicate that many eastern pagans retained an interest in politics in the fifth century and might even hold public office. Imperial prohibitions against pagans holding high office or rank,

[18] *Ibid.*, 26-27.

[19] *Ibid.*, 39-40.

[20] Zosim., *Historia nova*, L. Mendelssohn, ed. (Leipzig 1887) xi-xv.

[21] Rhetorius, *Catalogus codicum astrologorum graecorum*, P. Boudreaux, ed. (Brussels 1922) VIII, Pt. 4, 221-224. Cf. W. Ensslin, "Pamprepios," *RE*, 18 Pt. 2 (1949) 411-412; for critical translation and commentary: O. Neugebauer and H.B. Van Hoesen, *Greek Horoscopes* (Memoirs of the American Philosophical Society, 48 [Philadelphia 1959]) no. L 440, 140-141. Theophanes, *Chronographia* (I 128 De Boor); Suidas, "Pamprepios," *Lexicon* (IV 14 Adler).

[22] Zachariah of Mitylene, *Vie de Sévère*, Kugener, ed., *PO*, 2. 57-75).

[23] Photius, *Bibliotheca*, cod. 242 (*PG*, 103. 1,266-1,268) = Damascius, *Das Leben des Philosophen Isidoros* (40-42 Asmus).

although on the books since the reign of Theodosius II, were not always strictly enforced.

Not all pagan hopes for political success of their religion had died with the failure of Julian the Apostate (361-63), the abortive rebellion of his cousin Procopius against Valens and Valentinian I (365-66), and the collapse of the revolt of Eugenius against Theodosius (394).[24] There was no evidence of concerted pagan political activity in the early decades of the fifth century. Two possible explanations may be offered. The pagans may have felt so weak, still reeling from the stern anti-pagan measures of Theodosius I and the failure of Eugenius's revolt in 394, that they were unable to engage actively in any political movement. Second, pagan intellectuals (such as Olympiodorus of Thebes) may have hoped for imperial tolerance through the good offices of the Empress Eudocia.[25] Pagan hopes for tolerance and imperial understanding probably disappeared only after the removal of Cyrus (late 441) as consul and prefect, and the first (439) and second—the permanent—exiles of Eudocia to Jerusalem (443).[26]

Thus some fifth-century pagans held pronounced political opinions, which is consistent with reports of pagan involvement in political movements and pagan officeholding in the east during the fifth century. Some, therefore, were interested in Roman or Byzantine politics. One must modify

[24] In general on Julian: J. Bidez, *La vie de l'empereur Julien* (Paris 1930); J. Geffcken, *Kaiser Julianus* (Leipzig 1914); A. Piganiol, *L'Empire chrétien* (325-395) (Paris 1947) 110-145. On the revolt of Procopius, Stein, *Histoire du bas-empire*, I 175-176; A. Solari, "La rivolta procopiana a Constantinopoli," *Byzantion*, 7 (1932) 143-148; and the recent article, G. L. Kurbatov, "Vosstanie Prokopiia (365-366 gg.)," *Vizantiskii Vremennik*, N.S., 14 (1958) 3-26, stresses the wide social support for this uprising.

[25] Suidas, "Kyros," *Lexicon* (III 220 Adler); F. Gregorovius, *Athenaïs*, 144-193; Diehl, "Athénaïs," *Figures byzantines*, I 25-49.

[26] For the dates, Stein, *Histoire du Bas-Empire*, 2nd edn., revised J. R. Palanque (Paris 1959) I 293-297.

Johannes Geffcken's statement, "We now see no longer among almost all these renowned [fifth-century pagans] a series of prominent officials and rhetoricians who in addition diligently attended to religious services; instead, almost all known pagans are mystics and theosophists."[27] It is hardly surprising that some of those eastern pagans did not remain indifferent to the fifth-century crisis of the Roman Empire. The ill-founded hopes and bitter experiences of fifth-century eastern pagan communities markedly influenced the views of those eastern pagans who did record their interpretations of Roman decline.

III

The basic arguments pagans were to employ concerning Roman decline in the fifth century had far earlier antecedents. Roman pagans had long argued that the Roman state had thus far survived because men had worshipped the gods in the duly prescribed manner. Cyprian and Tertullian report this thesis. About 180 Celsus, in his *True Speech*, addresses the Christians, expressing concern over the possibly deleterious political consequences of Christianity for the Roman Empire:

> You will surely not say that if the Romans were convinced by you and were to neglect their customary honors to both gods and men and were to call upon your Most High, or whatever name you prefer, He would come down and fight on their side, and they would have no need for any other defense. In earlier times also the same God made these promises and some far greater than these, so you say, to those who pay regard to him. But see how much help he has been to both them [the Jews] and you [the Christians]. Instead of being masters of the

[27] Geffcken, *Der Ausgang des griechisch-römischen Heidentums* 2nd edn. (Heidelberg 1929) 178.

whole world, they have been left no land or home of any kind. While in your case, if anyone does still wander about in secret, yet he is sought out and condemned to death.[28]

Arnobius reports that at the beginning of the fourth century pagans were charging that various calamities, including plagues and wars and locusts, began with and were attributable to the Christian religion.[29] These arguments contained the seed of the more elaborate theses concerning the religious origin of Roman decline which the pagans of the late fourth and fifth centuries developed.

Emperor Julian (361-63), in his treatise, *Against the Galilaeans* (Christians), written in 362, attempted to demonstrate a connection between political failure and Judaeo-Christian religion. He maintains that the historical evidence showed the gods had granted the Romans sovereignty over the world while the Hebrew God had not prevented the Jews from being enslaved: "Now answer this for me. Is it better to have been free continuously and to rule over most of earth and sea for two thousand entire years, or to be a slave and live according to another's command?"[30] He

[28] Origen, *Die acht Bücher gegen Celsus*, 8. 69, P. Koetschau, ed. (Leipzig 1899) II 285-286; quote from English translation, *Contra Celsum*, H. Chadwick, tr. (Cambridge, England 1953) 505. For the date of composition see H. Chadwick, *Contra Celsum*, Introduction, xiv-xv; and G. Bareille, "Celse," *DTC*, 2 (1939) 2,090-2,092. In general: P. de Labriolle, *La réaction païenne: étude sur la polémique antichrétienne du Ier au VIe siècle*, 9th edn. (Paris 1950) 111-134. Also: Cyprian, *Ad Demetrianum*, 2-7, W. Hartel, ed., *CSEL* (Vienna 1868) III. 1. 352-356; Tertullian, *Apologeticum* 40. 1-15 (*Opera*: Corpus Christianorum, Series Latina, Turnholt, 1954, I. 1. 153-155).

[29] Arnobii, *Adversus nationes libri vii.*, 1. 1, 1. 3, C. Marchesi, ed., 2nd edn. (Turin 1944) 1, 4.

[30] Iuliani imperatoris *librorum contra Christianos quae supersunt*, 218 A, 218 B, C.I. Neumann, ed. (Leipzig 1880) 202. On this work see P. de Labriolle, *La réaction païenne*, 395-425. On Julian's political philosophy: F. Dvornik, "The Emperor Julian's 'Reactionary' Ideas of Kingship," *Late Classical and Mediaeval Studies in Honor of Al-*

triumphantly notes that the pagans had produced great military leaders while the Hebrews could boast of none: "show me one general like Alexander or one like Caesar among the Hebrews. You have none."[31] He also asserts that the gods had conferred exemplary laws, political institutions, and literary brilliance on the "Hellēnes" (he uses the term here to signify both Greeks and pagans) and asks: "were not those of the Hebrews miserable and barbarous?"[32] Julian's low opinion of the political rewards of Christianity is best summarized in an ironical question he puts to the Christians: "Why has it happened that you have deserted to the Jews, showing ingratitude to the gods? Is it because the gods gave imperial authority to Rome, but granted freedom to the Jews for only a short time, and forever after they were to be slaves and exiles?"[33]

A few years later, in 390, the pagan rhetorician and orator of Antioch, Libanius, stressed the importance of the assistance of the gods for the prosperity of the Roman state. In his *Pro templis*, addressed to Theodosius I, he asserts:

> It was with the assistance of these gods that the Romans attacked their enemies, gave them battle, were victorious, and made the condition of those who were defeated better than it had been before their defeat by freeing them from fear, and by sharing the Roman constitution with them.[34]

He again emphasizes these points in a subsequent passage:

bert Mathias Friend, Jr. (Princeton 1955) 71-81; W.E. Kaegi, "The Emperor Julian's Assessment of the Significance and Function of History," *Proc Phil Soc* 108 (1964) 30-32.

[31] Julian, *Contra Christianos*, 218 B (202 Neumann).

[32] *Ibid.*, 221 E (202-203 Neumann).

[33] *Ibid.*, 209 D (200 Neumann).

[34] Libanius, *Oratio*, 30. 5, R. Förster, ed., Libanii . . . *Opera* (Leipzig 1906) III 90. Cf. R. Van Loy, "Le 'Pro Templis' de Libanius" *Byzantion*, 8 (1933) 21.

For let one of those who has abandoned forceps, hammers, and anvils and who deems himself worthy to discuss heaven and those in heaven, tell us which gods the Romans followed to be able to achieve the greatest deeds from their small and ordinary beginnings—the God of those people [Christian monks]—or those gods who have temples and altars and from whom the Romans heard through diviners what must be done and must not be done?[35]

In his famous *Relatio* on the Altar of Victory, the western Roman *Praefectus urbis*, Q. Aurelius Symmachus, vainly attempted to convince Emperor Valentinian II (384) that the prosperity of the Roman state was dependent on the continuation of proscribed pagan religious ceremonies.[36] By the end of the fourth century there existed a firm tradition of pagan propaganda affirming that the survival and political fortunes of Rome were intimately connected with performing traditional pagan rituals.

IV

It was from this general pagan argument, common in the fourth and earlier centuries, that the fifth-century pagans molded their own intellectual response to the events which had overtaken the western Roman provinces. The sources indicate that inhabitants of the eastern provinces did not remain indifferent to Alaric's sack of Rome. In his *De civitate Dei* (written between 413 and 426), Saint Augus-

[35] Libanius, *Or.*, 30. 31 (103 Förster); 30-31 Van Loy.
[36] See the edition and commentary, Symmachus, *Relatio*, 3. 2-3 in J. Wytzes, *Der Streit um den Altar der Viktoria* (Amsterdam 1936) 48, 113-114. On Symmachus cf. H. Bloch, "A New Document of the Last Pagan Revival in the West, 393-394," *HThR*, 38 (1945) 209-219; D. N. Robinson, "An Analysis of the Pagan Revival of the Late Fourth Century, with Especial Reference to Symmachus," *TAPA*, 46 (1915) 96-101; N. Casini, "Le discussioni sull' 'Ara Victoriae' nella curia romana," *Studi Romani*, 5 (1957) 501-517; Rev. J.J. Sheridan, "The Altar of Victory—Paganism's Last Battle," *Ant Cl*, 35 (1966) 186-206.

tine tells the Romans: "as we hear, the eastern multitudes bewail your ruin and the greatest cities in the most distant lands are brought to grief and mourning."[37] Presumably some of those grief-stricken easterners were pagans.

Eastern Christian works appeared during the first quarter of the fifth century which were intended to refute pagan charges that the rise of Christianity, the neglect and pagan worship, and the decline of the Roman Empire were all interrelated. No specific, extant sources, however, indicate that eastern pagans exploited Alaric's sack of Rome for propaganda purposes. Nevertheless, it is clear that eastern pagans early in the century openly discussed the general religious significance of the barbarian invasions. Saint Nilus of Ancyra, who died in 430, wrote a letter refuting the pagan rhetorician Apollodorus' charge that, "hordes of barbarians frequently are invading the Roman Empire because all men are not willing or eager to worship the gods with sacrifices."[38] Nilus's lost treatise, *Against the Pagans*, may have contained additional references to pagan arguments about the religious causes for the decline of the Roman Empire.[39]

The passage from Nilus's correspondence shows that eastern pagans were using arguments similar to those which pagans employed in the western Roman Empire. Augustine characterizes the arguments of his pagan opponents in these terms: "they ascribe the calamities of the Roman state to our religion because it prohibits sacrifices to their gods."[40]

[37] Augustine, *De civ. D.*, 1. 33, E. Hoffmann, ed., *CSEL*, 40. 1 (Vienna, Prague, Leipzig 1899) 56.

[38] Saint Nilus, *Epist.*, 1. 75 (*PG* 79. 116).

[39] J. Quasten, *Patrology* (Utrecht, Antwerp, Westminster, Md. 1960) III 502.

[40] Augustine, *De civ. D.*, 1. 36 (58 Hoffmann). It is also possible that the *Historia Augusta* was written in the west during this period. See the important recent study by J. Straub, *Heidnische Geschichts-apologetik in der christlichen Spätantike: Untersuchungen über Zeit und Tendenz der Historia Augusta*, Antiquitas, Reihe IV, Bd. I (Bonn 1963).

The pagans in both east and west had staked much on the use of this issue. Recently battered by the oppressive measures of Theodosius I, they hoped it would enable them to recover the right to performance of public sacrifices, to strengthen the convictions of disillusioned and wavering pagans and to win back some pagans who had converted to Christianity. But it was the last effective issue pagans used in an attempt to rescue themselves from their desperate condition and prevent the slow death of their religion, albeit that it again made paganism relevant to the contemporary political situation.

Nilus's refutation of pagan arguments concerning the relationship between the neglect of pagan ritual and barbarian invasions of the empire is found only in one letter of the 1,061 letters attributed to him. Apparently the issue did not occupy much of his attention.

Another fifth-century treatise, entitled *Quaestiones et responsiones ad orthodoxos*, now generally attributed to Theodoret of Cyrus (east of Antioch, in Syria), or at least to one of his contemporaries,[41] also contains a rebuttal of pagan charges about the unfavorable political results of the neglect of pagan religious ceremonies. Theodoret reports that the pagans were asking the following questions:

[41] For the attribution to Theodoret of Cyrus see the arguments of A. Papadopoulos-Kerameus in his new edition: *Zapiski istoriko-filologicheski fakultet*, St. Petersburg University, 36 (1895) ii-xii. Also see B. Altaner, *Patrology*, H. C. Graef, tr. (New York 1958) 397-398. M. de Brok denies that Theodoret was the author of the treatise, but agrees that the author was a contemporary of Theodoret: "De waarde van de 'Graecarum affectionum curatio' van Theodoretus van Cyrus als apologetisch werk," *Studia Catholica*, 27 (1952) 210; Quasten, *Patrology*, III 548-549, also believes that Theodoret wrote the *Quaestiones et responsiones ad orthodoxos*. G. Bardy is not positive that Theodoret was the author, but agrees that the composition date is mid-fifth century: "La littérature patristique des *'Quaestiones et responsiones*,'" *Revue Biblique*, 42 (1933) 212. Additional evidence for the attribution to Theodoret is presented by M. Richard, "Les citations de Théodoret conservées dans la chaîne de Nicétas sur l'Évangile selon Saint Luc," *Revue Biblique*, 43 (1934) 88-96.

If God repays the faithful with prosperity in this life—
as Abraham and Isaac and Jacob and their descendants
received wealth and good children and a bounty of fruits
—why were these same things given to the pagans who
formerly worshipped idols everywhere? Why would not
paganism seem more holy, because as long as it prevailed in cities, all cities and fields enjoyed complete
prosperity and abundance, and these conditions existed
even though wars were more frequent at that time? But
as it is, ever since the Christian message has taken hold
of these cities they have become emptied of houses, inhabitants, and the rest of their prosperity, and these cities
appear to possess scarcely the remains of those buildings
of the former pagans. How can the causes of the former
prosperity and the present desolation be attributed to
anything but the change of religions?[42]

Theodoret, however, shows only limited interest in such
pagan charges, because only once—in this quotation above
—does he discuss the question of Roman decline. Nevertheless, he believed the pagan thesis required at least some
reply. He does not refer to any pagan arguments about
Roman decline in his longest and most important apologetical treatise, *Graecarum affectionum curatio*.[43] Saint Augustine and his disciple, Orosius, indicate that western pagans
were using arguments similar to those Theodoret refuted.[44]

[42] Theodoret, *Quaestiones et responsiones ad orthodoxos, quaes.*
136, Papadopoulos-Kerameus, ed., 125-126. The phrasing of this question may indicate that some Christians had even begun to wonder
whether in fact conditions had not been better before Christianity
supplanted paganism.

[43] Theodoret, *Thérapeutique des maladies helléniques*, P. Canivet,
ed., 2 v. (Paris 1958).

[44] Augustine, *De civ. D.*, 1. 1; 1. 6; 2. 3; 2. 23; 3. 8; 3. 17-20;
3. 23-24; 3. 27-30; 5. 1; 5. 22; E. Hoffmann, ed., *CSEL*, 40 Pt. 1
(Vienna 1899) 4-5, 11-12, 62-63, 95-97, 117, 135-147, 150-151, 153-
158, 209-211, 257-258; *Pauli Orosii presbyteri historiarum adversum
paganos*, I prol., C. Zangemeister, ed., *CSEL*, 5 (Vienna 1882) 3-5.

V

During the fifth century an important medium for spreading pagan propaganda was historiography. But apparently only two pieces of eastern pagan, historical apologetics have survived from the early part of the century, the histories of Eunapius of Sardis and Olympiodorus of Thebes in Egypt. Eunapius (b. Sardis, in Lydia, 345-46, d. ca. 420) studied at Athens under Prohaeresius, a Christian sophist, and at Sardis under the pagan philosopher, Chrysanthius. The only extant, complete work of his is the *Lives of the Sophists*, a collection of biographies of pagan philosophers who lived between A.D. the second century and the end of the fourth century. Scholars disagree whether our present text of the *Lives* is a second edition, and if so, whether the author of this later edition is Eunapius himself.[45]

Only a few fragments remain from Eunapius's other major work, his *History*. They constitute a continuation of the *History* Dexippus wrote late in the third century.[46] The Patriarch, Photius, wrote in the ninth century that Eunapius's *History* had existed in two editions:

> . . . in the first edition he sowed much blasphemy against our pure Christian faith, extolled pagan superstition, and assailed the pious emperors frequently. But in the second edition, which he entitled *The New Edition*, he deleted the worst insolence and licentiousness which

[45] The best edition of the *Lives of the Sophists* = *Vitae Sophistarum* is Eunap., *VS*, G. Giangrande, ed. (Rome 1956). See W. Schmid, "Eunapios," *RE*, 6 (1907) 1,121-1,127; W. von Christ, W. Schmidt, O. Stählin, *Geschichte der griechischen Litteratur*, 6th edn. (Munich 1924) II 1,034-1,035; M.E. Colonna, *Gli storici bizantini* (Naples 1956) I 42-44; G. Moravcsik, *Byzantinoturcica*, 2nd edn. (Berlin 1958) I 259-261; G. Giangrande, "Vermutungen und Bemerkungen zum Text der Vitae Sophistarum des Eunapios," *RhM*, N.F., 99 (1956) 133-153.

[46] There is a standard edition of Eunapius's *History* ('Υπομνήματα ἱστορικὰ) in *FHG*, C. Muller, ed. (Paris 1868) IV 11-56.

he had scattered against piety. But he strung together the rest of his work which . . . still contained many indications of its former fanaticism.[47]

Most extant fragments of the *History* probably survive from the second edition, which Eunapius completed no earlier than 414, and describe events which took place between 270 and 404.[48]

In line with his extreme hostility to Christianity Eunapius devotes considerable attention to pagan propaganda themes in his *Lives of the Sophists*. It is hardly surprising, therefore, that in this collection of biographies he referred to the recent neglect of pagan worship and the destruction of pagan temples. He encountered the problems of explaining the role of the pagan gods in the failure of Julian's attempt to restore paganism, and in Theodosius I's rigorous anti-pagan policies.

The destruction of pagan temples and the prohibition of sacrifices may have convinced the Christians that the pagan gods were nonexistent, or at any rate powerless to defend themselves, but the pagans were not so easily persuaded to abjure the worship of their deities. But how did Eunapius explain why the gods, if so powerful, permitted these humiliations for paganism? His description of the life of a pagan diviner, Antoninus, son of the remarkable woman philosopher, Sosipatra, is instructive. Eunapius characterizes Antoninus in these complimentary terms:

[47] Photius stated that there were two editions of Eunapius's History: *Bibliotheca*, c. 77, *Bibliothèque*, R. Henry, ed. (Paris 1959) I 159. On this question: W. Chalmers, "The Νέα ἔκδοσις of Eunapius's *Histories*," *CQ*, N.S., 3 (1953) 170. On Eunapius's bitterness towards Christians: V. Biagi, "Eunapio e il cristianesimo," *Les quarante années de l'activité de Théophile Boreas* (Athens 1940) II 179-182; A. Momigliano, "Pagan and Christian Historiography in the Fourth Century A.D." *The Conflict Between Paganism and Christianity in the Fourth Century*, Momigliano, ed. (Oxford 1963) 95.

[48] For the date of composition of the *VS*: Chalmers, "The Νέα ἔκδοσις of Eunapius's *Histories*," 165.

Although he himself still appeared to be human and associated with men, he foretold to all of his associates that after his death the temple would no longer exist and even the great and holy temples of the Serapis would withdraw to darkness and formlessness and become transformed. A fabulous and formless darkness would hold sway over the most beautiful things on earth. Time vindicated all of his predictions and the matter terminated with the force of an oracle.[49]

Eunapius explains to his readers how the predictions of Antoninus were fulfilled. He narrates the looting and demolition of the temple of Serapis during Theodosius I's reign and ridicules the establishment of monks ("who looked like men but lived like pigs")[50] in the area. He describes the relics these monks worshipped as "the bones and skulls of those who had been executed for their numerous crimes . . . they exhibited them as gods and spent time with the bones and considered themselves better for disgracing themselves at the tombs"[51] and concludes: "This at least contributed to Antoninus' great reputation for foreknowledge and accuracy, because he told everyone that the temples would become tombs."[52] In this way Eunapius demonstrates to his readers that the neglect and destruction of pagan rites and temples had been anticipated by the gods, who had informed some pious pagans of these impending developments. Eunapius clung to his pagan convictions because the successful prediction of events by seers indicated to him that the gods did exist, and were able even recently to foresee events and communicate knowledge of the future to selected men who worshipped properly.

[49] Eunap., VS, 6. 9. 17, G. Giangrande, ed. (Rome 1956) 36; cf. ibid., 6. 11. 10-12 (40 Giangrande).
[50] Ibid., 9. 11. 6 (39 Giangrande).
[51] Ibid., 9. 11. 8 (39-40 Giangrande).
[52] Ibid., 9. 11. 10 (40 Giangrande).

Eunapius similarly describes the powers of foresight possessed by the fourth-century Neo-Platonic philosopher, Chrysanthius. The pagan emperor, Julian, had invited Chrysanthius to come to Constantinople to participate in his new government. Eunapius reports that Chrysanthius, although a pagan, on finding the omens unfavorable, had declined the invitation. Instead:

> Chrysanthius accepted the high priesthood of the province. Knowing the future clearly, he did not use his authority oppressively, nor did he erect temples as everyone hotly and excitedly ran to do, nor did he give special injury to the Christians. His manner was so quiet that in Lydia the restoration of the temples was virtually unnoticed. Then when the leadership passed to the other party [the Christians, after Julian's death], no innovations appeared to have been made, nor was much overall change evident, but everything was properly smoothed in orderliness and calmness. Only he was admired, while all the others were tossed as though in rough water. Some cowered and others who were previously humbled rose up. He was admired for these reasons: not only was he wise in predicting the future, but he made use of what he had perceived.[53]

Eunapius apparently approves of Chrysanthius' course of action, for he contrasts it with that of another Neo-Platonic philosopher, Maximus of Edessa, who had disregarded or twisted unfavorable signs and had needlessly rushed to join Julian's government.[54]

This is significant, if not astonishing. Eunapius as a fervent pagan might well have condemned Chrysanthius for disloyalty to Julian's program for restoring paganism. Cer-

[53] *Ibid.*, 23. 2. 7-9 (93-94 Giangrande).
[54] *Ibid.*, 7. 3. 9-7. 4. 14; 23. 1. 3-23 2. 5 (47-51, 91-93 Giangrande).

tainly the refusal of such an influential pagan as Chrysanthius to participate in Julian's government must have hindered its effectiveness and contributed to the failure of the mid-fourth-century pagan reaction. Nevertheless, Eunapius professes admiration for Chrysanthius' cleverness and prudence in avoiding a commitment which would have exposed him to danger when Julian's government collapsed with the emperor's death in June 363. Instead of regarding the conduct of Chrysanthius as a denial of paganism, the pagan historian regards it as a reaffirmation of the wisdom of the gods and another demonstration of the efficacy of interpretation of pagan omens. Chrysanthius had shown that when properly practiced, pagan ritual could still be of great utility in ordering one's life.

Eunapius digressed from his general narrative to report various pagan prophecies which had been fulfilled. He says that a hierophant of Eleusis had declared in his own presence that in the hierophant's own lifetime both "the destruction of the temples and the ruin of Greece" and the election of an inexperienced and unfit hierophant of the Eleusinian Mysteries would occur. Eunapius was convinced that these predictions had proven to be accurate. He reports that a subsequent hierophant was illegally chosen, who proved to be unfit. This violation of the sacred laws, coupled with Christian actions, had grave consequences: "The gates of Greece [Thermopylae] were thrown open to Alaric by the impiety of those men wearing black clothing [monks] who entered Greece unhindered with him, and by the breaking of the law and restriction of the hierophantic precepts."[55] Eunapius clearly believed that the Christians had helped to ruin part of the Roman Empire, yet he unwittingly admitted that one cause for the devastation of

[55] *Ibid.*, 7. 3. 5 (46 Giangrande); G. E. Mylonas, *Eleusis and the Eleusinian Mysteries* (Princeton 1961) 186.

Greece was a sacrilegious act of pagans themselves in illegally choosing a hierophant.

Eunapius viewed the disasters which fell upon the Roman Empire and paganism in the last years of the fourth century as events foretold to men by the gods and therefore understandable as prophesied. But he neglects a question raised by this reasoning—if the pagan gods had foreknowledge of the impending destruction of pagan worship, why did they not prevent this development from taking place? to what extent did the gods will that these events should occur? Saint Augustine had raised these questions in refuting pagan arguments in his *De civitate Dei.*[56]

Eunapius dated the commencement of Roman decline from the reign of Constantine I (307-37). He found particular significance in the murder of Constantine's *assessor,* Sopater, a pagan philosopher, by the emperor's own orders.[57] He assesses the importance of Sopater's death in these terms:

> The entire state found misfortune through the murder of one man. For by calculating by the dates, one understands that from the violent death of Socrates nothing glorious was done any longer by the Athenians, but the city decayed and because of her decay all Hellas was also destroyed with her. It is possible to see that this also occurred through the plot against Sopater. . . . In our times, neither the multitude of ships from Egypt nor the useful amount of grain brought from all Asia, Syria, and Phoenicia and the other provinces as tribute income was able to fill and satisfy the drunken multitude which Constantine evacuated from other cities and moved to Constantinople. For the sake of applause in the theaters,

[56] Augustine, *De civ. D.,* 1. 2-6, 1. 15 (6-12, 27-30 Hoffmann).
[57] Eunap., VS, 6. 2. 1-3, 6. 3. 1 (18-19, 21 Giangrande). On Sopater: Seeck, "Sopatros," RE², 3 (1929) 1,006-1,007.

he organized drinking bouts of vomiting men close to himself, because he loved praises and mention of his name by foolish men who scarcely were able to pronounce his name due to their stupidity.[58]

Clearly Eunapius, as a pagan from Sardis in Asia Minor, detested the establishment of the new Roman capital at Constantinople, regarding the event as an element of decadence. He considered the murder of Sopater as a turning point, as important for Roman history as the execution of Socrates was for Athenian and Greek history.

Eunapius, in his *Lives of the Sophists*, comments bitterly and pessimistically on the contemporary condition of both pagan worship and the Roman Empire, but apparently resigned himself to the events the gods had foretold to the wisest of pagan philosophers. He did not believe human beings could have averted the fated disasters. Perceiving, he thought, a connection between the decline of philosophy and religion and the deterioration of the Roman state, he noted that harmful political developments followed the murders of both Socrates and Sopater and observed that the best philosophers and emperors flourished concurrently.[59]

Fanatically hostile to the Christians, Eunapius wrote for a pagan audience, under no illusions that the Christians might again tolerate the performance of pagan ritual. He did not attempt to appeal to Christians for toleration, as had a few decades earlier Symmachus, Libanius, and Themistius. Eunapius seems to have been resigned to passive contemplation of the destruction of pagan temples and the prohibition of public, pagan religious ceremonies, still con-

---

[58] Eunap., VS, 6. 2. 5-8 (19-20 Giangrande). On the question of the grain supply to Constantinople: J. Teall, "The Grain Supply of the Byzantine Empire, 330-1025" *DO Papers*, 13 (1959) 91-93, 135-137.
[59] Eunap., VS, 2. 2. 6-8; 6. 2. 4-12 (5, 19-20 Giangrande).

vinced of the validity of the pagan gods.[60] And he did not hesitate to openly express his bitter sentiments.

It is unfortunate that so little of Eunapius's *History* remains. In this work he airs his pessimistic views on the current status of the Roman Empire even more fully than in his *Lives,* where he laid more emphasis on the condition of philosophical studies and the destruction of pagan worship. In his *History* he concentrates much criticism on the policies and habits of the Emperors Valens and Theodosius I. The reign of Valens (364-78) had been ruinous for the Roman Empire:

> They say that love of money is the source of all evil and there is nothing pleasant or useful in this evil. For from that beginning and from that excessive desire for money, irrational contentiousness and conflict are fostered and produced in men's minds. And when contentiousness has grown, it sprouts into strife and murders. The fruits which grow from murders are the destruction and ruin of the race. These converged in the reign of Valens.[61]

Eunapius's judgment on the consequences of the reign of Theodosius I is equally severe:

> Emperor Theodosius, on succeeding to so great an empire, bore witness to the ancients concerning how great and evil power is, and that men are impervious to and steadfast against everything except good fortune. When he had just assumed power, he acted like a youth who has just become rich through an inheritance from a father who had amassed much money by prudence and thrift.

---

[60] On Symmachus, Libanius, and Themistius: A. Momigliano, "Pagan and Christian Historiography in the Fourth Century A.D.," *Conflict Between Paganism and Christianity,* 95. On Themistius' plea for tolerance of paganism: G. Downey, *A History of Antioch in Syria* (Princeton 1961) 411.

[61] Eunap., *Hist.* frg. 38 (Muller, *FHG* IV 29).

On suddenly gaining possession of affairs, he rages exceedingly destructively against what he finds. So at that time the intelligent observer saw from a perspective how he [Theodosius] neglected no manner of evil and licentiousness, to the general destruction of affairs.[62]

He states that due to Theodosius, "our age has risked being wholly kicked about by jackasses."[63] Eunapius disliked not only Theodosius I but the very concentration of power in one man's hands. His reference to the opinion of the "ancients" is unmistakable evidence that he had not fully accepted the autocratic power of the emperor in the later empire.

Eunapius was conservative in holding to pagan religious views and in adhering to ancient political attitudes. Fifty years before he wrote his *History* the pagan Emperor Julian had also exhibited an extremely conservative, almost Republican Roman, position on the emperorship. Julian did not favored the exercise of absolute authority by the emperor, but instead argued that the emperor should be circumspect and not encroach on the traditional powers of the other magistrates of the Roman state. Thus Eunapius, like Julian, had coupled his religious conservatism with conservatism in political theory.[64]

Eunapius's *History* provides interesting insights into the opinions of a fifth-century eastern pagan on Roman religious and political decline. A consciousness of Roman decay pervades his writings.[65] However, he did not attempt to de-

[62] *Ibid.*, frg. 48 (*FHG* IV 35).

[63] *Ibid.*, frg. 65 [*sic*: should be "56"] (Muller, *FHG* IV 39).

[64] See esp. F. Dvornik, "The Emperor Julian's 'Reactionary' Ideas on Kingship," *Late Classical and Mediaeval Studies in Honor of Albert Mathias Friend Jr.* (Princeton 1955) 71-81. Also S. Mazzarino, "La propaganda senatoriale nel tardo impero," *Doxa*, 4 (1951) 121-148; and A. Alföldi, *A Conflict of Ideas in the Late Roman Empire: The Clash Between the Senate and Valentinian* I, H. Mattingly, tr. (Oxford 1952) 96-124.

[65] Eunap., *Hist.* frg. 65 [*sic*: should be 56] (*FHG* IV 39).

velop a general theory to account for this process of decline. Indeed he was too close to the deteriorating situation to be able to place events in any large perspective. Because in his opinion the disintegration of the empire and religion had begun only comparatively recently and was still continuing, he could place no final judgment on the process. Eunapius's *History* covered only the period up to 404 and makes no direct reference to the sack of Rome. Both his *Lives of the Sophists* and *History* are representative expressions of pagan gloom in the post-Theodosian period.

The bitterness and pessimism of Eunapius contrast with the fervent optimism of Rutilius Namatianus, a contemporary western pagan and native of Gaul.[66] In his well-known poem, *De reditu suo*, in which he describes his voyage from Rome to Gaul in 416, Rutilius expresses pride in Rome's past: "The stars which pursue without release their constant revolutions have seen no empire more beautiful."[67] He adds that, "Through just causes in your wars and without arrogant peace your eminent glory has reached the highest wealth."[68] Most important, he remained confident in Rome's promising future:

Things which cannot be submerged rise again with greater force,/ impelled they leap higher from the lowest

[66] On Rutilius: Martin Schanz, Carl Hosius, G. Kruger, *Geschichte der römischen Literatur*, 2nd edn. (Munich 1959) IV. 2, 38-41; J. Vessereau, *Cl. Rutilius Namatianus . . . l'oeuvre et l'auteur* (Paris 1904); P. de Labriolle, *La réaction païenne* 470-478. His paganism: Vessereau, *Rutilius* 276-279. His paganism has been denied by H. Schenkl, "Ein spätrömischer Dichter und sein Glaubensbekenntnis," *RhM*, N.F., 66 (1911) 393-416, but his arguments have not been accepted: Schanz, *Gesch. röm. Lit.*, IV. 2. 38n5; Labriolle, *La réaction païenne*, 474-478.

[67] Rutilius Namatianus, *De reditu suo*, 1. 81-82; R. Helm, ed. (Heidelberg 1933) 8; *Sur son retour*, J. Vessereau and F. Préchac, eds. trs., 2nd edn. (Paris 1961) 6. Cf. commentary of E. Merone, *Rutilius Claudius Namatianus, De reditu suo: commento filologico-semantico* (Naples 1955) 35.

[68] Rutilius, *De reditu suo*, 1. 89-90 (9 Helm); Merone 37; Vessereau-Préchac 6.

depths./ Just as a torch turned downwards recovers new strength,/ so you from a low condition soar more brilliantly above./ Offer the laws which will live through the Roman ages,/ only you need not fear the distaffs of the Fates/ . . . the centuries which remain to you are subject to no limits,/ as long as the earth stands firm and the heaven supports the stars.[69]

VI

Not every pagan historian of the first half of the fifth century shared Eunapius's hostility to the Roman emperors. A. Momigliano has asserted that by the end of the fourth century, "even the most optimistic pagan could no longer nurture illusions about Christian tolerance."[70] Yet at least one pagan appealed to a Christian emperor, arguing for an understanding of the pagan position—the historian Olympiodorus of Thebes, whose "religion was pagan," according to Photius.[71] Nevertheless, Olympiodorus dedicated his history (which he regarded as a collection of materials for a history rather than a finished history) to the Emperor Theodosius II (408-50), an extremely pious Christian.[72] This work covered the years 407-25. Only those fragments of it which Photius preserved in his *Bibliotheca* are extant.[73]

[69] *Ibid.*, 1. 129-138 (13-14 Helm); Merone 45-47; Vessereau-Préchac 8-9.

[70] Momigliano, "Pagan and Christian Historiography in the Fourth Century A.D.," *The Conflict Between Paganism and Christianity*, 95.

[71] Photius, c. 80, R. Henry, ed., *Bibliothèque*, I 166. On Olympiodorus: M. E. Colonna, *Gli storici bizantini* (Naples 1956) I 93; Moravcsik, *Byzantinoturcica*, I 468-470; and esp. E.A. Thompson, "Olympiodorus of Thebes," *CQ*, 38 (1944) 43-52. W. Christ, W. Schmid and O. Stählin, *Geschichte der griechischen Litteratur*, 6th edn. (Munich 1924) II. 2, 1,035-1,036.

[72] Photius, *Bibliotheca*, c. 80 (167 Henry); for Theodosius II's piety: Socrates, *Hist. Eccl.* VII. 22 (*PG*, 67. 784-8).

[73] Photius, *Bibliotheca*, c. 80; the best edition of Olympiodorus is now found in Photius, *Bibliothèque*, R. Henry, ed. tr. (Paris 1959) I 166-187.

E. A. Thompson, the only scholar who thus far has studied
Olympiodorus carefully, believes this historian wrote a clear
and factual record, while Eunapius composed a subjective
narrative.[74] But Thompson did not investigate the extent to
which Olympiodorus expressed pagan views in his history.
My close reading of the fragments reveals that the Egyptian
historian was not absolutely objective in his reporting and
did allow his pagan sentiments to affect his choice of subject matter, even though he dedicated his work to a very
self-conscious, Christian emperor.

Olympiodorus asserts that Alaric had been prevented
from crossing from Italy into Sicily in 410 by the power
of a sacred pagan statue at Rhegium. Photius summarizes
Olympiodorus's account: "[Olympiodorus] says that a consecrated statue erected there barred the passage. It was
consecrated, as he told the story, by the ancients to avert
the eruption of Etna and to prevent the crossing of barbarians by sea."[75] Olympiodorus points out that after this
statue was pulled down (in 421) during the reign of the
western emperor, Constantius III, "Sicily received damages
from the eruption of Etna and from the barbarians."[76] It
appears likely Olympiodorus included this description of
the destruction of the statue in an attempt to convince Theodosius II that pagan religious objects were useful—even
necessary—for the security and welfare of the Roman state.

Olympiodorus inserts another instance of the preventive
value of pagan statues for the empire. He describes the
events surrounding the discovery of three pagan "statues
of silver consecrated to halt the barbarians." During 421 the
Prefect of Thrace, Valerius, learned that these objects had
been found in his jurisdiction:

Valerius arrived at the spot and learned from the local

[74] Thompson, "Olympiodorus of Thebes," 47, 52.
[75] Photius, *Bibliothèque*, R. Henry, ed., I 171.
[76] *Ibid.*

inhabitants that the place was sacred and that the statues there had been consecrated by an ancient rite. He next referred this to the emperor [Constantius III] and received a letter commanding him to remove the objects which had been disclosed. Having excavated the place they discovered three statues made wholly of silver . . . facing to the northern region, that is, against barbarian territory. As soon as they had been removed—after just a few days—the nation of Goths overran all Thrace. It was only a short time later that Illyricum and Thrace itself were overrun by the Huns and Sarmatians. For between Thrace . . . and Illyricum the three consecrated statues were deposited, and it appeared that they had been consecrated against every barbarian.[77]

Here again Olympiodorus is attempting to show Theodosius II what terrible results had followed when an emperor heedlessly removed objects with the ability to ward off danger. He firmly believed recent evidence (his *History* was written soon after 425, probably before 427) indicated that pagan religious statues were essential for the protection of the Roman Empire from its numerous external enemies.[78] Olympiodorus therefore followed the same line of argument as had the fourth-century pagan apologists, Libanius and Symmachus.

The *History* of Olympiodorus also provides important evidence for assessing the impact on eastern pagans of Alaric's sack of Rome, in that it contains the earliest known, specific reference from an eastern pagan to Alaric's attack. Olympiodorus gives a brief report that Alaric had besieged and plundered Rome because the Romans had murdered Stilicho and because they failed to meet his own demands.

[77] *Ibid.*, I 177.
[78] On the date of composition see Thompson, "Olympiodorus of Thebes," 44.

He states that Alaric not only removed "incalculable wealth" from the city but took away Galla Placidia, the sister of Emperor Honorius.[79] He adds that the Romans' alliance with Sarus the Goth helped to cement Alaric's enmity against Rome, and notes that during Alaric's first siege of Rome (408) starvation forced the Romans to turn to cannibalism.[80] He then describes the fortunes of Galla Placidia in Visigothic captivity.[81] Such a detailed narrative of the capture of Rome demonstrates a great interest in the fortunes of the western Roman Empire.

Although he lived in the east during the 430s Olympiodorus was still impressed by the former size and magnificence of old Rome:

> . . . each of the large houses of Rome possessed everything which a city might contain: race tracks, forums, temples, fountains and different baths. Therefore [Olympiodorus] exclaimed: "One house becomes a town; a city contains five thousand towns." There were also enormous baths. . . . The city wall of Rome, measured by the geometer Ammon at the time of the first Goth attack against it, was shown to have a circumference of 21 [Roman] miles.[82]

In similar fashion Olympiodorus emphasizes the immense wealth of the city's inhabitants: "many Roman households received annually revenues of about 40 centenaria of gold from their properties, without counting grain, wine and all the other wares, which if added, tripled their income in gold."[83] Clearly the splendor of Rome overshadowed anything with which he was familiar in the east. Rome, to Olympiodorus, was incomparable with any other city in the

[79] Olympiodorus = Photius, *Bibliothèque* (I 167-168 Henry).
[80] *Ibid.*, I 168. [81] *Ibid.*, I 167, 173-176, 179.
[82] *Ibid.*, I 185. [83] *Ibid.*, I 185.

world, hence, its destruction made such a sharp impression on him.

Olympiodorus also relates how the pagan magician, Libanius, came to Ravenna during the reign of Galla Placidia and Constantius (421) promising to defeat the barbarian enemies of the empire without the use of arms. He attempted to accomplish this, but Placidia learned of the attempt and had Libanius executed.[84] Photius tells us no more. Olympiodorus's reference to the subject suggests he wanted Theodosius to examine the record of pagan attempts to defend Roman security.

Theodosius II's renewal of prohibitions against sacrificing (423) probably moved Olympiodorus to discuss the prophylactic use of pagan cult objects.[85] Since Olympiodorus seems to have written his history soon after 425, he probably included references to the efficacy of pagan ritual and statues in the hope of persuading the emperor to tolerate pagan statues and to rescind entirely or to modify the enforcement of his recent anti-pagan legislation.

It may at first seem surprising that a pagan would dare openly to dedicate a history containing pagan themes to an emperor noted for his devotion to Christianity. Empress Eudocia, a convert from paganism,[86] may have directly or indirectly encouraged Olympiodorus to address such a history to the emperor.[87] And, apparently, Theodosius II himself was at times tolerant of pagans, despite his Christian piety.[88] In such a context, Olympiodorus might have be-

[84] *Ibid.*, I 182-183.

[85] *Cod. Theod.*, 16. 10. 22, 16. 10. 23, T. Mommsen and P. Krueger, eds. (Berlin 1954) I Pt. 2, 904.

[86] See Charles Diehl, "Athénais," *Figures byzantines*, I 25-49 (Paris 1939); on the origins of Eudocia, John Malalas, *Chronographia*, L. Dindorf, ed. (Bonn 1831) 353.

[87] Suidas, *Lexicon*, 2,776, "Kyros," A. Adler, ed., III 220.

[88] Possibly a reference to paganism: Sinuthii Archimandritae *Vita a Besa*, c. 80, H. Wiesmann, tr., *CSCO*, 96, 22. Cf. the acute observation of Miss Alison Frantz, "From Paganism to Christianity in

lieved he could dare to write a history demonstrating the value of paganism to the empire, the existing anti-pagan legislation notwithstanding. Furthermore, he may have even hoped to convince the emperor to adopt a more tolerant attitude toward the performance of pagan rites and to permit the preservation of existing pagan temples.

Olympiodorus, then, was not nearly as pessimistic and bitter as Eunapius; he never openly placed responsibility on the Christians for contemporary conditions. Neither did he attempt to discuss Roman decline in terms of any general framework or theory of development. He, of course, said nothing critical of the Theodosian dynasty (unlike Eunapius or Zosimus) because he was addressing one of its members. Instead, he endeavored to persuade a member of the dynasty to adopt his own views on pagan religious rites and statues. He perceived evidence of damage being inflicted on the empire whenever paganism and its sacred objects were neglected or treated sacrilegiously—but there is no suggestion in the extant fragments of his *History* that the empire was facing imminent destruction or irrevocable decline.

VII

No available evidence survives concerning mid-fifth-century views of eastern pagans on the condition of the Roman Empire and on the state of pagan worship. In the third quarter of the century, however, it seems some eastern pagans were quite concerned about the critical situation of the state. Only in the last half of the fifth century are there reports that the pagans again hoped to seize political power and

---

the Temples of Athens," *DO Papers*, 19 (1965) 192-193: "The lines between pagan and Christian in fourth- and fifth-century Athens were perhaps not always as sharply drawn as might be expected, and at least some of the officials of both church and state seem to have been chosen for their skill in diplomacy, rather than for the strength of their convictions."

permanently restore public pagan worship. The pagan, Damascius, asserts that "Anthemius Emperor of Rome was a pagan and was of the same opinion as Severus, who was wholly devoted to idols. He chose Severus as consul and both had a secret wish to renew the defiling idols."[89] Actually, Anthemius appears to have been a sincere Christian. Yet it is clear that contemporary eastern pagans did share the views of Damascius, who declares that Severus "was a Roman. When Anthemius offered hopes that through his efforts fallen Rome would again be revived, Severus, who had withdrawn from Rome, returned to it and took the rank of consul."[90] Severus had been living in Alexandria.[91] His decision to travel west again to Rome demonstrated that he had not lost all hope in a rejuvenation of the Roman state by means of a restoration of pagan religious ceremonies. Nevertheless, his expectations were soon dashed: "Failing in politics, he turned to the quiet and easy life, with hatred for the inconveniences in government"; subsequently he retired to Alexandria.[92] Ricimer's murder of Anthemius in 472 ended the hopes of eastern pagans that pagan worship might be revived, together with the western Roman Empire itself, by pagan activity in the west.

A decade later eastern pagan hopes were even more strongly aroused by the revolt of the *magister militum per Orientem*, Illus, and his candidate for the throne, Leontius (484-88). Illus was a sincere Catholic who was rebelling in

[89] Photius, *Bibliotheca*, cod. 242 (*PG*, 103 1,276-1,277) = Damascius, *Das Leben des Philosophen Isidoros* (65 Asmus).

[90] Photius, *Bibliotheca*, cod. 242 (*PG*, 103 1,265) = Damascius, *Das Leben des Philosophen Isidoros* (40-41 Asmus). The coinage of Anthemius, discussed in the first chapter, has distinct Christian iconography.

[91] Photius, *Bibliotheca*, cod. 242 (*PG*, 103. 1,265) = Damascius, *Das Leben des Philosophen Isidoros* (41-42 Asmus).

[92] *Ibid.*

part against the monophysitism of Zeno,[93] but he managed to attract the fervent support of pagans such as the philosopher, Pamprepius. Having mentioned that Anthemius and Severus had a "secret wish to revive the defiling idols," Damascius says that "Illus and Leontius, whom Illus chose as emperor instead of Zeno, held similar opinions and wishes for impiety, since Pamprepius led them to this."[94] Pamprepius, *magister officiorum* for Leontius,[95] tried in vain to win over the support of such Alexandrian Neo-Platonists as Isidore.[96] Other late-fifth-century easterners held the same views as Damascius.

In his *Life of the Monk Isaac* and *Life of Severus of Antioch*, Zachariah of Mitylene presents important information showing Palestinians and Carians expected that major religious changes would result from Illus's rebellion. During the revolt of Illus, who, according to Zachariah, "was said to lean to paganism," Christians in the Gaza district feared that if this rebellion against Zeno succeeded, "the temples of the gods would be opened to the pagans."[97] Zachariah quotes the former pagan, Paralius of Aphrodisias in Caria:

> Remember how many sacrifices we offered as pagans, he said, in Caria to the pagan gods, when we asked them (these pretended gods), while extracting livers and examining them through magic, to teach us whether we, together with Leontius, Illus, and Pamprepius and all those who rebelled with them, would conquer the Em-

[93] On Illus's revolt see Stein, *Histoire du bas-empire*, J.-R. Palanque, ed. (Paris 1949) II 23-24, 28-31.

[94] Photius, *Bibliotheca*, cod. 242 (*PG*, 103. 1,276-1,277) = Damascius, *Das Leben des Philosophen Isidoros* (65-66 Asmus).

[95] Theophanes, *Chronographia*, A.M. 5,976 (I 130 De Boor).

[96] Damascius, *Das Leben des Philosophen Isidoros* (104-106 Asmus).

[97] Zacharias Rhetor, *Vita Isaiae monachi*, E. W. Brooks, ed. tr., *CSCO*, 103 Scriptores Syri, Ser. III, v. 25 (Paris 1907) 7.

peror Zeno of pious memory [honorably deceased]. We received a multitude of oracles and also promises that the Emperor Zeno could not resist our shock, that the time had come when Christianity would break up and disappear, and the cult of the pagans would revive.[98]

This is evidence that some pagans as late as 484 believed that paganism might again become supreme and that Christianity would be annihilated. The revolt of Illus and Leontius, however, did not fare well. Together with Pamprepius, they were compelled to flee to the remote Isaurian fortress of Papirius, where Zeno besieged them for four years. Illus and Leontius became convinced that Pamprepius had betrayed them, and therefore executed him in late November 484. They themselves were captured and executed in 488.[99]

VIII

It is difficult to perceive how the success of the Catholic Illus's revolt would have fulfilled all the expectations. The failure of the revolt had, in fact, two unfortunate consequences for eastern paganism. First, some pagans became disillusioned with paganism and began to drift to Christianity voluntarily. Zachariah of Mitylene states that the former pagan, Paralius of Aphrodisias, had become bewildered when the sacrifices offered on behalf of the rebellion had no effect: "When we sacrificed in those places located outside of the city, we remained without a sign, any vision, any answer, although previously we were accustomed to experience some illusion of this type. Perplexed, we sought and we wondered what this meant. We changed

[98] Zachariah of Mitylene, *Vie de Sévère* (Kugener, *PO*, 2. 40).
[99] Theophanes, *Chronographia*, A.M. 5,976 (I 129-130 De Boor) on the revolt of Illus and Leontius and the execution of Pamprepius; cf. also Malalas, *Chron.* (388-389 Dindorf); Joshua the Stylite, *Chron.* c. 15-17, W. Wright, ed. tr., 10-12 (Cambridge, England 1882). On the capture of Illus and Leontius, Theophanes, *Chron.*, A.M. 5,980 (132 De Boor).

the places of sacrifice. In spite of this, the so-called gods remained mute and their religion stayed without effect."[100] Paralius mentions these facts in a letter in which he attempted to induce his brothers to convert to Christianity, as he himself had done. Thus the failure of the great pagan hopes placed in the rebellion of Leontius and Illus helped to erode pagan self-confidence. After 488 there are no reports of pagans participating in the politics of the Byzantine Empire.

The second result of the revolt's failure was a harsh persecution of pagan intellectuals, especially in Egypt. Zeno, in cooperation with the Alexandrian patriarch, Peter Mongus, attempted to extirpate those who had opposed him. His agents searched for Isidore, Heraiskos, Horapollon, Ammonius, and Harpocras, for questioning. Harpocras escaped and Heraiskos died while in hiding. Isidore was jailed twice for interrogation, but ultimately was released. Ammonius and Horapollon converted to Christianity.[101] It was at this same time that the pagan physician, Gesius of Petra, who had hidden Heraiskos, was also frightened into a nominal conversion. The monk, Sophronius, reports that the conversion of Gesius under imperial pressure was a disgraceful sham: "he was baptized because he feared the threat of the emperor [Zeno]. And arising from the baptismal fount, he impiously recited that Homeric verse, 'Ajax utterly perished, when he drank the briny water.'"[102] One may suppose that other eastern pagans regarded their conversion to Christianity with no greater degree of respect. Legislation and persecution could not change pagan hearts; it could only

[100] Zachariah of Mitylene, *Vie de Sévère* (Kugener, *PO*, 2. 40-41).
[101] Damascius, *Das Leben des Philosophen Isidoros* (109-112 Asmus).
[102] Suidas, "Gesios," *Lexicon* (I 520-521 Adler); Sophronius Monachus, *De Gesio iatrosophista* in *Narratio miraculorum SS. Cyri et Iohannis* (*Spicilegium romanum*, A. Mai, ed. [Rome 1840] III 304-305).

compel superficial religious conformity, thus bringing about a slow death.

Eastern pagans, however, had not even presented a united front during the Leontius-Illus-Pamprepius revolt. There was no general pagan uprising in support of the insurgents. The neo-Platonist, Isidore, disliked and held aloof from Pamprepius.[103] Most eastern pagans probably confined themselves to a policy of wait-and-see before making any commitment to Zeno's opponents. The absence of cohesion among eastern pagans prevented them from mustering their full strength at critical moments, and made it easier for individual pagans to change their allegiance to Christianity, while the lack of effective leadership and organization made them vulnerable to external, Christian pressures and to internal disintegration.

Nevertheless, paganism had not become a completely lifeless religion in the east during the fifth century. Most pagans had inherited their religious practices and convictions from their parents, but pagan doctrines had sufficient intrinsic attractiveness even as late as the fifth century to induce men of other religions to convert to paganism. The sophist, Apollodorus, originally a pagan, had temporarily converted to Christianity early in the century, but relapsed into paganism, according to Saint Nilus: "For lately you seemed for a few days to have been purged of idol-madness by the message of Christ, but now having changed again, you evilly redden the statues with loathesome sacrifices."[104] This was a very rare example of a Christian reconverting to paganism in the fifth century. Another convert to paganism was Marinus of Neapolis in Palestine, who was born a Samaritan but converted to paganism.[105] Throughout the

[103] Damascius, *Das Leben des Philosophen Isidoros* (105-106 Asmus).
[104] Saint Nilus, *Epist.*, I 75 *Apollodoro Rhetori* (*PG*, 79. 116).
[105] Phot. *Bibl.* cod. 242 (*PG*, 103. 1,284).

period there always lurked the possibility that paganism might make a major resurgence. In light of the persistence of pagans in many regions of the empire, and the pagan participation in the revolt of Leontius and Illus, and finally, the ability of paganism to attract occasional converts, it becomes possible to understand the necessity of anti-pagan legislation in the fifth-century Byzantine Empire. Furthermore, the substantial number of fifth-century Christian treatises which refuted pagan arguments (surveyed at the beginning of this chapter) indicates that pagans even at that late date still did not hesitate to publicize their own views. The extensive anti-pagan legislation promulgated by Theodosius I had not succeeded in silencing eastern pagans.[106]

IX

Although their political aspirations died only with the failure of Illus (484-88),[107] throughout the century eastern pagans encountered serious obstacles in attempting to relate their principles to the contemporary situation. They were uncertain about the degree to which the gods themselves had influenced the course of Roman decline. If the gods knew Christians would attempt to suppress pagan rites why did they not prevent this outcome? Eastern pagans disagreed whether they should let matters take their own course or endeavor to influence developments. Confronted with the official prohibition of worship, the seizure and possible destruction of pagan temples and statues, what were pagans to do in the east? And were they to remain passive as they watched the western Roman Empire collapse?

[106] I must respectfully disagree with the opinion of N. Q. King, who claimed very effective enforcement of the anti-pagan legislation of Theodosius I: "The Theodosian Code as a Source for the Religious Policies of the First Byzantine Emperors," *Nottingham Mediaeval Studies*, 6 (1962) esp. 17.

[107] Zachariah, *Vie de Sévère* (Kugener, PO, 2. 41).

Under such circumstances, the pagans needed a rationale for maintaining their old religious loyalties. They needed to develop a new political role in a state where once alien religion had become the official cult. Eastern pagans of the early part of the fifth century had not yet placed all of these developments in some larger rational frame of reference. They managed to see in the suppression of their religion a vindication of the predictions of their gods. At the same time, they believed the crisis of the western provinces was related to the official neglect and persecution of pagan public worship. Therefore they found even in such negative developments further justification for remaining firm pagans. Until virtually the end of the fifth century no eastern pagan whose writings have survived seems to have accommodated himself—while remaining a pagan—to the reality of a Roman Empire being basically limited to the eastern provinces, centered at Constantinople and dominated by Christians. Earlier fifth-century pagans of the east believed that if the Roman Empire were to survive, either the ruling Christians must be overthrown or at least traditional, public pagan ritual must be fully restored; otherwise the Roman state would surely continue to disintegrate. Indeed, it was not until the very end of the century that a different pagan attitude appears merging with and developing from older views, in the *New History* written by Zosimus of Constantinople.

chapter iii

ZOSIMUS AND THE
CLIMAX OF PAGAN HISTORICAL
APOLOGETICS

After the collapse of Roman political authority in the west late in the fifth century only one pagan historian, eastern or western, explored the topic of Roman decline—Zosimus of Constantinople.[1] Having held the offices of *Comes* and *exadvocatus fisci*, he wrote his *Historia nova* (that is, *The New History* or *Modern History*) in six books at the end of the fifth century, or more likely, during the first twenty years of the next. Zosimus' pagan leanings may have caused him to lose his position as *advocatus fisci*, which would perhaps explain his bitterness. Although his writing has frequently served as a source for third- and fourth-century events it has received relatively little attention as a tract of pagan political propaganda. More than twenty years ago

[1] Old but interesting on Zosimus: O. von Ranke, *Weltgeschichte* (Leipzig 1883) IV. 2. 264-284. For other general works on Zosimus: W. Christ, W. Schmid, L. Stählin, *Geschichte der griechischen Litteratur*, 6th edn. (Munich 1924) II. 2. 1,037-1,038; G. Moravcsik, *Byzantinoturcica*, 2nd edn. (Berlin 1958) I 577-579; M. E. Colonna, *Gli storici bizantini* (Naples 1956) I 142-144; C. Hoefler, "Kritische Bemerkungen über den Zosimos und den Grad seiner Glaubwürdigkeit," *SB* Vienna, Philosophisch-historischen Classe, 95 (1880) 521-565; J. Leidig, *Quaestiones Zosimae* (Ansbach 1900); E. Condurachi, "Les idées politiques de Zosime," *Revista Clasică* 13-14 (1941-1942) 115-127; E. Stein, *Histoire du Bas-Empire*, J.-R. Palanque, rev. (Paris 1949) II 707-708; the standard critical edition is *Zosimi comitis et exadvocati fisci historia nova*, L. Mendelssohn, ed. (Leipzig 1887). P. de Labriolle, *La réaction païenne*, 9th edn. (Paris 1950) 479-481 includes only a brief discussion of Zosimus. See also: S. Impellizzeri, *La letteratura bizantina da Costantino agli Iconoclasti* (Bari 1965) 149-151.

the eminent Rumanian historian Emilio Condurachi wrote a penetrating article in which he called attention to the need for an intensive study of Zosimus' *New History*. (His appeal has been ignored—save by one of his students, Zoe Petre, and by N. N. Rozental—perhaps because his article appeared in a Rumanian classical journal during World War II and therefore could attract little attention.) In particular, Condurachi and Petre have correctly noted the extreme political conservatism of Zosimus.[2]

Unlike Eunapius and Olympiodorus of Thebes, who lived when the empire was deteriorating rapidly, Zosimus lived after Roman decay had already taken place in the west and at a date when the whole process of Roman decline might be placed in a larger perspective. Zosimus was the only eastern pagan whose writings have survived who attempted to make a comprehensive historical analysis of the decline of the Roman Empire. He endeavored to survey a much larger section of Roman history than Eunapius. He described ancient events from the Trojan Wars and the wars of the Roman Republic up to Alaric's siege of Rome in 410.[3] He made this a sweeping survey of ancient history in the hope of

[2] For the controversial date of Zosimus: Mendelssohn in his preface, pp. v-xii; for arguments (convincing to me) that the historian wrote in the early sixth century: T. Mommsen, "Zosimus," *BZ*, 12 (1903) 533; F. Rühl, "Wann schrieb Zosimus?" *RhM*, N.F., 46 (1891) 147; cf. Moravcsik, *Byzantinoturcica*, I 577-578. For Condurachi's observation: "Les idées politiques de Zosime," 127; also see Zoe Petre, "La pensée historique de Zosime," *Studii clasice*, 7 (1965) 263-272, and N.N. Rozental, "Religiozno-politicheskaia ideologiia Zosima," *Drevnii mir: Sbornik statei*, N.V. Piguleskaia, ed., Akademiia nauk SSSR, Inst. narodov Azii (Moscow 1962) 611-617. On the office of *advocatus fisci*: Kubitschek, "Advocatus fisci," *RE*, 1. 1 (1893) 438-39.

[3] It is uncertain how much beyond 410 Zosimus originally extended his history; later writers such as Evagrius Scholasticus (594) in his *Ecclesiastical History*, 3. 41, J. Bidez and L. Parmentier, eds. (London 1898) 140, believed Zosimus lived in the reign of Arcadius and Honorius; if so, Evagrius read an edition which also contained no further record than our extant one.

demonstrating to himself and to his readers that the pre-Christian period of Roman history had been far more fortunate for the Romans than had the Christian-dominated one. His *Historia nova* or *New History* not only provides an insight into the opinions of a late eastern pagan but also permits one to read the reflections of a Constantinople official who had gained direct political experience that probably influenced his views. His shallow, inconsistent, and superstitious arguments indicate how intellectually impoverished eastern paganism had become by the year 500.

Nevertheless, the *New History* is the last and most highly developed eastern pagan interpretation of Roman history, and therefore marks the climax of pagan historical apologetics. It is an interesting yet not unfamiliar phenomenon that this most comprehensive statement of a pagan interpretation of Roman history appeared when eastern paganism was waning and the last real eastern pagan attempt to recapture political power had failed. Fortunately, unlikely the histories of Eunapius and Olympiodorus, Zosimus' *New History* is fairly complete; only the section on Diocletian and that part which described Alaric's capture of Rome and subsequent events are missing.[4]

[4] It is possible that the chapter on Diocletian was later struck out by a zealous Christian copyist. On the crystallization and formalization of thought in the declining stages of a civilization see J. Huizinga, *The Waning of the Middle Ages*, F. Hopman, tr. (New York 1948) 31-45, 136. Zosimus must be regarded as the last pagan historian, unless one maintains that Procopius of Caesarea was a secret pagan. The evidence on the pagan and Christian tendencies in Procopius has been carefully reviewed by G. Downey, "Paganism and Christianity in Procopius," *Church History*, 18 (1949) 89-102. Strong arguments for the Christian persuasion of Procopius have been presented by B. Rubin, *Prokopios von Kaisareia* (Stuttgart 1954) 56-70. Cf. also O. Veh, *Zur Geschichtsschreibung und Weltauffassung des Prokop von Caesarea* (Bayreuth 1952) II 30; E. Stein, *Histoire du Bas-Empire*, revised by J.-R. Palanque (Paris 1949) II 716n1. On balance, I believe Procopius can be classified as a Christian, although a skeptical one. In no sense was he an open pagan apologist.

More emphatically than either Eunapius or Olympiodorus, Zosimus made Roman decline the theme of his history. He had read and indeed borrowed data from the works of Eunapius and Olympiodorus, but the basic mood of his history differed from that of his pagan predecessor, Eunapius, who viewed Roman decay in terms of political incompetence and corruption, barbarian invasions, and the disappearance of pagan rites.[5]

Zosimus, however, could point to far more serious evidence of Roman decline visible in his own day. By the time he was writing his *New History* the last eastern military expeditions to aid the ailing western Roman government had failed and there were no more western emperors. Furthermore, the empire had lost by abandonment, barbarian occupation, or outright secession many former Roman provinces, including Italy, and was reduced to the eastern provinces. Zosimus, unlike Eunapius, not only sensed the deterioration of the empire but also realized that he was now isolated in a sea of barbarism. He primarily sought to explain "how the Romans destroyed their empire,"[6] or, as he restates his aim in another passage: "When I reach those times in which the Roman Empire gradually became something small, barbarized, and ruined, at that time I shall explain both the causes of this misfortune and the oracles which disclosed the events which occurred."[7]

Assuming it was obvious to his readers that the Roman Empire had declined Zosimus did not attempt to prove that decay had taken place. He employs strong language in discussing decline but never defines his terms. He simply uses

[5] Zosim., *Hist. nov.*, 5. 27. 1 (250 Mendelssohn) actually refers to Olympiodorus of Thebes. On Zosimus' use of Eunapius see A. F. Norman, "Magnus in Ammianus, Eunapius, and Zosimus: New Evidence," *CQ*, N.S., 7 (1957) 132.

[6] Zosim., *Hist. nov.*, 1. 57. 1 (41 Mendelssohn).

[7] The quotation: *ibid.*, 1. 58. 4 (42-43 Mendelssohn); cf. *ibid.*, 2. 7. 1-2 (65 Mendelssohn).

phrases similar to those quoted in the previous paragraph: "[the empire had] diminished little by little," "sank to its present observed condition," "piecemeal destruction." He refers to the contemporary situation as "our present misfortune" or "provinces have perished piece by piece."[8] Zosimus essentially was not expressing an opinion about decadence of Roman culture or spiritual and religious life, but instead about the reduction of the physical size of the Roman Empire and the barbarian occupation and plunder of former imperial provinces.

Contemplation of this phenomenon of Roman decline stirred Zosimus' anger, shocked and inspired him to write the *New History*. He believed the process of Roman decline was brief but that it had lasted longer than one imperial reign.[9] He seems to have been fascinated in a macabre way by the magnitude of this process of decadence, and endeavored to use all of his faculties to understand its causes. But Zosimus lacked the sophistication and intellectual acumen of his second century B.C. model, Polybius of Megalopolis.

II

Regarding himself as an historian of Roman decline Zosimus conceived of himself as a latter-day counterpart of Polybius: "For just as Polybius explained how the Romans had built their empire in a short time, so I set out to tell how in not much time they destroyed it by their presumptions."[10] He began Book I with a rapid survey of ancient history. Having mentioned the Trojan War he quickly reviewed the Roman victories over Carthage and Macedon and then proceeded

---

8 *Ibid.*, 4. 59. 3 (216 Mendelssohn); 1. 1 (2 Mendelssohn); 4. 38. 1 (193-194 Mendelssohn); 2. 7. 2 (65 Mendelssohn); 3. 32. 6 (154 Mendelssohn).

9 *Ibid.*, 1. 57. 1 (41 Mendelssohn).

10 *Ibid.*, 1. 57. 1 (41 Mendelssohn).

to reflect on the basic causes for these major Roman achievements. In conformity with the presentation of Polybius, Zosimus also discussed the causes for the cessation of Roman expansion.

Polybius, in a famous passage in Book VI of his *Histories*, describes the nature, advantages, and deficiencies of six basic forms of political constitutions. He regards the Roman constitution as a fortunate combination of three of these forms—monarchy, aristocracy, and democracy: "it is evident that we must regard as the best constitution a combination of all these three varieties. . . ."[11] He also states, "The three kinds of government that I spoke of above all shared in the control of the Roman state. And such fairness and propriety in all respects was shown in the use of these three elements for drawing up the constitution and in its subsequent administration that it was impossible even for a native to pronounce with certainty whether the whole system was aristocratic, democratic, or monarchical."[12] Polybius outlines a theoretical cycle of constitutional evolution through which all states must pass:

> Now the first of these to come into being is monarchy, its growth being natural and unaided; and next arises kingship derived from monarchy by the aid of art and by the correction of defects. Monarchy first changes into its vicious allied form, tyranny; and next, the abolishment of both gives birth to aristocracy. Aristocracy by its very nature degenerates into oligarchy; and when the commons inflamed by anger take vengeance on this government for its unjust rule, democracy comes into being; and in due

[11] Polybius, *The Histories* 6. 3. 7, W. R. Paton, tr., Loeb Classical Library (London, New York 1923) III 273; Buettner-Wobst (Stuttgart 1962) II 242.
[12] *Ibid.*, 6. 11. 11 (295-297 Paton); Buettner-Wobst, II 256-257.

course the licence and lawlessness of this form of government produces mob rule to complete the series.[13]

To what extent does Zosimus attempt to apply the schematic framework of Polybius to explain Roman developments? He ignores Polybius's opinion that the Roman Republic possessed a "mixed constitution," regarding the Roman Republic as simply an "aristocracy." He was convinced this particular constitutional form had made possible the remarkable Roman territorial expansion. Having observed that "fortune [*tychē*] had subjugated the rest of Europe to the Romans,"[14] and having briefly mentioned the Roman conquest of Asia and Egypt, he comments:

As long as the aristocracy was preserved, the Romans succeeded in adding each year to the empire, consuls competing among themselves to excel in virtues. But Sulla and Marius and then Caesar and Pompey the Great engaged in civil wars. Therefore these wars destroyed the constitution. Abandoning the aristocracy, the Romans chose Octavian as monarch. Referring the entire administration to the will of this man, they forgot themselves and threw dice for the hopes of all men by risking to entrust such a great empire to the energy and power of one man. For even if he chose correctly and justly to govern the empire, he would not be able to deal with

[13] *Ibid.*, 6. 4. 7-10 (275 Paton); Buettner-Wobst, II 243. See esp. F. W. Walbank, *A Historical Commentary on Polybius* (Oxford 1957) I 635-662; K. von Fritz, *The Theory of the Mixed Constitution in Antiquity: A Critical Analysis of Polybius' Political Ideas* (New York 1954) 60-95; P. Pedech, *La méthode historique de Polybe* (Paris 1964) 308-317; A. Roveri, *Studi su Polibio*, in Studi pubblicati dall'Istituto di Filologia Classica, 17 (1964), Università degli Studi di Bologna, Facoltà di Lettere e Filosofia, esp. 180-192.

[14] Zosim., *Hist. nov.*, 1. 5. 1 (4 Mendelssohn). In general on Zosimus and Polybius see Zoe Petre, "La pensée historique de Zosime," *Studii clasice*, 7 (1965) 268-271, for a good discussion.

everything as was required, not being able immediately to assist in very different matters, nor will there be found so many rulers who would feel ashamed if they did not accomplish the orders given to them nor otherwise conform to the different opinions of so many minds. Or being corrupted, the state will be carried beyond the limits of kingship into tyranny and the government will be thrown into confusion and will ignore its faults and exchange justice for money and consider those people who are governed as domestic servants. Most emperors are of this type, rather, virtually all become such a person. It is quite necessary due to the irrational power of the ruler.[15]

Zosimus' opinions on the office of emperor are a remarkable testimony to the tenacious adhesion of some pagans to outdated political assumptions as well as anachronistic religious values. Condurachi correctly called attention to this problem, but his opinions require modification. He is not wholly correct in asserting that Zosimus regards the transition to the empire as the beginning of Roman decadence. Zosimus believes that the end of an "aristocratic" form of government was a regrettable development which halted Roman territorial growth and exposed the Roman state to some dangerous internal risks:

> For flatterers, being rewarded with gifts and honors from this tyrant, will assume the highest offices, while the modest and quiet men not choosing this life, properly complain that they do not enjoy these [benefits]. For this reason cities are filled with uprisings and disturbances, and the political and military rewards are surrendered to inferior officials, and life in peacetime is made painful and distressing for the more accomplished men, and the willingness of soldiers for war is ended.

[15] Zosim., *Hist. nov.*, 1. 5. 2-3 (5 Mendelssohn).

That such things happened in this manner was shown clearly by the experience of these events and by that which occurred immediately in the reign of Octavian. For the pantomime dance was introduced at that time, not yet having existed, when Pylades and Babullus arrived, and, in addition, other causes occurred for many evils that exist until today.[16]

Zosimus believes that some "evils" (*kakōn*) began during the reign of Augustus, and that these evils continued to plague the Roman state thereafter, but he does not specifically declare that this Roman constitutional change to rule by an emperor began the collapse of the Roman Empire. He does, however, ascribe the beginning of Roman ruin to the reign of Constantine I. Although some "evils" had begun under Augustus, Constantine "himself brought the beginning and seeds of destruction for affairs up to today."[17]

Another question is the extent to which Zosimus really applied Polybius's cyclical constitutional theory to Roman decline. Although Zosimus openly admits inspiration from Polybius he never declares that he was attempting to apply Polybius's theories. Unlike Polybius, Zosimus does not mention any "mixed constitution" in the Roman state. He declares in the above passage that "tyranny" would naturally succeed "kingship"—as Polybius had stated—but does not attempt to show that the Roman state was passing through all of the Polybian cycle. For example, according to Polybius, aristocracy should be followed not by "kingship" or "monarchy" but rather by "oligarchy" and "democracy."[18] Zosimus does not follow this pattern. Beyond his general

---

[16] Condurachi, "Les idées politiques de Zosime," *Revista Clasică,* 13-14 (1941-42), 119-121. The quotation is from Zosim., *Hist. nov.,* 1. 5. 4-6 (5-6 Mendelssohn).

[17] *Ibid.,* 2. 34. 2 (92 Mendelssohn).

[18] Polybius, *Histories,* 6. 8. 1-6. 9. 3, T. Buettner-Wobst, ed., II 248-249; cf. K. von Fritz, *The Theory of the Mixed Constitution,* esp. 184-219.

discussion of the transition from the "aristocracy" to "monarchy" and "tyranny" in the first century B.C., Zosimus makes no effort to discuss the basic nature of imperial power. He makes only three references to Polybius in his entire *New History*.[19] In summary, Zosimus certainly received some general inspiration from Polybius's analysis of constitutional development, but did not succeed and probably did not strive to follow Polybius's analytical framework too closely.

These traces of republican sentiment were a natural inheritance not merely from Polybius but also from the hostility and misgivings about the office of emperor which the senatorial aristocracy (and even the pagan emperor Julian) had held in the fourth century. Such an outlook could eventually be traced back to the early years of the Roman Empire.[20]

III

Zosimus considered the pre-Constantine years, 200-300, as a happy age for the Romans, when the gods favored the empire with victory and prosperity. The civil wars of the third century notwithstanding, he took a favorable view of overall conditions at that time. Zosimus believed, for example, that the gods had favored Septimius Severus and had showered benefits on the Romans during his reign.[21] (Eunapius had also spoken favorably of Septimius.)[22] Zosimus

[19] Zosim., *Hist. nov.*, 1. 1. 1; 1. 57. 1; 5. 20. 4 (1, 41, 240 Mendelssohn).

[20] F. Dvornik, "The Emperor Julian's 'Reactionary' Ideas on Kingship," *Late Classical and Mediaeval Studies in Honor of A. M. Friend Jr.* 71-81; Alföldi, *A Conflict of Ideas* 96-124; cf. Tacitus, *Annales*, 1. 2. 1; 1. 9. 5; 4. 18. 3; 15. 18. 1; 15. 68. 3; also: R. Syme, *Tacitus* (Oxford 1958) I 408-419; II 547-565; M.L.W. Laistner, *The Greater Roman Historians* (Berkeley 1947) 117-118, 132-138; in general: G. Boissier, *L'Opposition sous les Césars*, 5th edn. (Paris 1905), and R. MacMullen, *Enemies of the Roman Order* (Cambridge, Mass. 1966) 1-94.

[21] Zosim., *Hist. nov.* 1. 8. 1-2 (8 Mendelssohn).

[22] Eunap., *VS*, 2. 2. 7-8, G. Giangrande, ed. (Rome 1956) 5.

also sought to demonstrate that the victorious campaign of Emperor Aurelian (270-75) against Queen Zenobia and her Palmyrenes in 274 had been predicted by the gods. He describes, for example, the oracles issued by the temple of Apollo at Seleucia, Cilicia. After first reporting how the temple had relieved the district of locust plagues ("these things I grant to the good fortune of the men of that time, since our generation has shrugged off every divine kindness"),[23] he proceeded to invoking the oracles. The Palmyrenes, who inquired whether they would achieve domination of the east, were rebuked and answered negatively: "Leave my shrine, deceptive and baleful men, who cause pain to the generation of immortals."[24] Concerning the outcome of Aurelian's expedition against the Palmyrenes, the oracle predicted: "A falcon leads many doves to cold groaning, and they shudder at the carnage."[25]

Zosimus also observed that the Palmyrenes encountered an unfavorable sign at a sacred lake of Aphrodite, between Heliopolis and Bilbis in Syria. If offerings sank to the bottom, the goddess accepted them, if they floated, however, the goddess signified her rejection of the presents:

> The Palmyrenes in the year before their downfall met together at the occasion of the festival in honor of the goddess and threw gifts of gold, silver and robes into the lake. All sank to the bottom. But in the following year at the time of the festival they all were seen floating. The goddess by this means disclosed the outcome.[26]

Zosimus comments on this incident and Aurelian's capture of Palmyra and Queen Zenobia: "Such, therefore, was divine favor to the Romans because the sacred ritual was

[23] Zosim., *Hist. nov.*, 1. 57. 3 (41 Mendelssohn).
[24] *Ibid.*, 1. 57. 4 (41 Mendelssohn).
[25] *Ibid.*, 1. 57. 4 (42 Mendelssohn).
[26] *Ibid.*, 1. 58. 3 (42 Mendelssohn).

observed."[27] Zosimus also perceived divine support for Emperor Probus (276-82) in his wars against the Burgundians and Vandals: "fortune concurred in the will of the emperor."[28]

Finally, Zosimus argues that Diocletian, the last important pagan emperor to rule before the accession of Constantine I, had succeeded in creating a very effective defense system for the empire:

> Everywhere the frontiers of the Roman Empire were provided at intervals with cities, forts and towers through the foresight of Diocletian in the manner which I already mentioned. As the whole army settled at these, passage was made impracticable for the barbarians, since everywhere there was an opposing defensive force able to repel the invaders.[29]

Unfortunately, no other comments by Zosimus concerning Diocletian and his policies are extant. At any rate, it seems apparent that Zosimus believed the Roman Empire had been brought to a sound condition by Diocletian. It was only his successor, Constantine I, who "destroyed this security."[30]

Such fourth-century pagans as Emperor Julian possessed no clear idea of what was the most ideal period in history, although they were dissatisfied with present conditions and were attempting to return to older customs. Zosimus similarly may have had no precise, ideal former period in mind.[31]

[27] Ibid., 1. 58. 4 (42 Mendelssohn).

[28] Ibid., 1. 68. 1-2 (49 Mendelssohn); his coverage of Probus in general: 1. 65. 1-1. 71. 4 (46-53 Mendelssohn).

[29] Ibid., 2. 34. 1 (91 Mendelssohn).

[30] Ibid., 2. 34. 2 (91 Mendelssohn).

[31] R. Andreotti, Il regno dell' Imperatore Giuliano (Bologna 1936) 127-128, observed that although the pagan emperor Julian (361-363) admired the past achievements of the Greeks and Romans, and although he sought to restore an earlier state of affairs, he seems to have been uncertain as to which particular period of ancient history enjoyed the ideal political constitution.

Zosimus attributes Roman success in the pre-Constantine period in establishing and maintaining an empire not to objective physical factors but to divine causes. The rise of the Romans to great political and military authority was not primarily for constitutional reasons (as Polybius had argued in his history); it was for religious ones: the most important force acting to promote Roman expansion had been *Pronoia* (Providence, or Foreknowledge). At the beginning of his *New History* Zosimus declares that the Romans had remained relatively stagnant and had accomplished little during their first 600 years of existence, but in less than fifty-three years they had mastered Africa, Italy, Spain, and then even Greece and Macedonia. As he observes in his first chapter:

> No person therefore can suppose that all of this proceeded from mere human causes, but rather it was due either to fatal necessity, or to the influence of the planets, or to the will of God who regards with favor all of our actions when they are just. For these provide for future contingencies by such a train of apparent causes, that thinking persons must conclude that the administration of human affairs is in the hands of a divine providence [*Pronoia*], so that when it guides souls there is prosperity, but if it is not present the affairs of state are brought to their current observable condition. It is necessary to make clear what I mean from the facts.[32]

It was divine *Pronoia* that had abandoned mankind when the Romans ceased to worship the gods according to the prescribed traditional religious ritual.

The meaning and nature of *Pronoia* was a subject of great concern to many of the intellectual elite, both Christian and pagan, of the eastern provinces of the Roman Empire during the fifth century. Christians such as Theodoret of

[32] Zosim., *Hist. nov.*, 1. 1. 2 (1-2 Mendelssohn).

Cyrus, Synesius of Cyrene and in Africa, Saint Augustine, discussed Providence, as did the century's most prominent pagan philosopher, Proclus.[33] Zosimus by his own admission conceived his role in writing the *New History* to be the tracing of the effectiveness of the *Pronoia* of the gods in human history, especially in the recent record of Roman events. Zosimus' notion of the causes influencing *Pronoia* is obscure. Although *Pronoia* might influence the course of human developments decisively, without regard for human conduct, human neglect of divine worship might also stir these gods to cease blessing men with their *Pronoia*. Nevertheless, despite man's failings and misconduct and omission of required duties, Zosimus believed that the gods could still mercifully continue to care for mortals and bestow *Pronoia* on them.[34] He never spoke in more precise terms about his conception of *Pronoia*.

Despite his criticism of the emperors Zosimus remained loyal to Rome. Indeed, the zealous attachment to Rome of Greek-speaking inhabitants of the eastern provinces such as Zosimus at a time when Rome could no longer dominate

[33] Theodoret of Cyrus, *De providentia* (*PG*, 83. 555-774). There is a modern translation with detailed analysis of the work, by Y. Azéma, *Discours sur la providence* (Paris 1954); Synesius, *Aegyptii sive De providentia*, critical edition found in Synesius Cyrenensis *Opuscula*, N. Terzaghi, ed. (Rome 1944) 63-131; cf. the analysis and commentary by S. Nicolosi, *Il 'De providentia' di Sinesio di Cirene* (Padova 1959); Saint Augustine discusses Providence esp. in Book V, *De civ. D.* (in particular Chapters 11 and 21). On Proclus' *De providentia*, preserved only in a Latin translation; see the edn. by H. Boese, *Procli Diadochi tria opuscula* (Berlin 1960) 109-171; for a brief discussion of this work, see: R. Beutler, "Proklos," *RE*, 23 Pt. 1 (1957) 200. See Hermann Dörries, *Das Selbstzeugnis Kaiser Konstantins*, Abh. Göttingen, Philologisch-historische Klasse, 3. Folge, Nr. 34 (Göttingen 1954) 353-355, for a lengthy discussion of the concept of *pronoia* in Late Antiquity.

[34] Zosim., *Hist. nov.*, 1. 58. 4 (42-43 Mendelssohn), for the gods' decision to cease protecting the Romans. But the gods might continue despite human frailty, to bestow their providence on men, for the gods do as they choose. *Ibid.*, 5. 24. 8 (247 Mendelssohn).

the Greeks was a remarkable tribute to the Empire's persistent ability to assimilate subject peoples and transform them into Romans.

Naturally Zosimus regarded Roman political decline as part of a much larger process involving the decay of religion, the deterioration of military strength, and the waning of moral strictness. His view derives not from any sophisticated perception of the interrelationship of all aspects of his society but from a primitive fear that impiety must adversely affect all elements of a society or civilization. His work is impressive testimony to the strong impact the disappearance of Roman government in the west made on an eastern pagan even several decades after the western provinces had fallen to the barbarians.

Zosimus does not openly address his *New History* to eastern Christians, nor does he attempt to debate the causes of Roman decline with any particular group of people. Clearly some Christians did read his work, for it made a sufficiently persuasive case to inspire Evagrius to insert a Christian refutation of Zosimus' thesis in his *Historia ecclesiastica*.[35] It is remarkable that a pagan dared to write such a bitter work at this late date. The existence of this history, let alone its zealous exposition of pagan propaganda, is evidence that individual pagans at the end of the fifth century remained quite as adamantly attached to their own religious views and as bitterly hostile to the Christians as any pagan had been in the fourth century or earlier. The very fact that Zosimus wrote this history when he did demonstrates that the apologetical labors of Saint Augustine and Orosius in the west, and the arguments of such eastern Christians as Theodoret of Cyrus and Saint Nilus of Ancyra, had not silenced or refuted the convictions of all eastern pagans.

[35] Evagrius, *Hist. Eccl.*, 3. 40-41, J. Bidez and L. Parmentier, eds. (London 1898) 139-144.

These pagans remained convinced that the critical situation of the Roman Empire in the fifth century was due to the failure to perform the necessary traditional pagan ceremonies (which had in the past secured divine protection for the Roman state). When Augustine had written (413-26) his *De civitate Dei*, he could rightly maintain that the Roman Empire had sustained some severe shocks recently, but certainly these shocks were no more serious than those it had received in the pre-Christian era, which did not at all indicate the state was collapsing. By Zosimus' time it was evident that half of the empire had disappeared from Roman authority, hence Roman decline was an established fact, the causes for which pagans and Christians might debate, but no one could deny that the western half of the empire no longer existed as Roman.[36]

IV

Although highly critical of the Roman emperors and convinced that many evils for the Roman state had begun with the establishment of the empire under Augustus Caesar,[37] Zosimus believed that Roman decadence truly began early in the fourth century A.D. Polybius himself had stated that governments were subject to two forms of decay, natural internal disintegration and change from one constitutional form to another, plus the possibility that some incalculable external force—chance or fortune (*tychē*)—might ruin the state.[38] Specialists disagree on the meaning Polybius assigned to *tychē*; sometimes he implied it was simply the

[36] Augustine, *De civ. D.*, 1. 1-2; 1. 6; 1. 30; 1. 33; 2. 3; 2. 23; 3. 8; 3. 17-20; 3. 23-24; 3. 27-30; 5. 1; 5. 22; E. Hoffmann, ed., *CSEL*, 40 Pt. 1 (Vienna 1899), 4-6, 11-12, 52-53, 56, 62-63, 95-97, 117, 135-147, 150-151, 153-158, 209-211, 257-258; *Pauli Orosii historiarum adversum paganos*, I, *prol.*, C. Zangemeister, ed., *CSEL*, 5 (Vienna 1882) 3-5.

[37] Zosim., *Hist. nov.*, 1. 6. 1 (6 Mendelssohn).

[38] Polybius, *Historiae*, 6. 57. 1-10, T. Buettner-Wobst, ed. (Stuttgart 1962) II 307-308.

unpredictable factor in a particular situation, while at other times he suggests it was a positive, divine force that actively shaped events.[39] Zosimus, attempting to be the Polybius of Late Antiquity, generally uses *tychē* or *Pronoia* in the second sense, that of a divine power actively shaping events in a particular direction. He did believe, however, that human beings might affect the working of this force by performing or neglecting traditional religious rites.[40]

Zosimus emphasized that the pre-Constantine Roman Empire had enjoyed good conditions because it had been blessed with divine favor.[41] The gods withdrew their favor, he observes, due to a chain of causes which originated in the reign of Constantine I (307-37). Zosimus devotes six chapters of his *History* to an account of the origin and nature of the Roman Secular Games which had taken place at Rome every 100 or 110 years as a religious ceremony to celebrate the beginning of the new "century" or "age."[42] In his view, performance of these games had gained the favor of the pagan gods, who reciprocated by protecting and preserving the Roman Empire. Zosimus notes that the last time the games had been duly held was during the reign of Emperor Septimius Severus in 204. (He fails to mention that Emperor Phillip, "the Arab," later celebrated an alternate series of Games.)[43] He observes:

When these [games] were held according to law, the empire of the Romans was protected and the Romans continued to possess what we call "the inhabited world." But because the festival has been neglected since Diocletian abdicated the throne, the empire has gradually de-

[39] See the important comments of F. W. Walbank, *A Historical Commentary on Polybius* (Oxford 1957) I 16-26.
[40] See Zosim., *Hist. nov.*, 1. 58. 4 (42-43 Mendelssohn).
[41] *Ibid.*
[42] *Ibid.*, 2. 1-7 (54-65 Mendelssohn).
[43] *Ibid.*, 2. 7. 1-2 (64-65 Mendelssohn).

clined and disappeared, having become largely barbarized, as events themselves have revealed to us. I wish to show the true explanation for this from the dates. For since the consulate of Chilo and Libo, when Severus held the festival of the Secular Games, up to the ninth consulate of Diocletian and the eighth consulate of Maximian, 101 years had passed. At that time Diocletian resigned as emperor and Maximian did likewise. When the third consulate of Constantine and Licinius arrived, the 110 years had passed according to which it was necessary to have held the festival, as prescribed by law. But since this was not observed, it was necessary for conditions to reach our present distressing ill fortune.[44]

This argument is a typical product of Zosimus' thinking. In it he demonstrates his preoccupation with the performance of traditional ritual: an oracle which had prescribed these games was ignored, an exact ceremony was not followed; consequently calamity struck the state.

Zosimus perceived a significant connection between Constantine's reign and the neglect of religious practices he deemed vital for the survival of Rome. He maintains that it was the sound advice of pagan soothsayers that had enabled Constantine to achieve power in the first place. He charges that Constantine himself had recognized the utility and perspicacity of pagan prophecies: "Because many successes had been prophesied to him and had been actually produced, he feared lest others would learn something predicted against himself. For this reason he applied himself to suppressing these [soothsayers]."[45] Zosimus further argues that Constantine chose to abandon paganism only when pa-

---

[44] *Ibid.*
[45] *Ibid.*, 2. 29. 4 (86 Mendelssohn). For the law: *Cod. Theod.*, 16. 10. 1. On Constantine's earlier reliance on pagan soothsayers see Zosim., *Hist. nov.*, 2. 29. 1 (85 Mendelssohn).

gan priests refused to grant absolution for the execution of his wife, Fausta, and son, Crispus. He declares that Constantine had been converted by an Egyptian Christian's promise that "those impious men who accepted Christianity would be at once delivered from all faults."[46]

The reference to Constantine's conversion is Zosimus' first direct mention of Christianity in his *New History*. Indeed it is one of his few characterizations of Christian doctrine, for he seldom discusses Christian beliefs. Perhaps he made a conscious decision to ignore the tenets of Christianity in his work. With the exception of this account of Constantine's conversion, he fails to provide his readers with any explanation for the appearance and eventual dominance of Christianity as the religion of the Roman Empire.

Zosimus maintains that Constantine I had contributed to the destruction of the Roman state not only by neglecting to hold the Secular Games but also by pursuing harmful, political, fiscal, and military programs—the establishment of the capital at Constantinople, the expenditure of large sums of state funds on its beautification and upkeep, the removal of troops from the frontiers and the concentration of them in cities far inside the borders where they became soft and a public burden, and finally, the institution of oppressive taxes, most notably the *chrysargyrum*.[47] Zosimus

---

[46] Zosim., *Hist. nov.*, 2. 29. 3 (86 Mendelssohn). The bibliography on the question of Constantine's conversion is too lengthy to cite in full. Some comparatively recent studies of significance: A. Piganiol, "L' État actuel de la question constantinienne," *Historia*, 1 (1950) 82-96; A. Alföldi, *The Conversion of Constantine and Pagan Rome*, H. Mattingly, tr. (Oxford 1948); H. Dörries, *Das Selbstzeugnis Kaiser Konstantins, Abh. Göttingen*, Philologisch-historische Klasse, 3. Folge, Nr. 34 (Göttingen 1954); H. Kraft, *Kaiser Konstantins religiöse Entwicklung* (Tübingen 1955) 1-61; P. Franchi de' Cavalieri, *Constantiniana*, Studi e Testi, 171 (Vatican City 1953) 5-50.

[47] Zosim., *Hist. nov.*, 2. 30-34, 2. 38 (87-92, 96-97 Mendelssohn). On the *chrysargyrum* see O. Seeck, "*Collatio lustralis*," *RE*, 4 (1901) 370-376; J. Karayannopoulos, *Das Finanzwesen des frühbyzantinischen Staates* (Munich 1958) 129-137.

concludes his catalogue of the policies of Constantine with: "he himself brought the beginning and seeds of destruction for affairs up to the present day."[48]

We may conclude that E. Condurachi exaggerated in declaring that Zosimus believed the beginning of Roman decadence occurred in the reign of Augustus Caesar.[49] The pagan historian, it is true, criticized Augustus for permitting mimes to perform in Rome, and he did comment that this was the commencement of evils that lasted up to his own time. But he used far stronger terminology in speaking of the consequences of Constantine's rule, and in asserting that "destruction" (*apoleias*) began at that time. There is another reason why Condurachi's argument should be rejected. Zosimus said clearly that he regarded the process of Roman decline as a short one ("in not much time the Romans by their presumptions destroyed [the Roman Empire]").[50] Because Zosimus believed the empire was ruined so swiftly he could not conceivably have thought that serious imperial decline began with Augustus—this would have stretched the process of decay over several centuries. He was unquestionably displeased with the substitution of an emperor for government by the consuls and the senate, but it seems clear from his language that he regarded the real crisis of the empire to have begun with the first Christian emperor.

Zosimus took a critical view of the course of events in the empire subsequent to the death of Constantine I in 337. He notes that Constantine's son and successor, Constantius II (337-61), "was unable to bear his fortune moderately." He furthermore observes that Magnentius, the imperial pretender in Gaul (350-53), "did nothing from good

---

[48] Zosim., *Hist. nov.*, 2. 34. 2 (92 Mendelssohn).
[49] E. Condurachi, "Les idées politiques de Zosime," *Revista Clasică*, 13-14 (1941-1942) 119.
[50] Zosim., *Hist. nov.*, 1. 57. 1 (41 Mendelssohn).

intentions."[51] He believed that the reign of Constantius' cousin and successor, pagan Emperor Julian (361-63), was an important landmark in the process of Roman decline, for in his eyes Julian's death brought in its wake greater political harm for the state than had occurred since the establishment of the empire. His chronicle of Julian's reign is largely a narrative of military campaigns; it contains almost no information concerning the emperor's restoration of pagan worship or data on his other internal policies (such passages may have been expurgated by Christian copyists).[52] He perceives religious significance in the death of Julian, who had proceeded to invade Sassanid Persia, "although the sacrifices were unfavorable to him."[53]

Zosimus saw important consequences for the empire arising from Julian's death. Other Roman leaders such as Crassus and Emperors Gordian and Valerian had been disastrously defeated by the Persians, but the Romans, even after these defeats, had never surrendered territory to this eastern foe:

> But only the death of the Emperor Julian was sufficient to destroy these provinces [Roman territories east of the Tigris, Nisibis, and part of Mesopotamia] so that until this day the Roman emperors have not been able to recover them. Furthermore, they have lost in addition the majority of the other provinces, some having become independent, others having been surrendered to barbarians while other provinces remained in extreme destitution.[54]

[51] On Constantius: *ibid.*, 2. 55. 1 (110 Mendelssohn); on Magnentius: *ibid.*, 2. 54. 2 (110 Mendelssohn).

[52] See the remark by A. Piganiol, *L'Empire chrétien* (325-395) (Paris 1947) p. vii.

[53] Zosim., *Hist. nov.*, 3. 12. 1 (128 Mendelssohn), stated that although he knew why Julian had continued on the Persian expedition despite unfavorable omens, he would pass over it.

[54] *Ibid.*, 3. 32. 6 (154 Mendelssohn).

Zosimus was convinced that a "divine force" (*daimōn*) was responsible for Julian's death.[55] As the above passage indicates, he also believed Julian's death brought in its wake the first in a long series of losses of Roman provinces. He perceived a relationship between the emperor's decease and the moribund state of the empire in his own day.[56]

V

Although Zosimus stated at the beginning of his history that he intended to demonstrate how Providence worked and how the empire declined so rapidly, he never expounded this thesis smoothly. He did not argue at every point in his narrative that neglect of traditional pagan worship had brought about Roman decadence. Instead, he abruptly inserts his thesis in the midst of a discussion of a particular event. He records the reigns of the brothers Valentinian I (western Emperor, 364-75) and Valens (eastern Emperor, 364-78) at some length. He notes carefully that the death of Valentinian was followed by a lightning flash in the city of Sirmium (in Illyricum) which burned down the local palace and marketplace: "it seemed to those men who were wise in discerning such things that it was not an auspicious portent for public affairs."[57] But in the same chapter he also describes how the gods might still protect mankind if men would observe their traditional pagan religious duties. Earthquakes occurred, he declares, in many places at that time, bringing destruction upon Greece and Crete in particular. Athens and surrounding Attica, however, were spared due to the favor of the pagan gods:

> They say that the city was saved for this reason. Nestorius had been appointed hierophant at that time and

55 *Ibid.*, 4. 4. 3 (161 Mendelssohn).
56 *Ibid.*, 3. 32. 6 (154 Mendelssohn).
57 *Ibid.*, 4. 18. 1 (172 Mendelssohn).

he had a dream in which he was ordered to give public honors to the hero Achilles, for this would be the salvation of the city. But when he shared his vision with those in authority, they thought that he was spinning a tale since he was a very old man. They put no trust in his words. But he reasoned out what was necessary and with divine inspiration created in a small house an image of the hero and placed it under the statue of Athena which stood in the Parthenon. And at that same time as he made the usual sacrifices to Athena, he did what he had been ordered to do on behalf of the hero. And, in this way, by fulfilling the advice of the dream in practice, when the earthquake occurred only Athens together with Attica (which also shared in the favor of the hero) were saved.[58]

To Zosimus this event demonstrated that paganism still had a meaning, purpose, and use in a society which had become largely Christian. It demonstrated that a pagan, acting on his own, following prescribed religious practices, might help to save his world from disaster. It showed that pagans still might have hope, optimism, and trust concerning their religion, even though its public practice was officially prohibited.

In general, however, Zosimus derived from fourth-century events only pessimistic conclusions which seemed to point to the climactic ruin of the Roman state in the fifth century. The *New History* is filled with omens and visions, none more sinister than the vision that appeared to Emperor Valens in 378 when he was marching to his fatal engagement with the Goths at Adrianople. Zosimus had no love for this emperor. He was critical in narrating Valens' persecution of soothsayers and pagans.[59] An important incident had oc-

[58] *Ibid.*, 4. 18. 2-4 (173 Mendelssohn).
[59] *Ibid.*, 4. 14-16 (169-172 Mendelssohn).

curred while Valens and his party were proceeding to Adrianople from Constantinople. A man was noticed "lying on the road completely motionless. He appeared to have been whipped from head to foot. His open eyes stared at those who approached. When they asked him who he was, where he came from, and at whose hands [he suffered this injury], he refused to answer everything."[60] Suddenly he disappeared. Zosimus remarks, "Many of those standing there were perplexed as to what should be done, but the wise agreed that this experience foretold the future condition of the government: afflicted and whipped, at its last gasp of breath, it would finally perish through the wickedness of its rulers and administrators"[61]—a brutally frank assessment of the contemporary condition of the Roman Empire.

V I

Zosimus was convinced that the deterioration of the empire had intensified and accelerated during the reign of Theodosius I (379-95).[62] As a stern guardian of morality Zosimus denounced the alleged licentious habits of Theodosius:

> The practice of luxuriousness nurtured this folly in him. For inasmuch as everything which sufficed for the destruction of character and life had such an increase, almost all who admired the pursuits of the emperor defined human happiness in terms of these. For there were mimes and dancers who were destined to a miserable end, and everything which contributed to filthy conduct and that

[60] *Ibid.*, 4. 21. 2 (176 Mendelssohn).
[61] *Ibid.*, 4. 21. 3 (176 Mendelssohn).
[62] See in general: N. Q. King, *The Emperor Theodosius and the Establishment of Christianity* (London 1961); W. Ensslin, "Die Religionspolitik des Kaisers Theodosius der Grosse," *SB Munich, Akademie der Wissenschaften*, Philosophisch-historische Abteilung, Heft 2 (Munich 1953).

strange and dissonant music which was performed in his reign.[63]

He cites the gluttony of Theodosius: "he introduced so much extravagance to the imperial table that because of the quantity of foods and their lavishness, populous legions of cooks, winepourers, and others were established which would require a lengthy book if one wished to count them."[64]

Many of Zosimus' indictments of Theodosius also deal with alleged mismanagement of the army and graft. He charges that Theodosius had needlessly multiplied, at the taxpayers' expense, the number of public officials. He criticizes the emperor for permitting the sale of government positions to the highest bidder regardless of merit, and remarks: "Since there was already such a great change for the worse in government, the army was reduced in a short time and became nothing. The cities were impoverished, on the one hand, because of the taxes which were imposed beyond moderation, and on the other hand because of the greediness of the rulers."[65] Finally, he criticizes the hiring of foreign mercenaries.[66]

Implacably hostile to Theodosius I, Zosimus nevertheless admits in another passage that this emperor at times had proven himself resourceful:

. . . because he so frequently dined on costly meals, busied himself with pleasures and took pride in theaters and race tracks, I am astounded at the other side of his character. For careless by nature, he surrendered to

[63] Zosim., *Hist. nov.*, 4. 33. 3-4 (188 Mendelssohn).
[64] *Ibid.*, 4. 28. 1 (183 Mendelssohn).
[65] *Ibid.*, 4. 29. 1 (184 Mendelssohn); for needless multiplication of commands: 4. 27. 1-3 (183 Mendelssohn); sale of offices: 4. 28. 2-4 (183-184 Mendelssohn).
[66] *Ibid.*, 4. 30. 1-5 (184-186 Mendelssohn).

every amusement. . . . When nothing painful or no pressing need troubled him, he yielded to his nature. But
when he was brought into such necessity that he was expected, according to custom, to fall, he said farewell to
luxury and withdrew to a more manly, suffering, and
harsh way of life.[67]

Although unable to demonstrate that Theodosius' leadership was always harmful to the state, Zosimus endeavored
to prove that the emperor's harsh religious policies had
grave consequences for the welfare of the Roman Empire.
Zosimus was especially disturbed by the conduct of Theodosius at Rome in 394. Having crushed the abortive revolt
of Eugenius, an imperial pretender in Italy who had enjoyed important pagan support, Theodosius had attempted
to persuade the pagan members of the Roman senate to
convert to Christianity.[68] But "None was persuaded by
his exhortation or chose to abandon those customs handed
down to them by their ancestors who had founded the city,
nor did they prefer the irrational creed [of the Christians]
(because by keeping these customs already for almost 1200
years the city had remained unsacked. They did not know
what would happen if they changed to other practices.)"[69]
Theodosius replied to the senators, announcing that due to
pressing financial demands on his government he found it
imperative to abolish state financial support for the maintenance of the pagan temples and sacrifices at Rome. The
senate protested that without this economic assistance it
would be impossible to perform the ritual acts required by

[67] *Ibid.*, 4. 50. 1-2 (207-208 Mendelssohn).
[68] On the revolt of Eugenius: N. Q. King, *Emperor Theodosius and
the Establishment of Christianity* (London 1961) 82-92. See Seeck,
"Arbogastes," *RE*, 2 (1896) 415-419.
[69] Zosim., *Hist. nov.*, 4. 59. 2 (216 Mendelssohn). Cf. on this
passage: E. Sihler, *From Augustus to Augustine* (Cambridge, England 1923) 247.

law. Theodosius ignored these dire predictions, thus no one observed the law concerning sacrifices or performed the other traditional religious rites. According to Zosimus, calamity ensued for the empire: "the Roman Empire was gradually reduced in size until it became a dwelling place for barbarians, lost its inhabitants, and fell into such a condition that no one could any longer recognize where there had once been cities."[70] In the passage immediately following this statement, Zosimus records the death of Theodosius himself. He probably sought here to suggest that there was a connection between the emperor's sacrilegious neglect of and opposition to pagan rites, and his death.[71]

Zosimus also attempts to show that the gods had been able to avenge a sacrilege committed by the western Emperor Gratian (375-83) who had himself named Theodosius as emperor of the eastern provinces. Gratian was assassinated on 25 August 383 after Maximus had usurped imperial power in the west.[72] Zosimus observes that Gratian had been the first Roman emperor to refuse the pagan priests' offer of the important traditional office of *Pontifex Maximus*, though even such zealous Christians as Constantine I and Valens had consented to hold this office. When Gratian rejected the offer of the position as unfit for a true Christian to hold, a pagan priest explained, "Even if the emperor does not wish to be named *Pontifex*, swiftly a *Pontifex Maximus* there will be."[73] Zosimus regarded these words as an unmistakable prediction that Maximus would succeed Gratian as emperor and as *Pontifex*, because Gratian had been disrespectful to the gods.

The gods were still able to provide protection for those

[70] Zosim., *Hist. nov.*, 4. 59. 3 (216 Mendelssohn).
[71] *Ibid.*, 4. 59. 4 (216-217 Mendelssohn).
[72] *Ibid.*, 4. 35. 4-6 (191 Mendelssohn).
[73] *Ibid.*, 4. 36. 5 (193 Mendelssohn); cf. G. Boissier, *La fin du paganisme*, 7th edn. (Paris 1922) II 259.

men and cities which might choose to favor them. Zosimus declares that when King Alaric approached Athens during his invasion of Greece in 397, he had every intention and expectation of capturing the city. Miraculously, however, the pagan gods intervened to save this citadel of Hellenism:

> But the antiquity of the city drew upon itself even in those impious times some divine providence (*Pronoian*) and remained inviolate. And it is worth not passing over in silence the cause by which the city was saved, for it is a divine miracle which summons the reader to piety. When Alaric marched against the city, he saw Athena Promachos walking about the wall of the city just as she is seen in statues, armed and appearing ready to resist the attackers. She stood like the hero Achilles in front of the wall, just as Homer portrayed him against the Trojans, when he fought in anger to avenge the death of Patroclus. It was reported that since Alaric could not bear this sight, he halted all assaults upon this city.[74]

Zosimus says that as a result of this vision Alaric agreed to negotiate with the Athenians, finally accepted gifts, and concluded a treaty which ended all hostilities. Alaric visited Athens personally but his army did not accompany him.

Zosimus regarded this settlement as a great triumph demonstrating unquestionably the ability of the pagan gods to

---

[74] The gods' defense of Athens: Zosimus, *Hist. nov.*, 5. 5. 8-5. 6. 1 (222-223 Mendelssohn); for the invasion of Greece by Alaric: *ibid.*, 5. 5. 4-8 (222 Mendelssohn); his approach to Athens: *ibid.*, 5. 6. 1 (222 Mendelssohn). Cf. F. Gregorovius, "Hat Alarich die National-götter Griechenlands zerstört?" *Kleine Schriften zur Geschichte und Cultur* (Leipzig 1887) I 60. In regard to Zosimus' account of the gods' defense of Athens, note the remarks of M. Le Nain de Tillemont, *Histoire des empereurs et des autres princes qui ont regné durant les six premiers siècles* (Paris 1701) V 433-434; E. Gibbon, *The History of the Decline and Fall of the Roman Empire*, J. B. Bury, ed. (London 1912) III 244.

successfully defend Roman cities against external attack. It seems very probable that he had in mind an implied contrast between the fortunes of two important imperial cities besieged by Alaric. Athens, a stronghold of paganism, was preserved by divine action against capture of Alaric. On the other hand, the gods permitted Alaric to capture Rome, where the proper pagan rites had been neglected and acts of sacrilege had been committed against sacred pagan objects and temples.[75] Zosimus viewed Athens as a city particularly blessed by the gods. He reminds his readers that the gods had also chosen to save it from the ravages of the severe earthquake which had struck Greece during the reign of Valens.[76]

VII

According to Zosimus' interpretation of events, the gods intervened in human history and actively worked to destroy Rome in the years immediately preceding Alaric's first siege of the city in 408.[77] Zosimus argues that the western *magister utriusque militiae*, Stilicho, who had labored so long and hard in the defense of the western provinces for Emperor Honorius (395-423), was murdered because of the gods' wrath.[78] Stilicho had ordered the golden doors removed from the Capitol in Rome. An inscription was found on the doors during their removal, which read, "Reserved for a wretched tyrant." Therefore the assassination of Stilicho fulfilled this prophecy.[79]

Observing that "In the absence of the divine, all human affairs are thrown into confusion," Zosimus concludes that

[75] Zosim., *Hist. nov.*, 5. 41. 7 (271 Mendelssohn).
[76] *Ibid.*, 5. 6. 3 (223 Mendelssohn).
[77] *Ibid.*, 5. 35. 5 (262 Mendelssohn).
[78] *Ibid.*, 5. 38. 4-5 (266 Mendelssohn); the best biographical study of Stilicho is by S. Mazzarino, *Stilicone. La crisi imperiale dopo Teodosio* (Rome 1942).
[79] Zosim., *Hist. nov.*, 5. 38. 5 (267 Mendelssohn).

the gods were dissatisfied with the mere death of Stilicho and added even more misfortune. At the news of Stilicho's death Roman soldiers offered a further display of violence by slaughtering the wives and children of the barbarian mercenaries. The barbarian troops who survived this massacre joined Alaric's forces to avenge the death of their kin.[80] Thus according to Zosimus, a divinely inspired chain of tragic events brought the fall of the city of Rome closer to reality.

Stilicho, Zosimus believed, may have met a violent death for another reason, one associated with the wrath of the gods against the commander's wife, Serena. The Roman senate suspected that Serena after the death of her husband had secretly conspired with Alaric, and she was ordered to be hanged. But the true reason for her execution, according to Zosimus, was that she had earned the fury of the gods by acting unwisely on a visit to the temple of the Mother of the Gods in Rome:

> Seeing the ornament—worthy of that rite—borne about the neck of the statue of Rhea, she removed it from the statue and placed it on her neck. And when an old woman, a Vestal Virgin who remained, reproached Serena to her face for her impiety, [Serena] insulted her and ordered her attendants to drive out the Vestal Virgin. When this old woman left, she prayed that everything worthy of this impiety should befall Serena, her husband, and their children. Paying no attention to these words, Serena left the temple, decorated with the ornament. Often, while asleep and awake, she was forewarned of her future death, and many others saw similar things. And so strong was the vengeance which pursued her in fulfillment of its duty, that Serena did not take guard, although she

[80] *Ibid.*, 5. 35. 5-6 (262-263 Mendelssohn).

knew the future, and she submitted her neck, on which had been hung the ornament of the Goddess, to hanging.[81]

Again Zosimus showed that in relatively recent times the gods had demonstrated their power and readiness to intervene in human affairs to punish with swift, divine retribution any act of disrespect towards them, the form of the punishment fitting the nature of the sacrilege.

Zosimus interprets the circumstances of Alaric's first siege of Rome (408) in the light of pagan values. He reports that some Etruscan magicians had visited Rome and offered to use their magical arts to produce lightning and thunder to repel the Visigoths: "they said that a certain city of Narnia had been freed from surrounding dangers by prayer to God and by religious services according to the ancestral customs. These were followed by extraordinary thunders and storms which chased away the attacking barbarians."[82] The *Praefectus urbis,* Pompianus, listened to their proposals and then consulted Pope Innocent I about the proper course of action. Zosimus declares that "Placing the safety of the city before [the cause of] his own religion [Pope Innocent] permitted them to perform their arts secretly." This was unsatisfactory, however:

> But [the Etruscans] said that the acts would not be effective for the city unless the senators fulfilled the lawful ceremonies in public by walking up to the Capitol and by performing the proper rites in the Forum. No one had the courage to participate in the ritual according to ancestral customs, however, and the Romans released the Etruscans who then turned to aid the barbarians. . . .[83]

Because no means was found for resisting the Visigoths

[81] *Ibid.,* 5. 38. 3-4 (266 Mendelssohn).
[82] *Ibid.,* 5. 41. 1 (269-270 Mendelssohn).
[83] *Ibid.,* 5. 41. 2-3 (270 Mendelssohn).

militarily, the Romans agreed to try to bribe Alaric and in this way avert the capture and destruction of their city. They chose to raise the required high ransom by a sacrilegious act of desperation—removing the valuable decorations from pagan altars throughout the city:

> This was nothing other than rendering lifeless and ineffective those statues which had been dedicated by holy rites and decorated properly in order to guard the eternal good fortune of the city. But since what was fated from all directions coincided for the destruction of the city, they not only stripped the statues, but they even melted down some of those made of gold and silver, one of which was of manliness, which the Romans called "VIRTUS." When this was destroyed, all of the manliness and excellence in the Romans were extinguished, according to those who devote themselves to interpreting divine matters and the ancestral rites.[84]

Zosimus explains the ultimate cause of the event: "the avenging deity who presided over affairs led those within the city who handled affairs to the summit of evils."[85]

These deeds of the Romans in 408 constituted for Zosimus the most important and climactic step in a long series of erroneous and sacrilegious acts stretching back to Constantine I's neglect of the Secular Games. Each pagan action had further diminished the supernatural protection of the city of Rome and its empire. Each injurious act had been committed by the Romans themselves. Zosimus did not say that the Christians had destroyed Rome; his emphasis was

---

[84] *Ibid.*, 5. 41. 6-7 (271 Mendelssohn). On the Roman negotiations with Alaric and their agreement to pay him 5000 pounds of gold and 30,000 pounds of silver and 4000 pieces of silk cloth: *ibid.*, 5. 41. 4 (270 Mendelssohn). Cf. H. Mattingly, *Christianity in the Roman Empire: Six Lectures* (Dunedin 1955) 72-73.

[85] Zosim., *Hist. nov.*, 5. 41. 5 (271 Mendelssohn).

on the neglect of pagan rites, not that many Romans happened to be Christian.

The Romans managed to save their city in 408, but two years later Alaric reappeared with his army. Zosimus' *New History*, as preserved, breaks off just at the point where Alaric has offered terms to the Romans after hostilities had resumed in 410. Jovius, the Pretorian Prefect of Italy, claimed that he could not make peace with Alaric since he had sworn a solemn oath to Emperor Honorius that he would not agree to a separate peace. Zosimus caustically exclaims that Jovius would have been willing to break an oath to God, but he was so overawed by the imperial majesty that he was afraid to violate a pledge given to a mere emperor; thus Jovius placed Rome in jeopardy.[86] This was a typical example of Zosimus' strong hostility toward Roman emperors.

Zosimus' account of the actual capture of the city on 24 August 410 is lost, as is the rest of his *New History*. It is uncertain just how far he originally carried his narrative of fifth-century events. The copy Evagrius Scholasticus consulted in the last decade of the sixth century covered no later period than does our extant edition (which led Evagrius to the erroneous conclusion that Zosimus had been a contemporary of Emperor Honorius).[87] At any rate, extant sections of Zosimus' work show that he regarded the fall of Rome to Alaric as the logical culmination of a vast number of impious acts and unwise policies of Roman emperors and officials beginning with Constantine I. His pessimistic estimate of contemporary conditions was not merely a typical pagan opinion; it also reflected the outlook of eastern

[86] On Alaric's second campaign against Rome: *ibid.*, 5.50. 1-3 (280-281 Mendelssohn). On Jovius' refusal to make peace with Alaric due to an oath which he had sworn to Honorius, see the critical remarks of Zosimus: *ibid.*, 5. 51. 1-2 (281 Mendelssohn).

[87] Evagrius Scholasticus, *Ecclesiastical History*, 3. 41 (140 Bidez-Parmentier).

Roman or Byzantine society generally. Joshua the Stylite, a contemporary Christian, expressed similar sentiments of political despair in his *Chronicle*, written in 507.[88]

VIII

Zosimus does not specifically blame the Christians for the misfortunes of the Roman Empire. Instead he charges that the general Roman neglect of the gods had caused them to cease protecting the state. He never discusses his own religious beliefs, but it is clear that his paganism was not primarily any neo-Platonic mystical syncretism such as that of Proclus and Iamblichus. Instead, he believed paganism consisted basically of observing the prescribed, traditional ritual practices the inhabitants of old Rome had followed for many centuries. There is no basis for asserting, as E. Condurachi does, that Zosimus was "indifferent" or "detached" in matters of religion and that he was a mere traditionalist.[89] In fact, the ancient Roman religion placed a strong emphasis on the performance of traditional ceremonies. Zosimus unquestionably was a zealous believer in paganism. He had a great respect for that which he regarded as divine and was convinced that religious ceremonies must be observed with precision or dreadful harm might come to mankind and to the Roman state.

Although Zosimus harbored unlimited hatred for the Christians he did not, as Julian did earlier, analyze Christian arguments in order to refute them.[90] He was, however, particularly critical of the Christian clergy and happily in-

[88] Joshua the Stylite, *Chronicle*, c. 3, W. Wright, ed. tr. (Cambridge, England 1882) 3-4.

[89] Condurachi, "Les idées politiques de Zosime," *Revista Clasică*, 13-14 (1941-1942) 118.

[90] Julian's considerable knowledge of Christianity is displayed in his treatise attempting to undermine Christian doctrines in general: *Iuliani imperatoris librorum contra Christianos quae supersunt*, C. Neumann, ed. (Leipzig 1880).

cluded in his history an account of the destructive fire in Constantinople caused by the rioting against Arcadius' exile of Patriarch John Chrysostom (403).[91] Naturally he has only bitter words for the Christian monks:

> These are persons who renounce legal marriage. They fill populous communities in cities and villages with unmarried men, and they are of service for neither war nor any other necessity. But proceeding in this way up to the present day, they have appropriated the greater part of the earth. On a pretext of giving everything to the poor they have, so to speak, made everyone poor.[92]

In general, Zosimus does not concern himself with details of Christian doctrine and internal disputes. One might expect him to have exploited for pagan advantage the divisive Trinitarian Controversy which rent the Church in the fourth century, but he does not mention it.

Zosimus believed Christians were immoral persons who adhered to a religion which permitted forgiveness for even such heinous offenses as Constantine's murder of his own son and wife.[93] The only feature of Christianity which enabled it to attract converts was its "promise of deliverance from every sin and impiety."[94] Zosimus gives no evidence of desiring any *modus vivendi* with the Christians nor does he make any special endeavor in his *New History* to persuade Christians to return to the performance of pagan rites. His principal objection to Christianity was not its advocacy of pernicious creeds but instead the fanatical intolerance it instilled in its adherents—intolerance that pre-

[91] Zosim., *Hist. nov.*, 5. 23-24 (243-247 Mendelssohn).
[92] *Ibid.*, 5. 23. 4 (244 Mendelssohn).
[93] *Ibid.*, 5. 29. 3 (86 Mendelssohn); cf. also his description of the remarks of Theodosius I to the Roman Senate, in which once again stress is laid upon the all-inclusive nature of Christian forgiveness: *ibid.*, 4. 59. 1 (215-216 Mendelssohn).
[94] *Ibid.*, 4. 59. 1 (216 Mendelssohn).

vented the observance of the traditional pagan ritual which was necessary, in Zosimus' eyes, for the security and prosperity of the Roman Empire.

Pessimism pervades the *New History*. Apparently Zosimus assumed that political and military conditions would not improve measurably in the future. He nowhere suggests the possibility that a pagan uprising might improve conditions. His attitude seems to have been that the decline of the Roman Empire had already occurred. He does not advocate any attempt to reverse the course of previous events, and voices no expectation that the lost western provinces would ever be recovered. His outlook differs from that of those eastern pagans who had hoped that the western Emperor, Anthemius, or the eastern rebel, Illus, would restore the public worship of the gods. He simply regards himself as an analyst of the past process of Roman decay.

By the end of the century, although pagans might still discuss the causes for Roman decline, the topic had become a subject for debate by historians and antiquarians rather than a live political issue. While assessing damages already inflicted on the Empire Zosimus never predicted that the remaining portion of the Roman Empire would suffer total destruction or complete enslavement to the barbarians. Although an easterner, he had a keen interest in the fate of the western provinces and especially in the fortunes of the city of Rome, the founder and capital of the empire, and in the source of the religious ceremonies and traditions which had such an attraction for him.

Zosimus, of course, does not mention many factors modern historians of Roman decline usually consider important. Like other ancient students of history he does not stress, or even consider, the possible role of population change, static and inadequate technology, an inflexible and nonexpansive economic and financial system, lack of sufficiently representative political institutions, the absence of any adequate and effective provision for the orderly succession to political authority, class conflicts and unrest of nationality groups, the narrow and conservative views of the ruling elite, the diversion of the army from external defense to involvement in internal politics, or the inherent difficulty in holding together an empire of such huge dimensions given natural geographic barriers, and the contemporary state of communications and transportation.[95]

Although Zosimus was deeply shocked and embittered at the barbarization[96] of provinces and the obliteration of cities,[97] he had not personally experienced the destruction of his own city, province, house, or personal property because of barbarian invasions. As a resident of Constantinople he knew of western developments only at second hand; he had not witnessed the barbarian occupation of his province, nor had he seen the Roman legions withdraw from the defense of his province. Zosimus was writing about such developments from a comparatively secure vantage point in the east.

I X

Zosimus realized that his thesis did not entirely fit the actual

[95] S. Mazzarino, *La fine del mondo antico* (Milan 1959); this is a brief but competent discussion. In addition: J. J. Saunders, "The Debate on the Fall of Rome," *History*, 48 (1963) 1-17; a short anthology of views has been compiled by M. Chambers: *The Fall of Rome: Can It Be Explained?* (New York 1963); S. Katz, *The Decline of Rome and the Rise of Mediaeval Europe* (Ithaca 1955) 71-84; A.E.R. Boak, *Manpower Shortage and the Fall of the Roman Empire in the West* (Ann Arbor 1955); F. Altheim, *Niedergang der antiken Welt: eine Untersuchung der Ursachen* (Frankfurt 1952). A recent contribution: R. MacMullen, *Soldier and Civilian in the Later Roman Empire* (Cambridge, Mass. 1963) 152-177. Finally a careful discussion of the problem is found in two works of A.H.M. Jones, "Decline and Fall of the Roman Empire," *History*, 40 (1955) 209-226; *The Later Roman Empire 284-602* (Oxford 1964) II 1,025-1,068.

[96] Zosim., *Hist. nov.*, 1. 58. 4 (42 Mendelssohn).

[97] *Ibid.*, 4. 59. 3 (216 Mendelssohn).

situation of the Roman Empire in the fifth century. Although he speaks of its "destruction," it was nonetheless obvious that at least a vestige of the empire—the eastern provinces —continued to survive.[98] The existence of the eastern section of the empire presented Zosimus (and indeed any pagan charging that the neglect of pagan rites had caused imperial ruin) with a difficult, logical problem: if indeed the gods had withdrawn their protection from the Roman Empire why had even a piece of the formerly huge empire continued to exist? This problem was compounded by the fact that the eastern half of the empire had not only been preserved but also enjoyed relative security, even prosperity and an overcrowded population.[99] Thus a pagan might well point to the ruptured and ruined condition of the western provinces and charge the responsibility for this situation to the Christians and to neglect of pagan rites. Yet how in the same breath could he explain to himself, his fellow pagans, and the Christians that these gods could have also tolerated the comparatively fortunate conditions of the eastern provinces?

The case of Constantinople illustrates Zosimus' views. Like his predecessor, Eunapius, he criticizes Constantine I for moving the imperial capital from Rome to the shores of the Bosphorus. He complains that Constantine and his successors had brought unnecessary hordes of people to Constantinople, so that overcrowded living conditions resulted: "the houses approached each other so closely that housekeepers and inhabitants of this city who were in the markets were cramped and walked in danger because of the great number of men and animals."[100] He also scores Con-

[98] *Ibid.*, and *ibid.*, 5. 41. 7 (271 Mendelssohn); 1. 57. 1 (41 Mendelssohn).

[99] Zosim., *Hist. nov.*, 2. 35. 2-36. 1 (92 Mendelssohn); cf. Isaac of Antioch, "Homily on the Royal City," C. Moss, tr., *Zeitschrift für Semitistik und verwandte Gebiete*, 8 (1932) 68.

[100] Zosim., *Hist. nov.*, 2. 35. 2 (92 Mendelssohn).

stantine's lavish expenditures on this city: "Remaining peaceful and surrendering his life to luxury, he distributed to the people of Byzantium a grain allowance which it continues to receive up to this day."[101] Constantinople, of course, became an impressive Christian city where no public worship of the pagan gods was permitted. For this reason, many pagans were extremely hostile to the city.[102]

Nevertheless, Constantinople had indisputably become a great city. Although pagan rites were not celebrated publicly, the city had not suffered any serious calamities as a punishment for the neglect. Zosimus and other eastern pagans therefore found it necessary to explain a phenomenon western pagans did not have to face when they ascribed imperial decline to the neglect of the gods. It is clear from his own writing that this problem bothered Zosimus personally and he felt compelled to wrestle with it. He reflects openly:

> And often I have come to wonder why Byzantium has grown to the extent that no other city may in prosperity and size be compared to it, and why no prediction of the gods concerning this city's superior fortune was given to our ancestors. With this in mind for a long time, having read many histories and collections of oracles, and having spent much time in doubt about these matters, I finally found a certain oracle said to be of the Sibyll Erythraea or of Phaenno of Epirus which Nicomedes, son of Prusias, trusted. Thinking that he was fulfilling this oracle he went to war against his father, Prusias. . . .[103]

[101] *Ibid.*, 2. 32. 1 (89 Mendelssohn); cf. *ibid.*, 2. 30. 1-31. 3 (87-89 Mendelssohn).

[102] For the prohibition of pagan worship within the city: A. Frolow, "La dédicace de Constantinople dans la tradition byzantine," *RHR*, 127 (1944) 61-127. Note the hostility of Eunapius to this city: *VS*, 6. 2. 4-12 (19-20 Giangrande).

[103] Zosim., *Hist. nov.*, 2. 36. 1-2 (92-93 Mendelssohn).

He then proceeds to quote at length the entire oracle which had predicted in obscure fashion all of the particular evils that were to befall Bithynia because of the heavy impositions laid upon it, foretelling: "Swiftly power shall come to those who inhabit the seat of Byzas."[104] Zosimus believed that this particular oracle from the second century B.C. (Nicomedes waged war against Prusias, his father, in 167 B.C.)[105] was actually predicting the greatness and prosperity of Constantinople in the fifth century A.D. He realized that there might be some difficulty in explaining how it had taken so long for the prophecy of the oracle to be fulfilled, for the oracle had stated that all these developments would occur "swiftly," but the pagan historian observed that "all time is brief to God ($τ\tilde{ω}$ Θείω) who always exists and will exist"; therefore he saw no real contradiction.[106]

Zosimus implicitly contradicts his own argument that the Roman Empire had declined to nothing. It is important to note that he admits Constantinople had grown to greater size and prosperity than any other city. He is therefore declaring that Constantinople had become greater than Rome herself—indeed, a remarkable confession for a fanatical pagan conservative to make about a city whose recent greatness was bestowed by the empire's first Christian emperor. Zosimus' pagan predecessor, Olympiodorus of Thebes, on the contrary had still been overawed by the size and wealth of the city of Rome. He had reported with astonishment impressive statistics about Rome.[107] Olympiodorus had clearly felt that there was nothing in the eastern provinces that could compare with the magnificence of Rome. In the decades between Olympiodorus and Zosimus the strength,

---

[104] Zosim., *Hist. nov.*, 2. 37. 1. 10-11 (94 Mendelssohn); the complete oracle: *ibid.*, 2. 37. 1 (93-95 Mendelssohn).
[105] *Ibid.*, 2. 37. 2 (95 Mendelssohn).
[106] *Ibid.*
[107] Photius, *Bibliotheca*, c. 80 (*Bibliothèque*, R. Henry, ed. tr. [Paris 1959] I 185-186).

wealth, and prestige of Rome had waned, while those of Constantinople had become so preeminent even pagans felt compelled to concede its good fortune. They sought to connect Constantinople's favorable situation with their own gods rather than to allow the Christians by default to claim the city as exclusively Christian and therefore so successful and renowned.

Constantinople's importance in the fifth century was a stubborn fact that robbed the pagan charges about Roman decline of some of their impact. They were forced to account for a new situation which did not easily fit into the old and traditional rigid categories of pagan thought—the emergence of a Roman Empire centered around Constantinople rather than Rome. To understand this new phenomenon and to reach a satisfactory interpretation of its significance, these pagans attempted to refer to materials within their own more familiar religious context. Hence Zosimus endeavored to demonstrate to himself and his readers that a pagan oracle had in truth predicted the city's growth. In this manner the rise of Constantinople would confirm, rather than call into question, the gods' *Pronoia*.

x

Zosimus did not confine himself to stating that the gods had prophesied Constantinople would someday become a great city. He lived there himself and its good fortune impressed him.[108] A passage in the *New History* reveals just how deep this conviction went. In reporting the course of events in the eastern half of the Roman Empire Zosimus describes the violence that accompanied the departure of the Patriarch of Constantinople, John Chrysostom, from the capital on 20 June 403. Chrysostom incurred the wrath of the Empress Eudoxia by calling her a Herodias because she had erected

[108] Zosim., *Hist. nov.*, 2. 36. 1.-2 (92-93 Mendelssohn).

a statue of herself near St. Sophia Church. Consequently, her husband, Emperor Arcadius, ordered Chrysostom into exile. The news caused a major riot. On the night John was exiled the Church was mysteriously set afire and the blaze spread throughout most of the city. The building which housed the Roman senate at Constantinople was engulfed in flames. This edifice had contained many very fine ancient statues which Constantine I had collected from all areas of the empire to beautify his new capital. Among them were statues of Zeus Dodona and Athena Lindia, which stood in front of the senate building. The burning of the senate left a symbolic message for posterity: "When the beauty was changed into a heap of rubbish, the general opinion supposed that these statues had become ashes. But when the place was cleared and made ready for restoration, only the statues of these gods were shown to have been stronger than that all-encompassing destruction."[109] Zosimus concludes in one of the most significant statements in his entire work: "This gave to all of the wiser men [*i.e.*, the pagans] hopes for the city, specifically, that these gods were willing for it to have their providence (προνοίας) forever. But let all these things proceed as pleases God (τῷ Θείῳ)."[110] Once again Zosimus points out that the pagan gods were still powerful in human history. His concept of *Pronoia* is prominently displayed here. But even more important, here is a passage in which a pagan frankly speculates that the pagan gods might protect Constantinople for all time.

Zosimus was not positive that the gods had bestowed their providence on the city forever—they would do as they

[109] *Ibid.*, 5. 24. 8 (246-247 Mendelssohn). On the statues cf. C. Mango, "Antique Statuary and the Byzantine Beholder," *DO Papers* 17 (1963) 56-58.

[110] Zosim., *Hist. nov.*, 5. 24. 8 (247 Mendelssohn). Zosimus fails to note that the statue of Athena Lindia was later destroyed by fire during the reign of the usurper Basiliscus (476?): Zonar., *Epit. Histor.*, 14.2 L. Dindorf, ed. (Leipzig 1870) III 257.

please, being gods—but he did recognize the definite possibility that Constantinople might have become a god-protected city, just as Rome had once been. Although throughout his *New History* Zosimus argues that because the gods
had ceased to defend the empire, Rome was declining, he
apparently refused to believe that the gods have totally
abandoned mankind. He continued to place some hope in
the future and in the eternity of at least the eastern vestige
of the Roman Empire.

Zosimus was convinced that Athena was one of the gods
who might be watching over Constantinople. In subsequent
centuries of Byzantine history, it was the Virgin Mary who
appeared to defend the city against its many besiegers.[111]
Interestingly, it was during the fifth century that the Virgin
Mary began to receive extensive veneration as the special
protectress of the Byzantine capital and her robe was carried to Constantinople and dedicated with appropriate
ceremonies.[112] Zosimus seemed to believe that Athena was
playing a role of city guardian comparable to that role
which the Christians attributed to the Virgin. Although bitterly hostile to each other, both pagans and Christians in
the eastern provinces during the fifth century sometimes
shared religious thought patterns.

Zosimus ignores a number of problems which his thesis

[111] See: N.H. Baynes, "The Supernatural Defenders of Constantinople," *Byzantine Studies and Other Essays* (London 1955, reprinted
1960) 248-249, 255-260. On the substitution of worship of the
Virgin Mary for worship of Athena/Minerva, cf. J. Seznec, *The Survival of the Pagan Gods*, B. F. Sessions, tr., Bollingen Series, 38
(New York 1953) 105n98.

[112] See: N. H. Baynes, "The Finding of the Virgin's Robe," *Byz.
Studies and Other Essays* (London 1955) 240-247. In this article
there is an important description of the discovery of the alleged
robe of the Virgin in Galilee and its conveyance to Constantinople
during the reign of Leo I (457-474), where it was properly housed
in the church of the Blachernae quarter which was specifically con-
structed to hold this relic.

raised. Why should the pagan gods have chosen to protect Constantinople—were a sufficient number of pagans in that city following the traditional pagan rites to warrant such a generous divine reward? Zosimus can only believe that whichever sections of the empire still survive must exist because the gods have so willed it. If the gods were so powerful, would they ever restore public pagan worship and perhaps also restore pagans to supreme political and religious authority?

XI

Zosimus gave himself a formidable task. In attempting around 500 to justify paganism, he had to explain in terms of his own religious values the existing political realities of the Roman Empire. He sought on the one hand to blame the Christians for the ruin of the western provinces, yet, on the other hand, he wished to ascribe the prosperity and vigor of the eastern provinces to the providence of the pagan gods. In attempting this task he tried to do more than any other known fifth-century easterner had done: he tried to reassess traditional pagan arguments in the light of the special conditions existing in the eastern provinces. He was therefore endeavoring to create a viable pagan philosophy of history for his eastern Roman contemporaries.

Zosimus must not be regarded as an absolutely pessimistic and despairing pagan who looked with nostalgia to the past achievements of Graeco-Roman antiquity; the most impressive and interesting feature of his work is that he still found it possible at such a late date to believe in the gods' protection of the Roman Empire and he believed that these gods might even guard Constantinople forever. Hence the Roman Empire might not necessarily fall into irrevocable decay. He was beginning to shift his loyalties to the "second" Rome.

Zosimus had in fact become a Byzantine pagan. Although

stunned and disgusted by the reduction of the Roman Empire to the dimensions of the Byzantine Empire, he came to believe that his gods might have taken the New Rome under their protection—for eternity. He could not suppress his respectful awe for Constantinople. He managed to reconcile with pagan values his attachment to the city. This was his most important achievement. He still found paganism to be a meaningful religion, although the majority of the empire's population had become Christian.

The political situation of the eastern Roman, or Byzantine, Empire by the end of the fifth century made it very difficult for a pagan to frame an explanation comprehending both eastern and western conditions. This was perhaps one reason for the apparent lessening of general debate between eastern Christians and pagans over the causes for the successive western Roman political and military catastrophes: the pagans also had to account somehow in their thesis for the general well-being of the east.

Zosimus' arguments were quite dated. The *New History* expressed a pagan outlook which had validity and appeal only during the fifty or sixty years between the final collapse of Roman authority in the western provinces and the Justinianic reconquest of Italy, Sicily, Sardinia, North Africa and even portions of Spain, from the Ostrogoths, Vandals, and Visigoths.[113] Most of Justinian's subjects probably shared the pride and satisfaction which John Lydus[114] and Cosmas Indicopleustes[115] voiced in the imperial restora-

---

[113] For a sound survey of Justinian's western conquests: E. Stein, *Histoire du Bas-Empire*, J.-R. Palanque, ed. (Paris 1949) II 311-368.

[114] John Lydus, *De magistratibus*, 3. 39 (R. Wuensch, ed., 126-127).

[115] Cosmas Indicopleustes, *The Christian Topography*, E.O. Winstedt, ed. (Cambridge, England 1909) 80; cf. 81. See the important new analysis of this work: W. Wolska, *La topographie chrétienne de Cosmas Indicopleustès, théologie et science au VIe siècle* (Paris 1962); and Altaner, *Patrology*, H.C. Graef, tr. (New York 1960) 624.

tion.[116] The military success of Justinian may account for the absence of references to Zosimus' work during his reign. Eustathius had referred to Zosimus during the reign of Anastasius, and Evagrius Scholasticus was to refute him (see below, Chap. V) many years later in 594.[117]

One may suggest that the inadequacy of the eastern pagan thesis on the religious causes of Roman decay may have been a factor contributing to the gradual disappearance of paganism itself in the eastern provinces. The pagans had to grasp some issue decisively in order to maintain the confidence and allegiance of existing adherents and to win back those who had lapsed. Zosimus made an attempt to develop an interpretation of world history that would demonstrate the relevance and necessity of paganism for the common welfare. Yet the pagan case, as he presented it, although intended to be forceful, still sounded unconvincing.[118] Even Zosimus himself confessed that he was perplexed by the prosperity of Constantinople and consequently pondered such a development was related to the actions

[116] There were some important men, of course, such as the historian Procopius of Caesarea, *Historia arcana*, 18. 1-35 2nd edn., J. Haury and G. Wirth (Leipzig 1963) 111-117 and Agathias, *Historiae*, 5. 14, L. Dindorf, ed., *Historici Graeci Minores* (Leipzig 1871) II 370-372, who after many unfortunate experiences ultimately became harsh critics of Justinian. Generally, however, most men accepted the imperial propaganda or remained silent: B. Rubin, *Das Zeitalter Iustinians* (Berlin 1960) I 146-167, for official propaganda during his reign. For a survey of opposition literature: *ibid.*, I 168-244.

[117] Evagrius Scholasticus, *Hist. Eccl.*, 3. 40-41, J. Bidez and L. Parmentier, eds. (London 1898) 139-144. It is important to note that he reports that earlier in the century the Christian historian Eustathius' had employed Zosim., 5. 24 (219 Bidez-Parmentier). Eustathius' history does not survive. On Evagrius: Altaner, *Patrology*, H.C. Graef, tr. (New York 1960) 277.

[118] P. Lemerle argues that it is incorrect to apply the term "decadence" to the Byzantine Empire's history: "La notion de décadence à propos de l'Empire byzantin," *Classicisme et déclin culturel dans l'histoire de l'Islam* (Paris 1957) 263-277. In my opinion, Zoe Petre, "La pensée historique de Zosime," 271-272 exaggerates the intellectual achievement of Zosimus.

of the gods. He possessed the emotional inspiration but lacked the intellectual ability to create a work which could stem the gradual but steady diminution of pagans through voluntary conversions, Christian proselytization, and legal harassment. Finally, his pagan interpretation of western Roman decline encountered another set of obstacles—competing eastern Christian explanations of recent Roman history.

chapter iv

THE DIVERSITY OF CHRISTIAN
REACTIONS

The eastern Christian clergy could not help but interpret the political and military collapse of Roman authority in the west in terms of their own religious values. Neither could they ignore the pagan charges that neglect of traditional pagan religious ceremonies—in particular, sacrifices —had caused the disasters. If a recrudescence of paganism were to be prevented Christians would need to make an effective reply to the pagan arguments.

In the west, Saint Augustine, Bishop of Hippo, and his faithful disciple, the presbyter, Paulus Orosius, wrote extensive tracts designed to disprove pagan charges. In his *De civitate Dei* Augustine summarizes the pagan position and points to historical facts which could disprove paganism's thesis:

> [the pagans] strive to demonstrate to the multitude that the disasters, which must strike the human race at fixed intervals of time and place, happen because of the Christian name which is being spread everywhere by its great renown and magnificent reputation against the gods. Let them, therefore, reflect with us on those various calamities which pounded the Roman state before Christ came in the flesh and before His name, which they in vain envy, had become known by Its glory to the nations. . . .[1]

[1] Augustine, *De civ. D.*, 2. 3; cf. 1. 36 and 3. 30 (E. Hoffmann, ed., *CSEL*, 40. 1, Vienna-Prague-Leipzig 1899, 62, 58, 157); cf.

Augustine contends the moral corruption of the Romans began under the pagans.[2] He denies that the pagan gods were able to prevent disasters: "For why did these gods permit these things which I am about to mention to happen to their worshippers before the proclamation of the name of Christ displeased them and prevented their sacrifices?"[3] He also argues that the status of the empire and of all temporal government was determined not by the fates or the pagan gods, but "In short, human kingdoms are managed by divine providence."[4] He observes that God had granted many temporal blessings to some Christian emperors, in particular, to Constantine I: "For the good God, lest men . . . might reckon that no one might attain these heights and earthly kingdoms unless he were a worshipper of demons . . . for this reason filled Emperor Constantine, not a demon worshipper but a worshipper of the True God, with more earthly gifts than one might dare wish for."[5] In this way Augustine strives to demonstrate that God could indeed protect the Roman Empire very effectively if He chose to do so.

The true worth of Christianity, Augustine feels, is not to be calculated in terms of earthly rewards: "the One and True God is to be worshipped not for earthly and temporal benefits, which divine providence concedes to good and to bad men, but for eternal life and for perpetual gifts and the society of this celestial city."[6] Augustine asserts that the

---

Augustine, *Epistula*, 138, c. 3. 16 (*PL*, 33, 532). See: J. Straub, "Christliche Geschichtsapologetik in der Krisis des römischen Reiches," *Historia*, 1 (1950) 65-74.

[2] Moral corruption: Augustine, *De civ. D.*, 2. 19 (86 Hoffmann); cf. *Epist.*, 138. 3. 16 (*PL*, 33. 532).

[3] Augustine, *De civ. D.*, 2. 3 (63 Hoffmann).

[4] *Ibid.*, 5. 1 (209 Hoffmann).

[5] *Ibid.*, 5. 25 (262 Hoffmann); cf. 5. 26 (263-266 Hoffmann).

[6] *Ibid.*, 5. 18 (251 Hoffmann).

welfare of the Church and the soundness of the Roman Empire are not necessarily connected.[7]

Paulus Orosius composed his *Historiae adversum paganos* at the request of Saint Augustine. He provided additional historical refutations of the pagan charges concerning Roman decline and strived to collect numerous references to misfortunes that had occurred in pagan times, ". . . whether burdens of wars, or ruin by disease, harshness of famine, or terrors of earthquakes, unusual floods, or dreadful eruptions of fire, or ferocious strokes of lightning or blows of hail or even the wretchedness caused by parricides and disgraceful acts. . . ."[8] He attempts to show that wars were numerous in pagan times,[9] concluding that ". . . past days [were] not only as painful as these, but even so much more dreadfully wretched the more distant they were from the medicine of the true religion."[10] Like Augustine, Orosius wished to prove

[7] *Ibid.*, 5. 24-25 (260-262 Hoffmann). See: Th. E. Mommsen, "St. Augustine and the Christian Idea of Progress," *Medieval and Renaissance Studies* (Ithaca 1959) 280-298. Augustine's patriotism: G. Combès, *La doctrine politique de Saint Augustin* (Paris 1927) 206-254; H. Deane, *The Political and Social Ideas of St. Augustine* (New York, London 1963) 94-104. Note also, K. M. Setton, *The Christian Attitude towards the Emperor in the Fourth Century* (New York 1941) 116-151, 188-195, 213-218, who argues that many prominent members of the Christian clergy in the east, especially Saint John Chrysostom, had come by the end of the fourth century to see a critical distinction between *imperium* and *sacerdotium* and defined a separate function for each. Also see the conclusions of K. F. Morrison, "Rome and the City of God: An Essay on the Constitutional Relationships of Empire and Church in the Fourth Century," *Transactions of the American Philosophical Society*, 54 Pt. 1. (Philadelphia 1964) 51-52; and F. Vittinghoff, "Zum geschichtlichen Selbstverständnis der Spätantike," *HZ*, 198 (1964) 556-572.

[8] Paulus Orosius, *Historiarum adversum paganos libri vii*, 1. prol. 10, (C. Zangemeister, ed., *CSEL*, 5 [Vienna 1882] 3). See esp. A. Lippold, *Rom und die Barbaren in der Beurteilung des Orosius* (diss. Erlangen 1952) 12-25, for Orosius' reaction to the sack of Rome in 410; for his views on the Roman state, *ibid.*, 33-62.

[9] Orosius, *Hist. adv. pag.*, 4. 12 (239-240 Zangemeister).

[10] *Ibid.*, 1. prol. 14 (4 Zangemeister); cf. *ibid.*, 7. 43. 17-18 (563 Zangemeister).

that the pagan gods had not prevented the occurrence of tragedies, that, on the contrary, material conditions had actually improved with the appearance of Christianity.

Augustine puts forth another argument against the pagan position by noting that Alaric's Visigoths had avoided harming those people who took refuge in Christian sanctuaries during the sack of Rome. Both Augustine and Orosius regard this phenomenon as an improvement over the wanton slaughter in former times of the populace of captured cities.[11] Augustine points out that the pagan gods in former times had not been able to save those who had taken refuge in their temples during the plundering of captured cities.[12] He denounces the ingratitude of pagans who themselves had been saved by taking refuge in Christian churches: "Thus escaped many who now disparage Christian times and who ascribe to Christ the calamities which that city bore."[13] "And yet are not those Romans hostile to the name of Christ whom the barbarians spared because of Christ? Witnesses of this are the places of the martyrs and the churches of the apostles that received both friends and foes who fled to it during that devastation of the city? Up to here the bloodthirsty enemy raged, but his furious slaughter went no further."[14]

II

Saint Jerome, a native of the west (born at Stridon on the borders of Dalmatia and Pannonia), was living at Bethlehem when he heard that Rome had fallen to Alaric. He speaks of that event with bursts of emotion: "We are unable to see without tears and groaning that the [city] which

---

[11] *Ibid.*, 7. 39. 3-14 (545-547 Zangemeister); Augustine, *De civ. D.*, 1. 1 (4-5 Hoffmann); 1. 3 (8-9 Hoffmann).
[12] *Ibid.*, 1. 4 (9 Hoffmann).
[13] *Ibid.*, 1. 1 (5 Hoffmann).
[14] *Ibid.*, 1. 1 (4 Hoffmann).

was once powerful and carefree has come to such indigence that it needs housing, food, and clothing."[15] He is convinced that the entire world was intimately involved in the sack of the city: "O horrid! The universe tumbles and yet our sins do not fall. A renowned city and head of the Roman Empire is consumed in one blaze."[16] Among the incidents which occurred in the siege he mentions the story of a Roman virgin. He reports that she successfully defended her chastity against the advances of a Visigothic soldier and ultimately found refuge in the Church of Saint Paul.[17]

Jerome not only grieves for Rome but also laments the devastation of other western provinces. He believes the fates of Rome and the rest of the empire were related: "What is safe if Rome perishes?"[18] His response demonstrates the impact of the attack on Rome on one western Christian who lived in the east. Can his reaction, given his western origins and western associations, be regarded also as a response typical of eastern clerics? Or was his reaction an isolated one?[19]

The evidence shows that eastern Christians, particularly

[15] Hieron., *Commentar. in Ezech.*, 7 (*PL*, 25. 199). On this work: M. Schanz, C. Hosius, *Geschichte der römischen Literatur*, 2nd edn. (Munich 1959) IV. 1. 462, 464.

[16] Hieron., *Ep.*, 128. 5 (*Lettres*, Labourt, ed. tr. [Paris 1961] VII 153); cf. his *Commentar. in Ezech.* 3 (*PL*, 25. 75).

[17] *Hieron., Ep.*, 127. 13 (Labourt, VII 147).

[18] *Ibid., Ep.*, 123. 15-16 (Labourt, VII 91-93); *Ep.*, 60. 15-18 (Labourt, III 105-109); cf. J.-R. Palanque, "St. Jerome and the Barbarians," *A Monument to St. Jerome*, F. X. Murphy, ed. (New York 1952) 173-199.

[19] G. Bardy, "St. Jerome and Greek Thought," *Monument to St. Jerome*, 97-98, 107-108. For a survey of Jerome's life: F. Cavallera, *Saint Jérôme sa vie et son oeuvre* (Louvain, Paris 1922); A. Penna, *S. Gerolamo* (Turin, Rome 1949); J. Steinmann, *Saint Jérôme* (Paris 1958); J. Forget, "Saint Jérôme," *DTC*, 8 (1947) 894-983. He was born at Stridon on the borders of Dalmatia and Pannonia: F. Bulic, "Stridone luogo natale di S. Girolamo," *Miscellanea Geronimiana* (Rome 1920) 253-300; cf. also the remarks of J.-R. Palanque, "St. Jerome and the Barbarians," *Monument* 174-197.

the clergy, were so zealous in their attempts to eradicate paganism from their provinces that Theodosius II forbade them by law to annoy those pagans who were not violating any laws. But the Christians did not rely solely on the emperor and imperial officials during the fifth century; they acted independently to convert the remaining pagans and refute pagan philosophical and religious arguments. Any extensive pagan propaganda arguing that neglect of the gods was causing Roman decline encountered zealous Christian replies.[20]

Both St. Augustine, in his *De excidio urbis Romae sermo*, and Orosius, in his *Historiae adversum paganos* refer to a recent event at Constantinople. Augustine states that during the reign of Arcadius (395-408) a fiery, sulphurous cloud appeared which God had sent to chastise that city. Augustine and Orosius report that the emperor, the bishop, and the entire populace abandoned the city and prayed—and, fortunately, through prayer the city was preserved from divine wrath.[21] Augustine and Orosius believe that this event caused a religious reformation in Constantinople.[22] They regard this affair as a marvel and contrast it with the fate of Rome, for Augustine notes that many there had also abandoned the city and thus found salvation.[23] At any

[20] On 8 June 423: *Cod. Theod.*, 16. 10. 24. 1 (476 Pharr), T. Mommsen and P. Krueger, eds. (Berlin 1954) I Pt. 2 904-905.

[21] Sancti Aurelii Augustini, *De excidio urbis Romae sermo* 7-8, Sis. M. V. O'Reilly, ed. tr., *Catholic University of America Patristic Studies*, 89 (Washington, D.C. 1955) 68-71. This work was written soon after 410. Cf. Paulus Orosius, *Hist. adv. pag.*, 3. 3. 2. (146 Zangemeister). Cf. two papers by J. Hubaux: "La crise de la trois cent soixante cinquième année," *AntCl*, 17 (1948) 344-352, and "Saint Augustin et la crise eschatologique de la fin du IVe siècle," *Bulletin de la Classe des Lettres et des Sciences morales et politiques, Académie royale de Belgique*, 40 (1954) 658-660.

[22] Augustine, *De excidio urbis Romae sermo* 8 (70-71 O'Reilly); Orosius, *Hist. adv. pag.* 3. 3. 2 (146 Zangemeister).

[23] Augustine, *De excidio urbis Romae sermo*, 7-8 (68-71 O'Reilly); Orosius, *Hist. adv. pag.*, 3. 3. 2 (146 Zangemeister).

rate, these two western Christians were impressed by the fact that in the face of that particular danger, Constantinople had been preserved from harm. They could not help but think of the sound condition of Constantinople as they contemplated the violent fate which Rome had recently suffered.

III

Contemporary writers report that eastern Christians responded in different ways to the deteriorating situation of the western Roman Empire. Certainly the "eastern multitudes" who wept for Rome in 410, according to Augustine, must have included many Christians.[24] Yet no definite information exists on the reaction of one of the most politically conscious eastern clerics: Synesius of Cyrene, Bishop of Ptolemais and a learned student of philosophy, who was born about 370 and died between 412 and 415. In his *Oration on Kingship* to Emperor Arcadius (A.D. 399) Synesius sketches a desperate picture of the empire's condition: "Now everything balances on a razor's edge and the state needs the assistance of God and the emperor to crush that danger which has been troubling the Roman Empire for a long time."[25] After writing this oration he continued to take an active interest in the condition of the Pentapolis. In his treatise, *Katastasis*, he fears the complete ruin of his province:

I do not know what I ought to say about the misfor-

---

[24] Augustine, *De civ. D.*, 1. 33 (56 Hoffmann). Cf. Saint Jerome, *Ep.*, 60. 16, J. Labourt, ed. tr. *Lettres* (Paris 1953) III 107: *Inmunis ab his malis uidebatur Oriens et tantum nuntiis consternatus. . . .*

[25] Synesius, *De regno*, 18 (*Opuscula*, N. Terzaghi, ed. [Rome 1944] 42). See also the commentary and translation of C. Lacombrade, *Le discours sur la royauté de Synésius de Cyrène* (Paris 1951) 61. On the dates of Synesius' birth and death: C. Lacombrade, *Synésios de Cyrène: Hellène et Chrétien* (Paris 1951) 13, 273.

tunes before my eyes. For there is no time for those to speak who must weep, nor would speech be appropriate to the subject. The ability to cry has deserted those who are stunned by the magnitude of the evils which have occurred.[26]

The general condition of the empire made him ". . . ashamed of fearing for myself, for the times, for the state. O for the courage of the ancient Romans!"[27] His pessimism is almost total concerning the situation in his province: "The Pentapolis has died, been extinguished, found its end, been assassinated, and has perished. It no longer exists at all either for us or for the emperor."[28]

Despite this concern for the empire's condition Synesius does not specifically refer in any of his known works to Rome in 410 or to other Roman reverses in the west. This is significant, given the relative proximity of his province to Italy and his general interest in the political affairs of the empire. Perhaps an important reason for the silence was Synesius' increasing preoccupation with the pressing problems of his own province, which faced serious nomadic raids; his correspondence contains repeated references to his labors on behalf of local defenses.[29] The news from other provinces became less important in his eyes. He admits in a

[26] Synesius, *Katastasis*, 1 (Terzaghi, *Opuscula*, 285).
[27] Synesius, *Katastasis*, 3 (Terzaghi, *Opuscula*, 288).
[28] Synesius, *Katastasis*, 4 (Terzaghi, *Opuscula*, 290-291). For pessimism in his correspondence: *Epist.*, 34, 57, 73 (*PG*, 66. 1,361, 1,384, 1,437).
[29] It is conceivable that Synesius was alluding to Alaric's capture of Rome in *Epist.*, 109 (*PG*, 66. 1,492), but E. Demougeot says this is unlikely: *De l' unité à la division de l'Empire romain* (Paris 1951) 484n246. On Synesius' positive sense of civic responsibility and defense of his province: *Epist.*, 104, 108, 125 (*PG*, 66. 1,477-1,481, 1,489-1,492, 1,504-1,505). See also C.H. Coster, "Synesius, A Curialis of the Time of the Emperor Arcadius," *Byzantion*, 15 (1940/1941) 17-37.

letter that he was happily isolated in his province from news about the emperor and the imperial court at Constantinople:

> But the emperor and the friends of the emperor and the dancing of divine fortune, which we hear when we meet, are certain names like the flames which are kindled to the height of splendor and then are extinguished. Here these names are kept silent and there is rest for the ears from such recitations. But perhaps it is known that there is always an emperor living, for we are reminded every year by those who collect taxes. But we do not know precisely who is emperor.[30]

This passage indicates how insulated some Roman provincials felt they were from the centers of political developments. It may help explain Synesius' silence concerning the western military reverses, also. But was his reaction typical of other contemporary Greek-speaking eastern clerics both at Constantinople and in the more remote provinces?

The earliest known reaction by an eastern cleric, or an eastern Christian layman, to Alaric's attack on Rome in 410 is the response of Arsenius the Great (354-445), a monk who lived at Scete in the Libyan desert.[31] Saint Arsenius, who was born into a senatorial family, had held a high position in the court of Theodosius I at Constantinople. Subsequently he resolved to break with the world and turned to the monastic life. About 411 a nomadic raid forced him and his monks to abandon Scete and move to Canopus, near Alexandria. He sobbed and exclaimed bitterly: "The world

---

[30] Synesius, *Epist.*, 147 (*PG*, 66. 1549).
[31] On Arsenius in general: J. David, "Arsène," *Dict. d'hist. et de géog. eccl.* (Paris 1930) IV 745-747; J. Martin, "Arsenius der Grosse," *Lexikon f. Theol. u. Kirche* I, 2nd edn. (Freiburg 1957), 907; O. Bardenhewer, *Geschichte der altkirchlichen Literatur*, 1st and 2nd edns. (Freiburg 1924) IV 94-95.

has lost Rome and the monks have lost Scete."[32] Even isolated as he was in the Libyan desert, Arsenius regarded the fall of Rome not as a local event affecting only the inhabitants of the city but as a loss for all of the world.

Another eastern cleric, Isaac of Amida (modern Diyarbekir), visited Rome during the reign of Emperor Arcadius, who ruled from 395 to 408 and returned to the east. He became a presbyter in Amida.[33] The *Pseudo-Dionysius Chronicle* states that in about 418 Isaac wrote poems on the "sack of Great Rome."[34] Some of his poetry has survived, including poems on calamities such as earthquakes, but unfortunately none on the sack of Rome have been preserved.[35] If we can trust the *Pseudo-Dionysius Chronicle*, however, the fall of Rome to Alaric greatly impressed this eastern Christian, who believed that the event was a worthy subject for poetry. Isaac, too, was an inhabitant of a fairly remote province of the empire, but he still felt sufficiently moved to compose such works. Perhaps the memories of his previous visit to Rome inspired him to compose verses on this subject.

Palladius inserts a mention of the sack of Rome in his *Historia Lausiaca* narrative of the life of Saint Melania

[32] *Zhitie izhe vo sviatykh ottsa nashego Arseniia Velikago* = *Bios kai politeia tou hosiou patros hēmōn Arseniou tou megalou*, G.F. Tsereteli, ed., *Zapiski, istoriko-filologicheski fakultet, St. Petersburg University*, 50 (1899) 22. For the date see David, "Arsène," p. 746.

[33] Jacob of Edessa to John the Stylite: *Epistola* in: *Sancti Ephraem Syri Hymni et sermones*, T.J. Lamy, ed. (*Mechlinae*, 1902) IV 362.

[34] *Chronicon Pseudo-Dionysianum*, J.-B. Chabot, tr., *CSCO*, 121, Scriptores Syri Ser. III, v. I (Louvain 1949) 143-144. This important statement, although known to Syriac specialists, has been ignored by students of Late Antiquity and Byzantium. On this chronicle: I. Ortiz de Urbina, *Patrologia Syriaca*, 2nd edn. (Rome 1965) 211-212.

[35] J.-B. Chabot, *Littérature syriaque* (Paris 1934) 33; A. Baumstark, *Geschichte der syrischen Litteratur* (Bonn 1922) 63-66; B. Altaner, *Patrology*, H. C. Graef, tr. (New York 1958) 406; Bardenhewer, *Gesch. altkirch. Lit.*, IV, 404-407; W. Wright, *A Short History of Syriac Literature* (London 1894) 51-54; I. Ortiz de Urbina, *Patrologia Syriaca*, 2nd edn., 101-102.

the Younger (written 419 or 420). He observes that contemporaries marvelled that Saint Melania had been so wise as to sell her properties in the west before Alaric destroyed them, and describes the capture of Rome:

A barbarian storm, of which prophecies long ago spoke, fell upon Rome, and it did not even spare the bronze statues in the Forum. Plundering with barbarian madness, it destroyed everything. Thus Rome, beautified for 1200 years, became a ruin.[36]

The *Vita S. Melaniae*, the original form of which may derive from the hand of Gerontius sometime between 440 and 450, also reports that many praised Saint Melania and her family for their wisdom: "Blessed are those who perceived and sold their property before the arrival of the barbarians." The author of this life notes with satisfaction that Pompeianus, the pagan Prefect of the City (Rome), who tried to seize her properties for the fisc, was through divine providence killed by the people in a riot during Alaric's siege of the city.[37]

Alaric's depradations also stimulated eastern-born Christians living in the west to consider returning to the eastern regions of their birth. Paulinus of Pella (Macedon) writes in his *Eucharisticos* that in the wake of the barbarian invasions he contemplated leaving Gaul (about 412) and returning to his estates in Argos and Epirus, but his wife, pointing to the hazards of the voyage, dissuaded him. It is significant that the east appeared to be a safe haven and that some westerners who owned property there did think of returning.[38]

[36] Palladius, *The Lausiac History*, 54, Don Cuthbert Butler, ed., *Texts and Studies*, VI, Pt. 2 (Cambridge, England 1904) 148.

[37] *Vie de Sainte Mélanie*, Denys Gorce, ed. tr. (Paris 1962) 164-166. On the violent death of Pompeianus: 166. For the identification of Gerontius: 54-62.

[38] Paulini Pellaei *Eucharisticos*, lines 406-430, W. Brandes, ed.,

IV

So far as is known, neither Arsenius, Isaac, nor Palladius discussed with eastern pagans the religious significance of the destruction of Rome or other barbarian invasions of the western provinces. Moreover, Augustine's own writings were virtually unknown in the east. It is very unlikely that his works, such as *De civitate Dei* and *De excidio urbis Romae sermo*, would have been either widely read or copied by eastern Christians.[39] Eastern Christians, accordingly, could not have relied much, if at all, on Augustine's works to answer any eastern pagan critics. They would have been forced to devise their own arguments suited to eastern conditions and shaped to refute the particular charges made by their local pagan opponents.

The earliest known eastern Christian rebuttal of pagan charges concerning Roman decline was probably written by Saint Nilus of Ancyra. A native of Galatia who had entered monastic life by 390, Saint Nilus became the founder and abbot of a monastery near Ancyra. He engaged in a voluminous correspondence with other Christian clerics and with imperial officials in many parts of the Byzantine Empire.[40] He died in 430.[41] In an undated letter to the pagan rhetorician, Apollodorus, Nilus declares:

CSEL, 16 (Vienna 1888) 307. On his eastern origin and extensive possessions in the east: lines 271-285. On Paulinus see: P. Courcelle, *Histoire littéraire des grandes invasions germaniques*, 3rd edn. (Paris 1964) 92-96.

[39] B. Altaner, "Augustinus in der griechischen Kirche bis auf Photius," *HJ*, 71 (1952) 53, 55, 76.

[40] B. Altaner, *Patrology*, 390. Disdier, "Nil l'Ascète," *DTC*, 11 1 (1931) 661-674; K. Heussi, "Untersuchungen zu Nilus dem Asketen," *Texte und Untersuchungen*, III. Reihe, Bd. 12, Heft 2 (Leipzig 1917); K. Heussi, *Das Nilusproblem* (Leipzig 1921).

[41] Disdier, "Nil l'Ascète," 661.

You have said that hordes of barbarians have often invaded Romania because everyone was not willing or eager to worship the pagan gods with sacrifices. Know, however, something more distinct and unveiled: inroads of the barbarians, earthquakes and conflagrations and all other grievous things are occurring for no other reason than the wickedness and foolishness of the superstitious and impious men among you who have not ceased your idolatry, but continue to sacrifice to worthless deities every day in the suburbs.[42]

Nilus says that Apollodorus had previously been converted to Christianity, but had now reverted to the worship of wooden objects.[43] His statement indicates that there still were pagans sacrificing widely outside the cities (imperial legislation had particularly emphasized the elimination of pagan worship within the cities).[44]

Nilus confronted the same pagan arguments concerning barbarian invasions of the empire as Augustine and Orosius. He, however, sought to disprove charges applying not specifically to the sack of Rome in 410 but to the general barbarian devastation of the empire early in the fifth century. He believed these pagan arguments required a written reply. He simply reversed the pagan thesis, arguing that calamities had stricken the empire not because the pagan gods were neglected, but because pagans had in fact continued to sacrifice to them. Consequently he expounded a thesis similar to that of Augustine: these disasters had befallen the empire as a divine punishment from the Christian God for wickedness.[45] Apparently Nilus did not regard pa-

[42] Saint Nilus, *Ep.*, 1. 75 (*PG*, 79. 116).
[43] *Ibid.*
[44] *Cod. Theod.*, 16. 10. 3, 4, 12, 19.
[45] Cf. Augustine, *De civ. D.*, 1. 29, 1. 1, 1. 33-34 (Hoffmann, 51, 4-5, 56-57).

gan charges about imperial decline as a major intellectual problem for himself and his Christian contemporaries, for only one of his extant 1,061 letters discusses this question.

Another Christian cleric, Bishop Theodoret of Cyrus, also sought towards the middle of the fifth century to rebut the pagan contentions.[46] Theodoret inserts a reply in his practical religious manual which he entitled *Quaestiones et responsiones ad Orthodoxos*:

> The destruction of cities also occurred when paganism prevailed. The devastation of Babylonia and Assyria and Nineveh and many other nations bear witness to this. But it cannot be shown that one famous city has been made desolate since Christianity became predominant. Yet it is impossible to judge the holiness of the better [religion] from prosperity, the abundance of houses, and from the devastation of cities and fields, because the Lord God furnishes these for the benefit of mankind and He may also withdraw them. But the holiness of the better [religion] is determined by the voluntary good deeds of the men themselves. But the sacrifice of humans to deities ("It is said that they sacrificed their sons and their daughters to deities") and idolatry occurred when the pagans were predominant. But one may judge the holiness of the Christians from their prevention of such impious pagan acts, and not from the prosperity of houses, cities, and fields. Christianity, moreover, is so much greater with regard to this point: many fewer wars have occurred

[46] In general, on Theodoret's apologetical activity against pagans: J. Schulte, *Theodoret von Cyrus als Apologet* (Vienna 1904); Bardenhewer, *Gesch. altkirch. Lit.* IV 219-247. For broad studies of Theodoret, see also N.N. Glubokovskii, *Istoricheskoe polozhenie i znachenie lichnosti Feodorita, episkopa Kirrskago* (St. Petersburg 1911), and his lengthy *Blazhennyi Feodorit* (Moscow 1890) I-II.

in the world since Christianity has become predominant than when paganism was predominant.[47]

Like Saint Augustine and Orosius, Theodoret maintains that far worse calamities had occurred while men still worshipped the false pagan gods.[48] As in his *Ecclesiastical History* he apparently ignores the sack of Rome by Alaric, or regards it as not permanently destroyed—and indeed by the time in which he wrote, the city had recovered. His omission of the year 410 in his history is puzzling and one can offer no easy explanation (except for the fact that he was primarily writing a history of the Church). Just as Augustine and Orosius had argued that Rome had survived Alaric's brief occupation, Theodoret notes that during the period of Christian supremacy no major city had been devastated.[49] He further observes, with reasoning similar to that of the fourth-century apologetic historian, Eusebius of Caesarea, and the fifth-century Augustine and Orosius, that less warfare had taken place in the world since Christianity had become preeminent. Augustine and Orosius had pointed out that the barbarians who captured Rome had been more moderate than the victorious captors of cities in previous sieges.[50]

[47] Theodoret, *Quaestiones et responsiones ad orthodoxos*, 136, A. Papadopulos-Kerameus, ed., *Zapiski, istoriko-filologicheski fakultet, St. Petersburg University*, 36 (1895) 126-127; cf. translation by A. Harnack, "Diodor von Tarsus: Vier pseudojustinische Schriften als Eigentum Diodors," *Texte und Untersuchungen*, N.F., VI, Heft 4 (Leipzig 1901) 142. On attribution to Theodoret, cf. the discussion in n. 41, chapter 2 of this study. Also: F.X. Funk, "Le Pseudo-Justin et Diodore de Tarse," *Revue d'histoire écclesiastique*, 3 Pt. 2 (1902) 967-971. Funk accepts Theodoret as the probable author.

[48] Cf. Orosius, *Hist. adv. pag.*, 1, prol. 9, 14; 7. 43. 17-18 (3-4, 563 Zangemeister); Augustine, *De civ. D.*, 1. 2 (6 Hoffmann); 1, 36 (58 Hoffmann), 2. 3 (62-63 Hoffmann); *ibid.*, 3. 10-3. 31 (119-161 Hoffmann).

[49] Cf. *ibid.*, 1. 33 (Hoffmann 56). Orosius, *Hist. adv. pag.*, 7. 39. 3-14 (545-547 Zangemeister).

[50] Augustine, *De civ. D.*, 1. 2. 1, 7 (Hoffmann 6, 12-13). Orosius, *Hist. adv. pag.*, 1. prol. 14 (4 Zangemeister); *ibid.*, 7. 39. 3-14 (545-547 Zangemeister).

Above all, Theodoret's thinking resembles that of Augustine because he emphasizes that the real standard for judging a religion is not its ability to confer material benefits on governments, cities, and people, but rather the high standards of worship which it demands, and the eternal rewards it offers its followers.[51] Yet Theodoret apparently was more satisfied with the existing political, economic, and military situation of the empire than were Augustine and Orosius. In no way does he suggest that the Roman Empire was faced with imminent and total collapse.

v

Theodoret of Cyrus, as noted above, does not mention the siege of Rome by Alaric in his Ecclesiastical History.[52] This omission should not, however, be interpreted to signify—as some historians have asserted—that Theodoret was indifferent to events occurring in the western provinces of the Roman Empire.[53] Quite the contrary. A substantial number of letters from Theodoret's correspondence are extant and provide useful information on various aspects of Byzantine political, economic, and ecclesiastical conditions during the first half of the fifth century.[54] Several of these letters con-

[51] Augustine, De civ. D., 5. 4-16, 2. 25, 2. 29, 5. 18 (63-80, 100-102, 106-109, 245-261 Hoffmann). These passages describe the alleged wickedness of the pagan deities.

[52] The best edition is Theodoretus, Kirchengeschichte, 2nd edn., L. Parmentier and F. Scheidweiler, eds. (Berlin 1954); Quasten, Patrology, III 550-551; G. Moravcsik, Byzantinoturcica, I 529-531; G. Bardy, "Théodoret," DTC, 15 (1950) 299-325; R. Hanslik, "Theodoret von Kyros," Die Religion in Geschichte und Gegenwart (3 Aufl., Tübingen 1962) VI 749-750; N. N. Glubokovskii, Blazhennyi Feodorit (Moscow 1890).

[53] J. B. Bury, Hist. Later Rom. Emp. 2nd edn., I 302n2; Demougeot, De l'unité à la division de l'emp. Rom., 483; J. Bidez, "L'Historien Philostorge," Mélanges offerts à Henri Pirenne (Brussels 1926) I 25; A. Lippold, Rom und die Barbaren in der Beurteilung von Orosius (diss. Erlangen 1952) 17.

[54] There are two collections, each containing different groups of letters: PG, 83. 1,171-1,494 has 181 letters; Yvan Azéma has made a new critical edn. of all correspondence; Correspondance I-III (Paris

tain valuable comments on the Vandal conquest of North Africa from the Romans (429-40).[55] As Bishop of Cyrus (Syria) Theodoret had become acquainted with lay and clerical refugees from Libya who had fled to the eastern provinces. He sought to provide them with assistance and endeavored to alleviate their misery by his own efforts and by securing for them the aid and understanding of influential eastern leaders in other cities.

Theodoret also is convinced that the catastrophe of the Romans in Africa had momentous significance for Christians in the eastern provinces as well:

If men had respected the laws of God, they would have enjoyed solid and lasting blessings. But as we have removed ourselves from the straight path and we have scorned the divine precepts, our lot is fatefully a life of sorrows. Our hardships spur us to ascertain their cause— Original Sin—and this discovery stimulates us to avoid sin and instead to attach ourselves to the laws of God. It is certainly He who causes men to see people not only lose their fortunes, but also [He causes] cities and nations to lose their prosperity and fall into the worst misfortune. Such is precisely the fate that has befallen ancient Libya, today called "Africa"—a country that had been full of every good thing suddenly was stripped of all of them. The plunderers were familiar only with cruelty and barbarism and they lacked any education. Therefore the greater part of the bishops dear to God have preferred foreign soil to the land of their fathers, having no other consolation than the hope which they put in God and no

1955-1965). Vol. I contains letters not found in Migne. Cf. Sis. M.M. Wagner, "A Chapter in Byzantine Epistolography: the Letters of Theodoret of Cyrus," *DO Papers* 4 (1948) 119-181.

[55] In general on Vandal conquest: C. Courtois, *Les Vandales et l'Afrique* (Paris 1955) 155-185. The date of these particular letters appears to be later than 442: *ibid.*, 281n11.

other means of satisfying their physical needs than by the hands of those who love God.[56]

This passage demonstrates Theodoret's belief that God had willed the Vandal conquest of North Africa as both punishment and reminder to mankind that swift reversals of fortune do take place in worldly affairs. He regards this event as a stimulus to greater piety and feels impelled to provide assistance to the western victims of this military disaster. In another letter he more explicitly expresses his views on the meaning of this tragedy for the inhabitants of the eastern Roman provinces:

> I believe that the God of all things, caring in His Providence for the common salvation, sends misfortunes as a potent medicine for sinners, as an exhortation to perseverance for the virtuous, and as a beneficial example for all observers. For we take fright when we see others punished. Therefore I regard the misfortunes of Libya as a common blessing. By contemplating the complete reversal of Libya's former prosperity, I perceive the swift changes in human affairs and I learn not to expect that good fortune will endure or to resent my difficulties.[57]

Here again Theodoret reiterates his conviction that the catastrophes that had befallen Africa should cause Christians in the eastern provinces to be wary of favorable material conditions, and to remember the instability of human affairs. He believes God had chosen to use these Africans as instruments for inculcating piety in both the Africans and others who had observed the African tragedy.

On the other hand, Theodoret did not fear that the down-

[56] Theodoret to Eusebius Bishop of Ancyra, *Ep.*, 22. (*Correspondance*, Azéma, ed. tr., I 92-93); on dispossession of Africans by the Vandals: Courtois, *Vandales*, 275-283.
[57] Theodoret, To Ibas Bishop of Edessa, *Ep.*, 52 (Azéma, *Corresp.* II 128).

fall of Roman authority in Africa also signified that all of the empire, including the eastern half, was about to collapse. The tragedy of Africa made a clear and deep impression on him; it can be said emphatically that he was not indifferent to events in the west, nor did he believe that others should view the African catastrophe with indifference. He believed that he and his friends as individuals could do something to aid the plight of the refugees, but did not consider the possibility of any political or military action to restore Roman domination of Africa. In short, he contemplated this disaster only in terms of its implications for Christian piety, not in relation to any further political or military consequences.

Probably no letter expresses more definitely how deeply moved Theodoret was by the Arian Vandal conquest of Africa than this letter to Apellion (who seems to have been a high official in Syria or Phoenicia) asking assistance for Celesticiacus, a refugee:

> It would require the tragedies of Aeschylus and Sophocles to describe the sufferings of the Carthaginians, and perhaps the magnitude of these misfortunes would even conquer [the tragedians'] tongues. For long ago Carthage was with difficulty captured by the Romans. She often fought Rome for primacy and brought her to the extremity of danger. But now Carthage has become the plaything of barbarians. And those men who adorned her far renowned senate now wander throughout the whole world receiving daily subsistence from the hands of friendly strangers. They [the refugee senators] move observers to tears and they teach the uncertainty and instability of human affairs. I have seen many others who have come from there and I have become afraid. For I do not know, as the Scripture says, "what the morrow

will bring forth." I am quite fond of the most admirable and most honorable Celesticiacus, for he nobly bears his fate, and he makes his change from prosperity an occasion for philosophy. He praises the Ruler of all things and regards as beneficial whatever God either ordered to happen or did not prevent from happening. For the reasoning of Divine Providence is indescribable. May your excellency give hospitality like that of Abraham to him and to his wife and children. Trusting in your generosity, I have introduced you to them and I have revealed to him your hospitality.[58]

In other letters Theodoret requests aid and sympathy for African refugees; all were written in a tone of compassion for the victims and with the conviction that the Africans' misfortune represented a divine punishment for themselves and a warning for others.[59] Indeed the emotional reaction of Theodoret to these western misfortunes is comparable to these sentiments of Jerome on seeing refugees from Alaric's assaults on Rome:

Who would believe that Rome, built on victories over the whole world, would tumble, would be mother and tomb for the nations, that the coasts of the east, Egypt, and that Africa which lately belonged to the mistress city would be filled with her male and female servants, that daily holy Bethlehem would receive as beggars former nobles of both sexes who had abounded in riches? Since we cannot give relief to them, we suffer with them and join our tears to theirs. . . .[60]

Certainly Theodoret was at least as moved on seeing west-

[58] Theodoret, *Ep.*, 29 (Azéma, *Corresp.* II 86-88); on Celesticiacus: Courtois, *Vandales*, 281-282; n. 11 p. 281.
[59] For example: *Ep.*, 23 (Azéma, *Corresp.* I 94); *Ep.*, 30-36, 53 (Azéma, *Corresp.* II 88-100, 128-130); cf. n. 54, Chapter 6.
[60] Jerome, *Commentar. in Ezech.*, 3 (*PL*, 25. 79).

ern refugees as had been Jerome, and moreover, Theodoret did actually assist them and devote himself to finding assistance for them. One may suppose that he would also have reacted compassionately to reports of barbarian invasions, plundering, and occupation of other western provinces of the empire.

Nevertheless, Theodoret's most ambitious apologetical tract, *Graecarum affectionum curatio*, contains no reference to the pagan thesis that neglect of the traditional pagan rites was causing imperial ruin.[61] His published opinions on the political and military position of the empire under Theodosius II were completely favorable.[62] He specifically noted that this emperor had received divine protection against external threats.[63] At a later point in his life, when he was accused of Nestorian tendencies, Theodoret became more critical of the emperor's religious policies and handling of justice. But he never complained about the record of Theodosius II in international affairs.[64]

VI

Theodoret's reaction to western Roman disasters was the response of an important church leader who is generally regarded as belonging to the orthodox fold.[65] Certainly the other Christian reactions discussed above were orthodox. Arians also took an interest in fifth-century western events. They developed their own particular interpretations of the religious significance of Alaric's sack of Rome and other

[61] Theodoret, *Thérapeutique des maladies helléniques* 2 v., P. Canivet, ed. tr. (Paris 1958); also a discussion: P. Canivet, *Histoire d'une entreprise apologétique au V*ᵉ *siècle* (Paris 1957).

[62] Theodoret, *Hist. Eccl.*, 5. 37 (340 Parmentier-Scheidweiler).

[63] Theodoret, *Hist. Eccl.*, 5.36. 2-5, Parmentier-Scheidweiler, eds., 338-339; 5. 37. 4-6 (340 Parmentier-Scheidweiler).

[64] Theodoret, *Ep.*, 169 to Alexander of Hierapolis (*PG*, 83. 1,473-1,476); cf. *Ep.*, 163-168 (*PG*, 83. 1,464-1,473).

[65] E. Peterson, "Teodoreto di Ciro," *Enciclopedia Cattolica*, 11 (Rome 1953) 1927.

western political and military calamities.[66] One adherent of the Eunomian faction of Arians, Philostorgius (370?-425?),[67] wrote a *Historia ecclesiastica* comprising twelve books and covering the years 306-425.[68] Fortunately some fragments of the *Historia ecclesiastica* survive. After describing Alaric's siege of Rome[69] Philostorgius reflects on the significance of the capture of the city: "And then the vastness of such great glory and the wide renown of her power were torn to pieces by alien fire and enemy sword and by barbarian captivity. The city lay in a heap of ruins. . . ."[70]

Another group of fragments from Philostorgius' *Historia ecclesiastica* contains lists of recent calamities. During the reign of Arcadius (395-408) many terrible experiences occurred:

> . . . about the eighth hour, the sun was so fully eclipsed that the stars shone forth. So much drought accompanied the incident that it caused everywhere an extraordinary destruction of many men and other animals. The sun having eclipsed, a light [meteor] appeared in the heaven shaped like a cone. . . . This became the sign of great wars and inexpressible human destruction. In the following year, earthquakes began which were not comparable to the previous ones. The simultaneous breaking out of

[66] On Arianism: J.N.D. Kelly, *Early Christian Doctrines* (London 1958), 223-251; X. LeBachelet, "Arianisme," *DTC*, 1 (Paris 1937) esp. 1,779-1,849; A. Fliche and V. Martin, *Hist. de l'église* (Paris 1947) III 69-176, 237-276; H. M. Gwatkin, *Studies of Arianism* (Cambridge, England 1900).

[67] Date: Fritz, 1665; "Philostorge," 1,495.

[68] Best edition: Philostorgius, *Kirchengeschichte*, J. Bidez, ed. (Leipzig 1913); on this author: G. Fritz, "Philostorge," *DTC*, 12 (1935), 1,495-1,498; Moravcsik, *Byzantinoturcica*, I 473-474; J. Bidez, "L'Historien Philostorge," *Mélanges d'histoire offerts à Henri Pirenne* (Brussels 1926) I 23-30; Bardenhewer, *Gesch. der altkirchl. Lit.*, IV 132-135.

[69] Philostorgius, *Hist. Eccl.*, 12. 3 (141 Bidez).

[70] *Ibid.*, 12. 3 (142 Bidez).

earthquakes and fires cut off all hopes of safety. But human destruction was not accomplished, for divine favor sent down a strong wind which drove away the fire and cast it into the sea.[71]

He adds that "other such kinds of calamities were produced at that time, showing that these did not proceed from some physical sequence, as children of the pagans tell the story, but were scourges discharged out of divine anger."[72]

Philostorgius also describes miraculous phenomena which appeared at the accession of Theodosius II:

> In my time there was such human destruction as had not ever been known. This was demonstrated by a star appearing as a sword. For not only was the army consumed as in ancient wars, and the calamities took place in every part of the earth, but also all races were destroyed, the whole of Europe and no small part of Asia was ruined, and even much of Libya and especially as much as was subject to the Romans. For the barbarian sword produced most of the destruction, but famines, plagues, flocks of wild beasts combined and earthquakes pulled up large cities and houses from their foundations and cast them down to inevitable ruin . . . deluges of rain from heaven, and among other things a searing drought, and hurricanes made the horror varied and unbearable. Yes, then hail bigger than a rock fell everywhere . . . a mass of snow and excessive frost extinguished the lives of those whom previous scourges had not killed, and clearly proclaimed divine anger.[73]

Philostorgius declares that such occurrences do not happen naturally: ". . . earthquakes are contrived . . . only by

---

[71] *Ibid.*, 12. 8 (145-146 Bidez).
[72] *Ibid.*, 12. 9 (147 Bidez); cf. *ibid.*, 12. 8 (146 Bidez).
[73] *Ibid.*, 11. 7 (137 Bidez).

divine will to convert and correct sinners."[74] From the extant summaries of his chapters, there is no specific statement of the exact cause of this "divine anger" which he mentioned twice. It is likely, however, given his well-known Arian convictions, that he believed this divine anger was directed against Arcadius, Theodosius II, and their subjects for not confessing the Arian form of Christianity.[75]

VII

Nestorius[76] (d. ca. 451) wrote a tract entitled *The Bazaar of Heracleides*[77] in which he defended his Christological beliefs.[78] An anonymous fifth-century Nestorian—perhaps an immediate disciple—interpolated a section called *Enumeration of some part of the ills which happened in the world because of the transgression against the true faith of God impassible, with a prophecy.*[79] Concerned with contemporary western Roman disasters, this Nestorian author charges that the calamities had occurred because the Romans had failed to worship God in the proper Nestorian fashion:

[74] *Ibid.*, 12. 10 (147 Bidez).

[75] Cf. J. B. Bury, *A History of the Later Roman Empire*, 2nd edn. (London 1923, reprinted New York 1958) I 302n2.

[76] In general: M. Jugie, *Nestorius et la controverse nestorienne* (Paris 1912); M. V. Anastos, "Nestorius was Orthodox," *DO Papers*, 16 (1962) 117-140; J.N.D. Kelly, *Early Christian Doctrines*, 310-317; C. E. Braaten, "Modern Interpretations of Nestorius," *Church History*, 32 (1963) 251-267; Fliche and Martin, *Hist. de l'Église*, IV 163-196; É. Amann, "Nestorius," *DTC*, 11 (1931) 76-157.

[77] Nestorius, *The Bazaar of Heracleides*, G. R. Driver and L. Hodgson, tr. and notes (Oxford 1925); French tr. by F. Nau, *Le livre d'Héraclide de Damas* (Paris 1910); for his other works: F. Loofs, *Nestoriana* (Halle 1905).

[78] Authenticity and date (original, 449-451; Syriac translation, 525-526): L. I. Scipioni, *Ricerche sulla cristologia del "Libro di Eraclide" di Nestorio* (Freiburg 1956) 1-2; L. Abramowski, *Untersuchungen zum Liber Heraclidis des Nestorius*, CSCO, Subsidia, 22 (Louvain 1963) 127-132. Cf. I. Ortiz de Urbina, *Patrologia Syriaca*, 2nd edn., 243.

[79] Nestorius, *Bazaar* (362-380 Driver-Hodgson).

But because they abode not by what they had been forced to confess and had not believed in God the mighty and immortal, who is able to make even wars to cease, they had [not only] become the slaves of the barbarians and been subjected unto slavery to tribute unto them by the confession of written documents, but were also giving [it] unto those who were warring on his side. And there was naught that he, who showed the barbarian [to be] master and the Romans slaves, did not. And thus the supremacy had changed over unto the barbarians, as though the Romans themselves had not God who [is] over all, holy and mighty and immortal. For this reason the rest also of the peoples fled unto him but fled from the Romans, so that they were not even able to rescue themselves.[80]

In another passage the author expresses similar opinions:

. . . for what reason do you suppose that they who possessed the inhabited world [as] their home became the spoil of the barbarians? Was it not because they made not use of the supremacy which was given unto them as was right, that the peoples might know the grace which was given unto them, in such wise that they might learn as slaves what was required, because they learnt not as masters? For what reason again heard they the word of the Gospel, not from the orthodox but from the worshippers of creatures? They were brought into subjection neither to the supremacy of the Empire nor yet under the religion wherein they were, that they might know that, when they took the supremacy of the Empire, they preserved not even in the Empire the supremacy of their religion in God; for this reason also they were not supreme in aught else, in that the supremacy changed over to [their] enemies.[81]

[80] *Ibid.*, 368.   [81] *Ibid.*, 372.

The author also states that a great number of recent disasters had befallen the Romans in reprisal for the wrongs that had been committed against Nestorius:

> . . . hear therefore also the things which thou knowest and testifiest concerning the truth of the things which are said. . . . [thou seest] that the cities of Africa and Spain and of Muzicanus [uncertain] and great and glorious islands—I mean Sicily and Rhodes and many other great ones—and Rome itself have been delivered over for spoil unto the barbarian Vandal.[82]

The author is referring to the capture of Rome in 455 by Geiseric. Once again this passage is clear evidence that eastern Christians were aware of and concerned about the significance of military disasters in the western provinces. The author of this passage attempts to exploit those western disasters for the profit of Nestorianism.

VIII

A third, indeed, the largest, group of Byzantine religious dissenters—the Monophysites—also interpreted the Roman Empire's misfortune as visible evidence of divine displeasure with imperial religious policy. Not surprisingly, some Monophysites related Roman decline to Emperor Marcian's calling and favoring the Council of Chalcedon (451). The contemporary fifth-century sources on Monophysite views on Roman decline are scarce, but the twelfth-century historian, Michael the Syrian, the Jacobite Patriarch of Antioch, 1166-99, reports in his *Chronicle* (and there is no reason to doubt that Michael had access to fifth-century sources or traditions for this quotation) that immediately following the Council, Mar John, a disciple of Peter the

---

[82] *Ibid.*, 378-379. Is "Muzicanus" possibly "Muzuca," a city in Africa between Proconsularis and Byzacena? Cf. J. Andrée, "Muzuca," *RE*, 16 (1933) 989-990.

Iberian, had warned of probably disastrous consequences of the Council:

> If because of the sin of only one person such a great punishment struck the Jews, what then will be that [punishment] of the pestilential synod of Chalcedon, where took place an assembly of bishops and numerous people, who scorned and transgressed not a simple commandment, but the faith itself and its confession? Would they not call the anger of God upon the whole earth? That is why the Lord God told them as formerly: "I shall not be with you any more if you do not cause the anathema to disappear from your midst."[83]

Michael the Syrian comments: "And the outcome of events clearly proved this. Since that time, the empire of the Romans has been broken and the barbarians have become powerful."[84] Michael elaborates this interpretation in a later passage of his *Chronicle* where he dates the division and decline of the Roman Empire from the Council of Chalcedon:

> The Roman Empire has been divided since that time. Just as the churches split apart, each country's citizens giving themselves pastors (thanks to dogmatic schism which resulted from the synod of Chalcedon)—so in the same manner a just vengeance divided the empire. The impious Marcian himself was the cause of this whole rift which divided the Roman Empire. It had been an imperial law that when the emperor of Rome died, the emperor of Constantinople replaced him with his own candidate, and when the emperor of Constantinople died,

---

[83] Michael the Syrian, *Chronique*, J.-B. Chabot, ed. tr. (Paris 1901) II 87-88. On this chronicle, see: I. Ortiz de Urbina, *Patrologia Syriaca*, 2nd edn., 221.

[84] Michael the Syrian, *Chronique*, II 88.

the emperor of Rome chose and installed the one who seemed good to him. Now, as the account has disclosed above, Marcian began to reign—without the assent of the emperor of Rome—by the choice of Pulcheria who had disgraced herself in a secret debauch with him. Thus the unity of the empire was broken by Marcian just as he also divided the faith. And since the time of Marcian, the Romans and the whole western region have not been in accord with the emperors who reigned in the city of Constantinople. Moreover the empire was divided among several [emperors]. This is why the names of the emperors who existed there [in the west] at that time are not even mentioned among us; for the chroniclers were concerned only with the emperors who existed successively at Constantinople whom they called "the emperors of the Romans."[85]

Therefore, Monophysites followed the practice of the other Christian dissident groups, the Arians and Nestorians, in attempting to show that the misfortunes of the Roman Empire resulted from an erroneous imperial religious policy. They fixed the commencement of Roman decline in the year 451 and regarded the disasters as a vindication of their own views and policies.

These passages from the *Chronicle* of Michael the Syrian, from *The Bazaar of Heracleides*, and from the writings of Philostorgius, indicate that in the eastern provinces of the Roman Empire in the fifth century, the discussion of the religious significance of Roman decline could not remain, as it had in the western provinces, a simple dialogue between Christians and pagans. In the east there was no united front of Christians against the pagans: Christian

[85] *Ibid.*, II 122. Cf. *Chronicon Pseudo-Dionysianum*, J.-B. Chabot, tr., *CSCO*, 121, Scriptores Syri, Ser. III, Vol. I *Versio* (Louvain 1949) 165-168.

views on Roman decline were divided, mirroring factional and doctrinal disagreements in general among Christians in the eastern provinces. Disputes over Arianism, Nestorianism, and later, over Monophysitism, which so stirred the east, were not so serious in the western provinces.[86] The particular eastern religious situation in the fifth century therefore helped to shape the specific reactions of eastern Christians to news of Roman military, political, and economic calamities. Eastern Christian members of "heretical" sects, resentful of their mistreatment by the state and the orthodox majority, sought to find in reports of Roman misfortunes documentation of divine wrath against erroneous belief and a further proof of the correctness of their own views and conduct.

In this way, such eastern Christian heretics as the author of the cited sections of *The Bazaar of Heracleides* really were offering arguments very similar to those of pagans throughout the empire: these Roman political and military disasters are the result of divine anger at the Romans' failure to believe the proper religious doctrines and the failure to worship the deity in the correct manner.[87] Moreover, the Trinitarian and Christological Controversies that rent eastern Christendom during the fifth century attracted so much of the attention and energies of prominent eastern Christians that they found little time to engage in controversies with eastern pagans on the religious meaning of contemporary Roman calamities.

[86] In general on these controversies: A. Fliche and V. Martin, *Histoire de l'église* (Paris 1937) IV 163-240; J. Kelly, *Early Christian Doctrines* (London 1958) 223-400; R.V. Sellers, *The Council of Chalcedon: A Historical and Doctrinal Survey* (London 1953); J. Hefele, *Histoire des conciles* (Paris 1908) II 219-880; *Das Konzil von Chalkedon. Geschichte und Gegenwart*, 3 v., A. Grillmeier and H. Bacht, eds. (Würzburg 1951-1954).

[87] Cf. M. Simon, "Christianisme antique et pensée païenne: rencontres et conflits," *Bulletin de la Faculté des Lettres de Strasbourg*, 38 (1959-1960) 314-323.

In sum, the eastern Christian clergy were not at all indifferent to the political and military disasters which befell the western Roman Empire during the fifth century. Every major group of eastern Christians showed an interest in the misfortunes of the western provinces. The orthodox clergy, represented by such figures as Saints Arsenius and Nilus, and Bishop Theodoret of Cyrus, lamented the course of contemporary western Roman events. In defense of Christianity Theodoret and Nilus tried to refute pagan charges that these unfortunate events were caused by neglect of the pagan gods who had for so long protected the Roman Empire.

It is evident that the eastern Christians' arguments were not overwhelmingly persuasive, for the pagan historical apologist Zosimus of Constantinople still believed at the end of the fifth century that he could make an excellent case for the pagan thesis from an account of historical events. The orthodox Christian clergy was defensive in its explanations of Roman disasters, but the heretical eastern Christians eagerly attempted to interpret fifth-century calamities to the benefit of their particular sects. They found the weak condition of the Empire a worthy topic to exploit to prove the truth of their own religious tenets. On the other hand, a more affirmative Orthodox Christian interpretation of recent Roman history appeared in a group of ecclesiastical histories, including one which Theodoret wrote. Our attention must now turn to these historiographical developments.

chapter v

DIVINE PROVIDENCE
AND THE ROMAN EMPIRE:
A POSITIVE EASTERN CHRISTIAN
INTERPRETATION
OF RECENT HISTORY

The *Ecclesiastical Histories* of the *scholastici* Socrates, Sozomen, and Evagrius, and of the Bishop Theodoret of Cyrus, all Orthodox Christians, have been carefully studied
for their data on church history, but not for their valuable
information on early Byzantine political ideology. The favorable opinions the three writers delivered on the government of Theodosius II may be insincere statements inserted
to please the emperor and his officials. Today it is impossible
to ascertain the personal convictions of these historians.
Even so, their published affirmations are an important record of official Byzantine attitudes on Roman decline. Because of their basic similarity in scope and outlook, these
Ecclesiastical Histories—all continuations of Eusebius' *Ecclesiastical History*—deserve collective study.

One measure of these historians' interest in western Roman events is the attention they gave to Rome in 410.
Some Orthodox Christian laymen in the east left a record
of their reactions to Alaric's sack of Rome and to the general condition of the Roman Empire in the fifth century.
They wrote ecclesiastical histories which cover the events
of the previous century. As residents of Constantinople, and
frequently as holders of some public position such as *scho-*

lasticus (lawyer),[1] *sophist*[2] or *rhetor*,[3] they were exposed to, and indeed expressed, the outlook of the imperial court. Far more than the eastern clergy they were inclined as lay-men to see not only the religious significance of events but also to perceive their political implications for both the eastern Roman Empire and the office of the emperor.

Socrates Scholasticus, born about 380 at Constantinople and died about 450, wrote an ecclesiastical history comprising seven books, which cover the period 306 to 439.[4] He explains to his readers that he felt compelled to include political as well as religious matters in this work,[5] but devotes only one short chapter to Alaric's capture of Rome. After sketching how Alaric and his Visigoths had marched from the east into Illyricum and Italy, Socrates states:

[1] On the meaning of *scholastikos*: Seeck, "*Scholastikos*," *RE*, 2nd edn., 2 (1923) 624-625; E.A. Sophocles, *Greek Lexicon of the Roman and Byzantine Periods*, rev. edn. (New York 1900) 1,064; C. Du Cange, *Glossarium ad scriptores mediae et infimae Graecitatis. . . .* (Paris, 1688, reprinted Vratislav 1891) II 180; J. Gothofredus, *Codex Theodosianus cum perpetuis commentariis. . . .* (Leipzig 1737) II 627 [discussing *Cod. Theod.* 8. 10. 12].

[2] On *sophist* and the training of the *sophist* in Late Antiquity: W. Kroll, "Rhetorik," *RE, Supplementband*, 7 (1940) 1,043-1,048; O. Seeck, *Geschichte des Untergangs der antiken Welt* (Stuttgart 1922) IV 170-176.

[3] On the *rhetor*: W. Kroll, "Rhetorik," esp. 1,039-1,041; Seeck, *Gesch. d. Untergangs d. antiken Welt*, IV 176-202. Also, G. Kennedy, *The Art of Persuasion in Greece* (Princeton 1963) 3-68.

[4] Edition used: Socratis Scholastici *Historia ecclesiastica . . .* (*PG*, 67 1-842). Unfortunately no good critical edition of this work has yet been published, although one has been commissioned for *Die griechischen christlichen Schriftsteller*, and for "Sources Chrétiennes": *Bulletin d'Information et de Coordination*, II (Association Internationale des Études Byzantines 1965) 21. On Socrates Scholasticus: Eltester, "Sokrates Scholasticus," *RE*, 3 A (1927) 893-901; W. Nigg, *Die Kirchengeschichtsschreibung: Grundzüge ihrer historischen Entwicklung* (Munich 1934) 28-29; G. Bardy, "Socrate," *DTC*, 14 (1941) 2,334-2,337; Quasten, *Patrology*, III, 532-534; G. Moravcsik, *Byzantinoturcica*, 2nd edn., I 508-510; G. Downey, "The Perspective of the Early Church Historians," *Greek-Roman-and-Byzantine Studies*, 6 (1965) 59-63.

[5] Socrates, *Hist. Eccl.*, 5, *proem.* (*PG*, 67. 564-565).

. . . finally they took Rome. And having plundered it, they burned many of the most wonderful sights and robbed the city of its wealth. They killed many members of the senate by subjecting them to different punishments. And mocking the empire they proclaimed as emperor a man by the name of Attalus. One day he was ordered to be placed on a shield and made emperor, but on another day he was ordered to appear in the dress of a slave.[6]

Socrates remarks that there seemed to be a mysterious force which moved Alaric to capture and plunder Rome: "It is said that when he was proceeding to Rome, a certain monk risked his life and urged him not to take pleasure in such great misfortune nor to rejoice in death and blood. But Alaric said 'I am not going by my own will to that place, but each day something tortures and moves me and says, 'Go destroy Rome.'"[7]

Socrates, who is regarded as one of the most reliable church historians of the fifth century, provides no further observations or information about this event. However, this anecdote about Alaric's motivation again illustrates the eastern interest and rumors concerning the sack of Rome. Socrates obviously regards the event as important and a manifest demonstration of the vanity of worldly power.[8]

II

Sozomen, another *scholasticus*, also wrote an *Ecclesiastical History* of nine books covering the events of the years from the accession of Constantine I in 306 to 439, though the

---

[6] *Ibid.*, 7. 10 (*PG*, 67. 756).　　[7] *Ibid.*, 7. 10 (*PG*, 67. 757).

[8] On the general reliability of Socrates: Quasten, *Patrology*, III 533; Sozomen, *Hist. Eccl.* 9. 6. 6 (398 Bidez-Hansen), also reported this story about the monk and concluded that it illustrated that a divine power was behind the fall of the city.

section on the years 426 to 439 is no longer extant.[9] In dedicating the work to the Emperor Theodosius II, he asks the emperor to read it carefully and add or delete whatever he wished.[10] Presumably, therefore, Sozomen expresses views that were favored, or at least not specifically disapproved, by Theodosius II. His history is thus a priceless source for the attitude of the eastern Roman government and court towards Alaric's attack on Rome and the condition of the Roman Empire in the first half of the fifth century.

To gain an appreciation of Sozomen's narrative of Alaric's capture of Rome one must examine his record in the broader perspective of his treatment of fifth-century developments. Book IX of his *Ecclesiastical History* contains a narrative and interpretation of numerous events that had occurred during the reign of Theodosius II. In the first chapter Sozomen briefly sketches the early years of the emperor's reign. He declares that the very record of the reign of this young emperor and his able sister, Pulcheria,[11] taught an important lesson: "By these events it seems to me that God showed that piety alone (*monēn eusebeian*) suffices for the security of emperors, and without piety armies and the power of an emperor and all other armament are nothing."[12] Ensuing passages recount how the pious Pulcheria had trained her brother to pray, how well she had attended to affairs of

[9] Critical edition employed: Sozomenus, *Kirchengeschichte*, J. Bidez and G. C. Hansen, eds. (Berlin 1960). On Sozomen: Moravcsik, *Byzantinoturcica*, 2nd edn., I 510-512; Quasten, *Patrology*, III 534-536; (Eltester, "Sozomenos," *RE*[2] 3 (1927) 1240-1248; G. Bardy, "Sozomène," *DTC*, 14 (1941) 2,469-2,471; Downey, "The Perspective of the Early Church Historians" 64-66.

[10] Sozom., *Hist. Eccl.*, *prologium* (1-5 Bidez-Hansen).

[11] On Pulcheria: E. Stein, *Histoire du Bas-Empire*, I 275-276; but esp. W. Ensslin, "Pulcheria," *RE*, 23 Pt. 2 (1959) 1,954-1,963. On Theodosius II in general: A. Güldenpenning, *Geschichte des oströmischen Reiches unter den Kaisern Arcadius und Theodosius II* (Halle 1885). A new study is needed.

[12] Sozom., *Hist. Eccl.*, 9. 1. 2 (390 Bidez-Hansen).

state, how she founded numerous charitable institutions, and how greatly she respected the clergy.[13]

Sozomen further amplifies his praise of the piety of Theodosius II and his family in the succeeding chapters of Book IX. In the second chapter he reports how the relics of forty-two martyrs were discovered during Theodosius II's reign and he relates how Pulcheria gave proper honors to these remains.[14] He describes in chapter three the charity, piety, and virginity of Pulcheria and her sisters and significantly concludes: "For these reasons clearly the favors of God, who fights on behalf of their house, have been given to the emperor because of his age. The empire has been increased and every plot and war organized against him has ceased spontaneously."[15]

Sozomen observes in chapter four that the Persians had made peace with the Romans on the eastern frontier, while in Italy the able western *magister utriusque militiae*, Stilicho, had been murdered.[16] He recounts in chapter five how the Huns had threatened the empire of Theodosius II, but declared that "God showed what forethought (*promēthei-an*) He had for the present reign"; therefore many of the Huns suddenly had deserted to the Romans while the rest had simply dispersed. Numerous Huns were enslaved and shipped to Anatolia to serve as manual laborers.[17]

Up to this point in Book IX Sozomen has been illustrating how God had blessed Theodosius II and the particular section of the Roman Empire which he ruled, the east. He begins to discuss Alaric's campaigns against the empire in chapter six: "Thus the eastern part of the empire was freed

[13] *Ibid.*, 9. 1. 1-13 (390-392 Bidez-Hansen).
[14] *Ibid.*, 9. 2. 1-18 (392-394 Bidez-Hansen).
[15] *Ibid.*, 9. 3. 3 (395 Bidez-Hansen).
[16] *Ibid.*, 9. 4. 1-8 (395-396 Bidez-Hansen).
[17] *Ibid.*, 9. 5. 1-7 (396-397 Bidez-Hansen). The quote: *ibid.*, 9. 5. 3 (397 Bidez-Hansen).

from wars and was ruled in a very orderly manner, contrary to the expectations of many people, for the emperor was still young. But affairs in the west were in disorder because many usurpers rebelled."[18] In Sozomen's mind there could be only one explanation for this miraculously favorable situation in the east: God was bestowing special aid on this section of the Roman Empire.[19]

Sozomen gives the immediate background of Alaric's assault. Alaric had sent an embassy to Honorius, which the western emperor subsequently rejected; therefore the Visigoths undertook the siege of Rome:

> After the siege had continued for some time, famine and plague struck the city and many slaves (especially those of barbarian origin) deserted to Alaric. The pagans in the senate believed that it was necessary to perform sacrifices in the Capitol and the other temples. Some Etruscans, having been summoned by the Prefect of the City to do this, promised by means of thunder and lightning to drive off the barbarians. They asserted that they had done this at Larnia, a city of Etruria, which Alaric did not capture when he was marching to Rome. But the outcome showed that they were to be of no assistance to Rome. For to right-thinking [Christian] persons it appeared that these things befell Rome because of divine anger and were a punishment for her excessive ease and licentiousness and because she sinned unjustly and impiously against both her fellow citizens and strangers.[20]

Sozomen's inclusion of this incident again testifies to the

[18] *Ibid.*, 9. 6. 1 (397 Bidez-Hansen).
[19] *Ibid.*, 9. 3. 3 (395 Bidez-Hansen).
[20] Sozom., *Hist. Eccl.*, 9. 6. 3-5 (397-398 Bidez-Hansen). In general on the importance of astrology and divination at Rome in the pagan period: F. H. Cramer, *Astrology in Roman Law and Politics*, Memoirs of the American Philosophical Society, 37 (Philadelphia 1954) 281-283.

impact of the fall of Rome in 410 on the inhabitants of the eastern provinces. To justify his thesis about divine punishment of Rome he also cites the story Socrates had related: "It is said at all events that some monk in Italy urged Alaric, who was speeding to Rome, to avoid the city lest he cause many evils. But Alaric told him that he did not voluntarily attack this city, but something constantly troubled, compelled and commanded him to destroy Rome, and therefore he completed its destruction."[21]

Sozomen stresses, as had Socrates Scholasticus, that Rome had fallen to Alaric by God's will. He was aware of the proposals of the Etruscan magicians to save Rome. Contemporary eastern pagans were probably using this incident in debate with Christians. Zosimus inserted it in his *New History* (cf. Zosim. *Hist. nov.* 5. 41. 1-3). Sozomen felt compelled to combat these charges by arguing that the pagan rites were powerless and foolish in this situation. He endeavors to offer evidence that would undermine any pagan argument that the Roman failure to worship the gods properly had caused this disaster. He shows, as had Saint Nilus of Ancyra,[22] that the pagans in fact had been resorting to worship of their gods, and attempts to demonstrate that these measures had clearly been proven useless and vain when real danger threatened.

Although he was a citizen of the Roman Empire Sozomen exhibits in the above passage a very low, almost hostile, opinion of the city of Rome. He shared his conviction that Rome had suffered for her immorality with Saint Augustine and the presbyter, Paulus Orosius.[23] Sozomen showed in-

---

[21] Sozom., *Hist. Eccl.*, 9. 6. 6 (398 Bidez-Hansen); cf. Socrates, *Hist. Eccl.*, 7. 10 (*PG*, 67. 757).

[22] Saint Nilus, *Ep.*, 1. 75 (*PG*, 67. 116).

[23] Orosius, *Historiae adversum paganos*, 7. 39. 1-14 (Zangemeister, ed., 545-547); Augustine, *De civ. D.*, 1. 3, 1. 7-9 (Hoffmann, ed., 8, 12-18). On the views of Orosius: A. Lippold, *Rom und die Barbaren*

terest in the religious significance of the city's disaster. He perceived in this event a confirmation, not a repudiation, of the power of the Christian God. There is, however, no indication that he felt that the capture and sack of Rome in any way endangered himself or the eastern half of the empire.

Sozomen gives more details about the siege. In chapter seven of Book IX he describes Alaric's demands for rank, money, and provisions from Emperor Honorius;[24] in chapter nine how displeased the pagans were with the fall from power of the imperial pretender, Attalus, puppet of Alaric. Sozomen observes that the pagans had expected Attalus to restore their temples, altars, and festivals, and that the various Christian heretics had expected Attalus to restore their former churches to them.[25] To explain the immediate causes for Alaric's assault on Rome, he states that a group of Gothic mercenaries dispatched by the Romans had attacked Alaric and that in reprisal for this attack Alaric besieged Rome.[26]

Sozomen does not give details about the method by which Rome was actually captured.[27] He simply asserts that "having besieged Rome he took it by treachery":

He [Alaric] yielded to each man in his hordes what he was able to obtain from robbing the Romans of their

---

in der Beurteilung des Orosius (diss. Erlangen 1952), 18. On Augustine's opinions: J. Straub, "Christliche Geschichtsapologetik in der Krisis des römischen Reiches," *Historia*, 1 (1950) 76-78. Cf. also Saint Augustine, *De excidio urbis Romae sermo*, c. 8, Sis. M.V. O'Reilly, ed. tr. (Washington, D.C. 1955), p. 70.

[24] Sozom., *Hist. Eccl.*, 9. 7. 1-5 (398-399 Bidez-Hansen).

[25] On the elevation of Attalus: Sozom., *Hist. Eccl.*, 9. 8. 1 (399 Bidez-Hansen). On Attalus: Seeck, "Priscus Attalos," *RE*, 2 (1896) 2,177-2,179. On his deposition by Alaric: Sozom., 9. 8. 9-10 (400-401 Bidez-Hansen). On the resulting disappointment of the pagans and heretics: *ibid.*, 9. 9. 1 (401 Bidez-Hansen).

[26] *Ibid.*, 9. 9. 2-4 (401 Bidez-Hansen).

[27] *Ibid.*, 9. 9. 4 (401 Bidez-Hansen).

wealth and despoiling their houses. But out of reverence to the Apostle Peter he ordered that the church which surrounded Peter's tomb, which was large and encompassed a great area, was to be an asylum. And it happened for this reason that Rome did not utterly perish, because those who were saved inside (and they were numerous) rebuilt the city.[28]

Once more Sozomen stresses the religious significance of the sack of Rome. Augustine, Jerome, and Orosius also emphasize in their writings that only Christian sanctuaries had been left inviolate by the city's conquerors, and, like Sozomen, they point out that many Romans had saved themselves by fleeing to such churches.[29]

Sozomen further develops in chapter ten of Book IX this point that Christian sanctuaries had been havens of refuge for many Romans during the ordeal of the sack of the city. He repeats an interesting anecdote:

> Since it is natural that in the capture of such a great city many wondrous events occurred, I decided to record one worthy of an ecclesiastical history. Outstanding was the pious deed of a barbarian and the courage of a Roman woman in defending her virtue. They both were Christians but not of the same creed, as he was Arian and she esteemed the faith of Nicea. A certain young man among Alaric's soldiers on seeing this very beautiful woman was conquered by her beauty and tried to drag her to intercourse. But she tugged against him and strove that she might not suffer outrage. Baring his sword, he threatened to kill her, but because he loved her pas-

---

[28] *Ibid.*, 9. 9. 4-5 (401 Bidez-Hansen).
[29] Orosius, *Historiae adversum paganos*, 7. 39. 1-14 (545-547 Zangemeister); Augustine, *De civ. D.*, 1. 1 (Hoffmann, ed., 4-5); Hieron., *Ep.*, 127. 13-14, Labourt, ed. tr., *Lettres*, VII 147-148.

sionately he cautiously struck the skin of her neck. But although she lost much blood, she held out her neck to the sword, believing it better to die with honor than to live in carnal knowledge of another man since she was legally married. But wrestling and approaching her more threateningly, but still accomplishing nothing more, he became astonished at her virtue and led her to the Church of the Apostle Peter. On delivering her to the guard of the church together with six pieces of gold for her upkeep, he ordered the man to protect her.[30]

Once more in this passage Sozomen emphasizes that even in such adverse circumstances as the sack of Rome, Christian piety had vindicated itself. Orosius and Saint Jerome repeat similar stories about women successfully defending their honor during the sack of the city.[31]

Although Sozomen clearly stresses that divine wrath had caused the capture and plunder of Rome by the Visigoths, he is very careful to avoid leaving the impression that God had decided to destroy Rome because of any anger towards the western Emperor Honorius, the uncle of Theodosius II, the ruler to whom Sozomen had dedicated his *Ecclesiastical History*.[32] Immediately following his account of the fall of Rome he begins chapter eleven by observing that various unsuccessful revolts were attempted against Honorius.[33]

[30] Sozom., *Hist. Eccl.*, 9. 10. 1-4 (401-402 Bidez-Hansen).

[31] Saint Jerome, *Ep.*, 127. 13-14, Labourt, ed. tr., *Lettres*, VII 147-148; Oros., *Historiae adversum paganos*, 7. 39. 3-7 (545-546 Zangemeister).

[32] On Honorius: E. Stein, *Histoire du Bas-Empire*, I 224-228, 249-259, 262-275; E. Demougeot, *De l'unité à la division de l'Empire Romain (395-410)* (Paris 1951) 9-10, 97-112; O. Seeck, *Geschichte des Untergangs der antiken Welt* (1913) V 267; Seeck, "Honorius," *RE*, 7 (1913) 2,277-2,291. For the dedication: Sozom., *Hist. Eccl.*, prol. (1-5 Bidez-Hansen).

[33] Sozom., *Hist. Eccl.*, 9. 11. 1 (402 Bidez-Hansen).

In chapter sixteen Sozomen once more stresses that Honorius and Theodosius enjoyed divine favor:

> It is not the opportune moment to list these [deaths of usurpers]; nevertheless I must recall them in order that we might know that it is sufficient for an emperor to retain power merely by giving careful honor to the divine, as this emperor [Honorius] did. . . . And in this period, the eastern part of the empire was freed from wars and was ruled in a very orderly manner, contrary to the expectations of many people, because the emperor [Theodosius II] was still young. And it appeared that God himself was known conspicuously in this present reign, not only because wars were unexpectedly settled, but because there were revealed the holy bodies of many men who were long ago most conspicuous in piety.[34]

Sozomen sought to make two points in this passage: (1) that the eastern half of the empire under Theodosius II had successfully survived the external wars and domestic crises which had ravaged the west during the first half of the fifth century, that the excellent condition of the east during this period was unquestionable evidence of divine favor; and that there was (2) some proof that God had also blessed the western Emperor Honorius.

This latter is a significant and neglected point, for it suggests that both the government of Theodosius II (who had read and presumably approved of this particular historical presentation) and eastern intellectuals such as Sozomen were by no means cool or hostile to the western Roman Empire which Honorius ruled.[35] In chapter one of this study, other historical evidence indicating that Theodosius II did assist Honorius in 410 was reviewed. No positive evidence

---

[34] *Ibid.*, 9. 16. 1-4 (406-407 Bidez-Hansen).
[35] Cf. the conclusions of Chapter I of this study.

exists to demonstrate that Theodosius II was either hostile or indifferent to the fortunes of the western Roman Empire under Honorius in 410 or the following years.[36]

Sozomen, who is writing his *Ecclesiastical History* in the 440s, clearly does not believe the capture of Rome signified that the end of the Roman Empire was approaching.[37] Indeed, the combination of the fall of the old city and the secure condition of the east gives him greater confidence in the government of the eastern provinces. He believes it was a divine miracle that the east had managed to pass through this critical period without being troubled. Furthermore, it is obvious from the attention which Sozomen gives to the siege and sack of Rome that he regards that event as a very important calamity which deserved proper coverage in his history. Even though he is writing essentially a history of the Christian Church, he devotes considerable space to a description of this event and the circumstances surrounding it. His narrative is another testimony to eastern interest in the news of Rome.

III

But does the absence of detailed narratives of Alaric's sack of Rome in the works of the fifth-century Byzantine ecclesiastical historians Theodoret, Socrates, and Sozomen constitute evidence of an eastern lack of concern and an indifference to the fate of the west in general?[38] In the first place, it must be emphasized that Sozomen refers extensively to that event in Book IX, though it is true that Socrates inserts only a

[36] Demougeot, *De l'unité à la division de l'Empire Romain* 483-485, 487.

[37] For the date: Quasten, *Patrology*, III 534.

[38] J. B. Bury, *Later Roman Empire*, 2nd edn., I 302n2; Demougeot, *De l'unité*, 483-485, 487; A. Lippold, *Rom und die Barbaren in der Beurteilung des Orosius* (diss., Erlangen 1952) 17 and n72 on p. 101; J. Bidez, "L'Historien Philostorge," *Mélanges d'histoire offerts à Henri Pirenne* (Brussels 1926) I 25-26.

short discussion of that event in his *Ecclesiastical History*. But does the relatively brief notice Socrates gives to the sack of Rome indicate anything definite about his appreciation of the event's significance?

The primary goal of Socrates', Sozomen's, and Theodoret's works is the narration of the fortunes of the Christian Church.[39] At times they include some mention of political events, at other times they do not. Socrates even apologizes to his readers for his inclusion of secular affairs. He states that at times it was necessary to mention political affairs to make more comprehensible his account of ecclesiastical developments.[40] But given the fact these historians intended to write histories of the Church, their omission or only brief coverage of the fall of the city of Rome in 410 does not necessarily mean that they—let alone all eastern intellectuals—regarded this event as politically insignificant. They simply did not strive to provide a general political history of the years which they covered.

Why was no *De civitate Dei* written in the east during the fifth century, either in response to Alaric's sack of Rome or in reaction to other political and military calamities which plagued the western Roman Empire during that century? One may suggest some possible reasons beyond the obviously unique personality and mind of Saint Augustine himself. The eastern and western halves of the Roman Empire had different political and military experiences during the fourth and fifth centuries, which helped produce different attitudes among eastern and western intellectuals concerning the degree to which God might be expected to protect and promote the material interests of the Roman Empire as

[39] Sozom., *Hist. Eccl.*, *prol.*, 17, 19-21 (4-5 Bidez-Hansen); Socrates, *Hist. Eccl.*, 1. 1 (*PG*, 67 33); Theodoret, *Hist. Eccl.*, 1. 1. 1-4 (4 Parmentier-Scheidweiler).
[40] Socrates, *Hist. Eccl.*, 5, *proem.* (*PG*, 67 564-565).

a reward for the Christian piety of her citizens and in particular of her emperors.

During the fifth century the attitudes of Augustine on the one hand, and the eastern Christian *scholastici* Socrates and Sozomen on the other, differed very radically in respect to the Roman Empire and the significance for Christians of political and military affairs. After surveying the history of the empire since the early fourth century, when Christianity had become the official religion, Augustine concludes that there was not necessarily a relationship between the piety of a Roman emperor and his subjects and the well-being of the state.[41] He maintains that Christians should not expect divine political and military rewards for pious beliefs and actions. Instead, they should hope for the proper eternal rewards in heaven for living a Christian life.[42]

Augustine draws a contrast between the Heavenly and the Earthly City and he does not hesitate at points within his *De civitate Dei* to identify the Earthly City with the Roman Empire.[43] Although admittedly a citizen of the Roman Empire he did not believe the survival and prosperity of Christianity was dependent on its existence.[44] Likewise he rejects the notion that the condition of the empire was

[41] Theodor E. Mommsen, "St. Augustine and the Christian Idea of Progress: The Background of the City of God," *Medieval and Renaissance Studies* (E. F. Rice, Jr. ed. [Ithaca 1959] 281-287); G. Combès, *La doctrine politique de Saint Augustin* (Paris 1927) 112.

[42] Augustine, *De civ. D.*, 5. 25 (262 Hoffmann); 5. 24 (260-261 Hoffmann).

[43] Cf. F. E. Cranz, "The Development of Augustine's Ideas on Society Before the Donatist Controversy," *HThR*, 47 (1954) 285-316; also by Cranz, "Kingdom and Polity in Eusebius of Caesarea," *HThR*, 45 (1952) 64-66; G. Ladner, *The Idea of Reform: Its Impact on Christian Thought and Action in the Age of the Fathers* (Cambridge, Mass. 1959) 239-268; N. H. Baynes, "The Political Ideas of St. Augustine's 'De Civitate Dei,'" *Byzantine Studies and Other Essays* (London 1955) 298-304.

[44] On the Roman patriotism of Augustine: G. Combès, *La doctrine politique de Saint Augustin*, 201-254.

inevitably connected with Christianity. As noted earlier, in the east Bishop Theodoret similarly argues that the particular physical situation of the empire is not a proper standard by which to judge the veracity and effectiveness of the Christian faith.[45]

I V

To discover and understand the contrast between the views of Augustine and those of Socrates and Sozomen, one must examine the ecclesiastical histories of these two historians. Again, it is significant that Socrates and Sozomen, although eastern church historians covering a subject and period comparable to that Theodoret described in his *Ecclesiastical History*, were *scholastici* (lawyers), not clerics. Since they had received such legal training and since they lived at Constantinople, the center of eastern political decision-making, they were more likely to offer interpretations of historical events more favorable to the emperor than would Augustine and Theodoret, who lived in the provinces.[46] The influence of the eastern emperor is nowhere more apparent in fifth-century Byzantine historiography than in the *Ecclesiastical History* of Sozomen—who dedicated his work to Theodosius II.[47]

Both Socrates and Sozomen regarded themselves as continuators of the *Ecclesiastical History* of Eusebius.[48] They not only continued his history from the point at which the

[45] Theodoret of Cyrus, *Quaestiones et responsiones ad orthodoxos,* no. 126, Papadopoulos-Kerameus, ed., *Zapiski, istoriko-filologicheski fakultet,* St. Petersburg University, 36 (1895) 126.

[46] Saint Augustine was Bishop of Hippo, in North Africa. Theodoret was Bishop of Cyrus (or Cyrrhus), a small town near Antioch in Syria.

[47] Sozom., *Hist. Eccl., prol.* (1-5 Bidez-Hansen).

[48] On this work: Quasten, *Patrology,* III, 314-317. Standard edition: Eusebius, *Historia ecclesiastica* = *Kirchengeschichte* (E. Schwartz, ed., 3 Pts. [Leipzig 1903-1908]).

narrative broke off (324), but they also followed the distinctly Christian interpretation of historical events which Eusebius had developed.

Cranz asserts that Eusebius ". . . establishes an essential parallelism between the Empire and Christianity."[49] He also says of Eusebius: "In the first place he assumes that the Christian society on earth is to be an image of the kingdom and polity of heaven. In the second place he assumes that the Christian society on earth is a unity embracing all aspects of civilization and that in this unity the function of an emperor, for example, is as Christian as that of the bishop. The whole of human society should be Christian and holy, and it becomes Christian and holy when it is an image of heaven."[50] Baynes describes the political philosophy of Eusebius as "the conception of the imperial government as a terrestrial copy of the rule of God in Heaven."[51] Saint Augustine, on the other hand, believed the interests and fortunes of the empire and the Eternal City were not necessarily identical.[52]

Socrates Scholasticus in his *Ecclesiastical History* unquestionably accepts Eusebius' viewpoint. In his introduction to Book V, Socrates explains why he found it necessary to include some references to political affairs in his account of the history of the church:

[49] Cranz, "Kingdom and Polity in Eusebius of Caesarea," *HThR*, 45 (1952) 55.

[50] Cranz, "Kingdom and Polity" 64; Eus., *Hist. Eccl.*, 10. 8. 2-5 (892 Schwartz); cf. Ladner, *Idea of Reform*, 119-125.

[51] N. H. Baynes, "Eusebius and the Christian Empire," *Byzantine Studies and Other Essays* (London 1955) 168.

[52] Ladner, *The Idea of Reform*, 130, 132, 267-68; Cranz, "Kingdom and Polity in Eusebius of Caesarea" 64-65; Baynes, "The Political Ideas of St. Augustine's 'De Civitate Dei,'" *Byzantine Studies and Other Essays* 302-306; J. Sirinelli, *Les vues historiques d'Eusèbe de Césarée durant la période prénicéenne* (Dakar 1961) 409; Augustine, *De civ. D.*, 5. 24, 5. 19 (260-261, 253-254 Hoffmann).

We have included such accounts primarily to show that when public affairs were disturbed, as though by some connection the affairs of the church were also disturbed. For whoever searches will find that the public evils and the misfortunes of the church have been interconnected. For he would find that they were simultaneously moved or that one followed the other. Sometimes church affairs were first affected and then state affairs followed, and sometimes the opposite occurred. It is impossible to believe that these alterations occurred from some common fate, but rather they began from our sins so that we would bear evils as a punishment. . . . For this reason we have interwoven many state matters with our church history.[53]

Socrates arrived at this interpretation of history, as he recommended others to discover it, by examining the record of recent events.

It was significant for the development of Byzantine historiography and political ideology that historians such as Socrates, Sozomen, and even to some extent, Theodoret of Cyrus, found it possible to accept a view of history which emphasized the interrelationship of the fortunes of the empire and the Church. Eusebius of Caesarea (and indeed, Constantine I himself) had interpreted history in this manner and Eusebius' fifth-century continuators naturally attempted to apply his political philosophy to the subsequent historical events they described. As will be shown, they found that the concepts of Eusebius did provide a meaningful standard for the comprehension of later fourth- and fifth-century events. Eusebius' conception of the intimate connection of church and empire in human history continued to survive in Byzantium, no doubt in part because these fifth-

---

[53] Socrates, *Hist. Eccl.*, 5, *proem.* (*PG*, 67. 565).

century ecclesiastical historians preserved and repeated his outlook and passed it on to subsequent Byzantine generations.[54]

Socrates, Sozomen, and Theodoret believed they saw a relationship between the state of the Roman Empire and that of the Church from the reign of Constantine I up to and including the reign of their own eastern Roman Emperor, Theodosius II in the fifth century. They note, in line with the views of Eusebius, how Constantine I had enjoyed divine favor in his military campaigns both against domestic and foreign enemies. They believe God's Providence (*pronoia*) had aided the emperor.[55] Constantine's son, Constantius II (337-61), however, had favored the Arians; consequently he did not prove to be a successful emperor. He died while marching to combat the rebellion of his cousin Julian. Theodoret comments: "He did not possess that assistance which his father had left to him, because he did not guard undisturbed the inheritance of his paternal piety. Therefore he bitterly bewailed his change of faith."[56]

The fifth-century ecclesiastical historians understandably perceive a relationship between the condition of Christianity and the state of the Roman Empire under Julian the

[54] Cf. the comments of Baynes, "Eusebius and the Christian Empire," *Byzantine Studies and Other Essays* (London 1955) 168; K. M. Setton, *Christian Attitude towards the Emperor in the Fourth Century* (New York 1941) 46-56; and R. Jenkins, *Byzantium and Byzantinism* (Cincinnati 1963) 3-6. On Constantine's views: F. Dvornik, "Emperors, Popes and General Councils," *DO Papers* 6 (1951) 5-11; in general: G. Ladner, *The Idea of Reform* (Cambridge, Mass. 1959) 107-132.

[55] On Providence: H.-D. Simonin, "La providence selon les pères grecs," *DTC*, 13 (1936) 941-960; D. Amand, *Fatalisme et liberté dans l'antiquité grecque* (Louvain 1945) 277, 391-392, 402-404, 504-507; and in general the excellent work of H. Koch, *Pronoia und Paideusis: Studien über Origenes und sein Verhältnis zum Platonismus* (Berlin, Leipzig 1932).

[56] Theodoret, *Hist. Eccl.*, 2. 32. 6 (Parmentier-Scheidweiler 174); esp. Sozom., *Hist. Eccl.* 1. 7. 4-5 (16 Bidez-Hansen); Socrates, *Hist. Eccl.* 1. 16 (*PG*, 67. 117).

Apostate (361-63).[57] Theodoret believes Julian was killed by someone, "but whether it was a man or angel who wielded the sword, it was clear that he who did this was an agent of divine will."[58] Sozomen is convinced that God had demonstrated his wrath against Julian during that emperor's reign: in response to Julian's order for a statue of Christ to be mutilated, lightning struck at the statue of Julian himself which had been erected in its place.[59] He also states that God had shown his might and wrath in sending fire, which prevented the rebuilding of the Jewish temple at Jerusalem that Julian sanctioned and encouraged.[60]

Sozomen also presents a number of proofs for his thesis that Julian's violent death in Persia was due to divine wrath against his persecution of the Christians. He cites visions and Christian predictions that Julian would meet a violent end.[61] He also asserts: "It is obvious that throughout the reign of this emperor, God was shown to be angry. He permitted many kinds of disasters to fall upon the Roman provinces. For the earth was shaken repeatedly by the worst earthquakes and houses toppled and everywhere there were such terrible quakes that it was not safe to be inside or outside."[62] The consequent failure of Julian's attempt to restore official pagan worship, and his death after such a short reign, seemed to those fifth-century historians a definite proof that God would thwart pagan emperors and protect only Christian ones.

The Christian Emperor Jovian succeeded Julian. Jovian's

---

[57] On Julian: Theodoret, *Hist. Eccl.*, Bk. III (177-206 Parmentier-Scheidweiler); Socrates, *Hist. Eccl.*, 3. 1-3. 3; 3. 10-3. 23 (*PG*, 67. 368-388, 409-449).

[58] Theodoret, *Hist. Eccl.*, 3. 25. 5-7 (204-205 Parmentier-Scheidweiler).

[59] Sozom., *Hist. Eccl.*, 5. 21. 1-3 (227-228 Bidez-Hansen).

[60] *Ibid.*, 5. 22. 7-14 (230-232 Bidez-Hansen).

[61] *Ibid.*, 6. 2. 1-12 (236-238 Bidez-Hansen).

[62] *Ibid.*, 6. 2. 13 (238 Bidez-Hansen).

reign was extremely short (363-64), but even in his case
these historians demonstrate that the emperor was rewarded
in this world for his good faith. Theodoret declares that
Jovian had enjoyed God's Providence as a reward for his
piety. God had extricated Jovian and his army safely from
the precarious situation in the middle of Persia where Julian had led it. Theodoret regards the request for peace by
the Persian King Shahpur as divinely inspired.[63] Socrates
Scholasticus even asserts: "But the Roman Empire would
have fared well, both with respect to public and to ecclesiastical affairs, prospering so much from a good emperor,
if not suddenly death had come and taken away such a man
from the state."

The Christian historians do not find it difficult to explain
why such a pious Christian emperor as Jovian should have
died so quickly after his accession. Theodoret explains that
this was a sign from God that He bestows and takes away as
He chooses, and thus this should serve as a stimulant to
strive for a better life.[64] Saint Augustine places a more radical interpretation on the brevity of Jovian's rule, maintaining that this event demonstrates that one should not expect
concrete political and military rewards from God in return
for one's piety: "Lest, however, any emperor should become
a Christian in order to merit the felicity of Constantine—
for one ought to become a Christian for eternal life—He
took away Jovian much more quickly than Julian."[65]

Jovian was followed in the eastern provinces by the Emperor Valens (364-78) who favored Arianism.[66] Fifth-cen-

[63] Theod., *Hist. Eccl.*, 4. 2. 2 (211 Parmentier-Scheidweiler);
Socrates, *Hist. Eccl.*, 3. 26 (*PG*, 67. 457). I owe thanks to Mr. Doug-
las Greene, my student at the University of Chicago, for pointing out
this reference to me.

[64] Theodoret, *Hist. Eccl.* 4. 5. 2 (216-217 Parmentier-Scheidweiler).

[65] Augustine, *De civ. D.*, 5. 25 (262 Hoffmann).

[66] On Valens: W. Ensslin, "Valens" *RE*, 2nd edn., 7. Pt. 2 (1948)
2,097-2,147.

tury Orthodox eastern historians assert that the erroneous religious policies of Valens had manifestly incurred divine anger. Socrates Scholasticus states:

> On July 2, in the following year, in the consulate of Lupicinus and Jovinus, hail the size of a man's hand fell on Constantinople, similar to stones. Many said that the hail had fallen due to the anger of God because the emperor had exiled many of the clergy who were unwilling to be in communion with Eudoxius. . . . In the following consulate, which was the second of both Valentinian and Valens, an earthquake occurred in Bithynia and ruined the city of Nicea on the eleventh of October. This was the twelfth year after the fall of Nicomedia. Shortly after this earthquake, even many parts of Hellespontine Germa trembled because of another earthquake. Although these things took place, they did not restrain either Eudoxius, the bishop of the Arians, or of Emperor Valens. For they did not cease persecuting those who disagreed with them. The earthquakes appeared to be signs of the upheaval of the churches.[67]

The death of Valens at the battle of Adrianople in 378 was viewed as a divine retribution for his persecution of the orthodox Christians. Sozomen relates an interesting story to illustrate the theme of divine punishment of Valens:

> Isaac, a very good monk, approached Valens who was leaving Constantinople. Scorning his own danger for the sake of the divine, he said: "Give back, O emperor, the churches which you took away from the orthodox who guard what was done at Nicea, and you shall be victorious." But the emperor became angry and ordered him to be seized and guarded in chains until he returned and

[67] Socrates, *Hist. Eccl.*, 4. 11 (*PG*, 67. 481-484).

exacted punishment for his audacity. But Isaac replied:
"But you shall not return unless you restore the churches."
And such was the issue.[68]

Theodoret repeats this story. He adds that Valens' commanders warned the emperor that by fighting against God
in his religious policies he had caused God to join with
the Goths against him.[69] He says the death of Valens at the
hands of the Goths (who had surrounded and ignited the
house in which he had taken refuge) had religious significance: "Therefore in this manner he even received punishment in this present life for those whom he had wronged."[70]
By emphasizing the retribution Valens had suffered, the historians demonstrate the close connection between an emperor's religious policies and his political fortunes. As Theodoret observes, "The conduct and fate of Valens taught
clearly how the Lord God bears at great length those strug-
gling against Him and how He punishes those who abuse
His patience."[71]

Valens was succeeded by Theodosius I, a loyal Catholic.
Naturally the fifth-century eastern Christian historians, who
were writing during the reign of his grandson, Theodosius II, attempted to show Theodosius' adherence to correct
religious beliefs was rewarded by success in his political
and military undertakings. Theodoret reports that Theodosius enjoyed divine assistance in his campaign to overthrow
the imperial usurper Eugenius: in the decisive engagement
God sent a high wind into the faces of the insurgents and
blew back their arrows. He observes: "Such a man he was
in both peace and war, always asking for divine assistance

[68] Sozom., *Hist. Eccl.*, 6. 40. 1 (301 Bidez-Hansen).
[69] Theod., *Hist. Eccl.*, 4. 34. 1-2 (272 Parmentier-Scheidweiler);
ibid., 4. 33. 1-2 (271-272 Parmentier-Scheidweiler) on remarks of the
commander Trajan to Valens before the battle.
[70] Theod., *Hist. Eccl.*, 4. 36. 2 (273 Parmentier-Scheidweiler).
[71] *Ibid.*, 5. 1. 1 (278 Parmentier-Scheidweiler).

and always receiving it."[72] The historian relates that before the battle Theodosius had seen a miraculous vision, "two men clad in white borne on white horses, who ordered him to take courage, to expel his fear, to array his army facing eastward, and to marshal them in formation. They said that they were his allies and champions. One said that he was John the Evangelist and the other said that he was the Apostle Philip."[73]

Socrates and Sozomen reiterate the theme that the piety of Theodosius earned political and military dividends. Socrates asserts that Theodosius' efforts to conciliate the various Christian sects had their reward: "I believe that this public declaration by the emperor was the cause of benefit to him. For by some divine providence (*pronoia*) in those times, the races of barbarians were subjected to him."[74] Adding some details he repeats the report that God had sent a powerful wind to aid Theodosius in his engagement against Eugenius:

> The emperor became anxious when he saw his barbarian [mercenaries] being destroyed, and throwing himself on the ground, he called on God for help and he did not fail in his request. For Bacurius his commander . . . routed those who shortly before had been the pursuers. There followed another event worthy of wonder. For a very strong wind blew the arrows sent by Eugenius' men and turned them back on their senders. But the arrows of their opponents [the Romans] were sent with much greater force against them. The prayers of the emperor had such great force.[75]

Sozomen also reports that Theodosius' victory over Eugeni-

[72] *Ibid.*, 5. 24. 17 (327 Parmentier-Scheidweiler).
[73] *Ibid.*, 5. 24. 5-6 (325 (Parmentier-Scheidweiler).
[74] Socrates, *Hist. Eccl.*, 5. 10 (*PG*, 67. 584).
[75] *Ibid.*, 5. 25 (*PG*, 67. 652-653).

us was miraculous, and adds that the arrows of the rebel forces were mysteriously turned back.[76] He repeats the popular tale that John the Baptist had aided the emperor.[77]

Socrates and Sozomen were convinced that ample evidence existed to show that during the reign of Arcadius (395-408), the son of Theodosius I and the father of Theodosius II, God had intervened to influence the course of events. Sozomen asserts that Eutropius, the Pretorian Prefect of the East, quickly found death as punishment for his injustices against the Church.[78] When the barbarian commander, Gainas, and his Goths attempted to seize Constantinople in 400 angels appeared who so frightened the Goths that they fled from the city and were massacred.[79]

Sozomen notes that when Gainas and his force, after leaving Constantinople, had attempted to cross on rafts from the Chersonese to Lampsachus, "Even here the Romans were aided by divine power. . . . Suddenly a large wind blew and broke up their rafts with force and drove them against the Roman ships. Most of the barbarians with their horses were drowned, but some were killed by the Roman soldiers."[80] Socrates also narrates this event and describes it as "an astounding deed of divine providence."[81]

Fifth-century eastern ecclesiastical historians believed their present emperor, Theodosius II, had been particularly blessed with divine protection. For example, Theodoret declares:

[76] Sozom., *Hist. Eccl.*, 7. 24. 6 (338 Bidez-Hansen).
[77] *Ibid.*, 7. 24. 8-9 (338 Bidez-Hansen).
[78] *Ibid.*, 8. 7. 5-6 (360 Bidez-Hansen).
[79] Sozom., *Hist. Eccl.*, 8. 4. 12-14 (355-356 Bidez-Hansen). On Gainas: Seeck, "Gainas," *RE*, 7 (1912) 486-487; Seeck, *Geschichte des Untergangs*, V 308-310, 318-325; and esp. E. Demougeot, *De l'unité à la division de l'Empire Romain* 256-262; Bury, *Later Roman Empire*, 2nd edn., I 127-135. Gainas was killed while in flight by the Hunnic leader Uldin.
[80] Sozom., *Hist. Eccl.*, 8. 4 18-20 (356-357 Bidez-Hansen).
[81] Socrates, *Hist. Eccl.*, 6. 6 (*PG*, 67. 680).

But the God of his parents and ancestors did not allow his orphanage to be a hardship. God provided for him to share in a pious upbringing. He guarded his empire unshaken and He restrained rebellious intentions. Always remembering these favors, Theodosius and his sisters sing hymns to Him. His sisters have practiced virginity throughout their lives and believe that the greatest luxury is care for the divine scriptures and that care of the needy is an inviolate treasure. Theodosius adorns his reign with many other things, not the least love of mankind (*philanthropia*), gentleness, perpetual calmness of mind, and a pure and proper faith.[82]

One specific example of divine aid to Theodosius, according to Theodoret, was God's dissipation of the Hunnic menace in 434:

> [Theodosius II] continuously gathers the fruits of his good works. For he has the protection of the Lord of the Universe. Therefore when Roilas [= Rua or Rugila or Ruas], Chief of the nomad Scyths, crossed the Danube with an especially large army, wasted and plundered Thrace, threatened to besiege, capture and lay waste the imperial city [Constantinople] with a mere shout, God with thunderbolts and lightning from above burned him and consumed his entire army.[83]

Theodoret expresses satisfaction with the political and military situation of the eastern Roman Empire under Theo-

[82] Theod., *Hist. Eccl.*, 5. 36. 3-5 (Parmentier-Scheidweiler 338-339). *On philanthropia* (love of mankind): G. Downey, "Philanthropia in Religion and Statecraft in the Fourth Century after Christ," *Historia*, 4 (1955) 199-208.
[83] Theod., *Hist. Eccl.*, 5. 37. 3-4 (340 Parmentier-Scheidweiler). On Roilas or Rua: E. A. Thompson, *A History of Attila and the Huns* (Oxford 1948) 63-73; Roilas died in 434, *ibid.*, esp. 72-73. Cf. Isaac of Antioch, "Homily on the Royal City," C. Moss, tr., *Zeitschrift für Semitistik und verwandte Gebiete*, 8 (1932) 67-70.

dosius II. He anticipates no collapse of the state nor does he perceive any indications of Roman decline.

Socrates Scholasticus similarly maintains that God had given special protection to the eastern Roman Empire during the reign of Theodosius II. He portrays Theodosius as a priest-king, able to intervene personally with God through prayers in order to procure certain desired benefits for his empire. He states that in the campaign of Aspar to crush the western usurper John, "the prayer of the God-loving emperor again prevailed. For an angel of God in the dress of a shepherd guided Aspar and his men through the swamp adjacent to Ravenna."[84] In this manner the Romans were able to approach and seize the city together with the usurper John.[85] Socrates also attributes the destruction of the Huns in 434 to the power of the prayers of Theodosius II:

> For after the death of the usurper [John], the barbarians [Huns] whom he had summoned for assistance against the Romans were ready to overrun the Roman Empire. Having learned this, the emperor repeatedly turned his mind to God. Having spent time in prayers, he accomplished in no short time what he had sought to receive. It is good to hear what happened to the barbarians. For their chief, whose name was Rougas [= Rua or Rugila or Ruas], died when struck by lightning. Then a plague destroyed most of the men who served under him. And even this did not suffice. For fire descended from heaven and consumed many of those who remained. And this caused the greatest fear among the barbarians, not because they dared to raise arms against such a noble race as the Romans, but more because they perceived them to be aided by a powerful God. . . . But because of his

---

[84] Socrates, *Hist. Eccl.*, 7. 23 (PG, 67. 789); cf. W. W. Hyde, *Paganism to Christianity in the Roman Empire* (Philadelphia 1946) 221.
[85] Socrates, *Hist. Eccl.*, 7. 23 (PG, 67. 789-792).

gentleness the providence of God conferred many other benefits on the emperor.[86]

Socrates recounts another instance of a favorable response by God to the prayers of the emperor. In 421 the empire was locked in war with the Persians:

> The emperor, on seeing the Persian make preparations with his whole army, placed all of his hopes for the war in God, and sent forth his largest force. Because he had faith, the emperor immediately found benefit from God. It was evident from this: while the people at Constantinople in the Hippodrome were standing in uncertainty about the fortune of the battle, angels of God were seen in Bithynia by some persons coming to Constantinople on business. The angels ordered them to urge the people of Constantinople to have courage and pray, and to trust in God that the Romans would be victorious, for they said that they were sent by God as arbiters of the war.[87]

In the battle which resulted God struck fear into the Saracen mercenaries of the Persians and a general Persian rout resulted.[88] Socrates observes that God had given so many victories to the Romans during Theodosius II's reign that the people composed panegyrics to the emperor.[89]

In general, Socrates Scholasticus highly esteems the character of Theodosius II: "The Emperor Theodosius is more gentle than all other men on earth. Because of this gentleness, God twice in military contests subjected his enemies to him, as the said victory over John the Usurper and the subsequent destruction of the barbarians demonstrate. For

----

[86] On the prayers of Theodosius II which secured divine aid against the Huns: Socrates, *Hist. Eccl.*, 7. 43 (*PG*, 67. 832-833).

[87] On God's answer to the prayers of Theodosius II for aid against the invading Persians: *ibid.*, 7. 18 (*PG*, 67. 776).

[88] *Ibid.*, 7. 18 (*PG*, 67. 776-777).

[89] *Ibid.*, 7. 21 (*PG*, 67. 784).

the God of the Universe now gives to the most God-loving emperor such benefits as were given in ancient times to the just."[90] Socrates was convinced the empire was being ruled wisely and was far from irreparable decline. God was bestowing political and military rewards on the empire in return for the pious actions of the present emperor.

Sozomen in his *Ecclesiastical History* also proclaims the good fortune of the eastern provinces of the Roman Empire under Theodosius II[91] and, adhering to the concepts of Eusebius and other eastern fathers, he praises the emperor as an imitator of God: "You therefore are humane and gentle both to neighbors and to all, imitating your Protector the Heavenly Emperor since He loves to send rain and cause the sun to rise upon the just and the unjust and furnishes other things ungrudgingly."[92] Such views are strikingly different from those of Sozomen's western contemporary, Saint Augustine, who rejects the notion of any real parallel between an emperor and God.[93] Sozomen makes this statement in the preface to his history, and in this address he also lists many of the virtues of Theodosius II:

To summarize, it is possible, in the fashion of Homer, to address you as more imperial than the emperors before you. For we have heard of some possessing nothing to be admired, and others honoring the emperor's office with only one or two virtues. But you, O most powerful, gathering all of the virtues, you have excelled everyone in piety, love of mankind (*philanthropia*), courage, temperance, justice, love of honor, greatness of soul (*megalopsychia*) proper for the imperial dignity. Eternity will boast of

90 *Ibid.*, 7. 42 (*PG*, 67. 832).
91 Sozom., *Hist. Eccl.*, 9. 6. 1 (397 Bidez-Hansen).
92 *Ibid.*, *prol.*, 9 (3 Bidez-Hansen).
93 Cf. F. E. Cranz, "*De civitate Dei* XV, 2, and Augustine's Idea of the Christian Society," *Speculum*, 25 (1950) 218-221.

your government because it is less tainted with blood or murder than all of the reigns of your predecessors.[94]

He concludes this preface by expressing a hope that God might always preserve Theodosius II and allow his "pious empire" to be transmitted to his sons' sons.[95] These passages from Sozomen's work all illustrate how pleased and undisturbed eastern orthodox Christians were concerning the state of the empire in the first half of the fifth century; they found no reason to doubt that God would continue to reward the Christian piety of emperors with prosperity and military security.

Such opinions were virtually official expressions of imperial propaganda. Sozomen openly requests Theodosius to give official approval to his history:

> Come, O omniscient possessor of every virtue, especially piety which the Holy Word says is the beginning of wisdom, receive from me this work. Organize it and purify it, and add and delete material through your exact knowledge and efforts. For whatever seems pleasing to you will appear completely useful and brilliant to the readers and no one will raise his finger to what you have approved.[96]

V

Basically it was far more difficult for western Romans to perceive any divine political and military rewards for imperial piety than it was for eastern Romans. They could discern no such clear connection between the fortunes of Catholic, western Roman emperors and their empire, and

[94] Sozom., *Hist. Eccl.*, *prol.*, 15-16 (4 Bidez-Hansen). On the significance of *megalopsychia* in Late Antiquity: G. Downey, "The Pagan Virtue of *Megalopsychia* in Byzantine Syria," *TAPA*, 76 (1945) 279-286.

[95] Sozom., *Hist. Eccl.*, *prol.*, 21 (5 Bidez-Hansen).

[96] *Ibid.*, *prol.*, 18 (4 Bidez-Hansen).

the degree of piety of these emperors. Although pious Catholics, the western Emperors Constantine II and Constans had both met violent deaths.[97] The pagan Julian had only briefly enjoyed imperial power, but his Catholic successor Jovian had ruled for an even shorter period.[98] Even under the Catholic Emperor Valentinian I the west had suffered serious invasions.[99] The Catholic Gratian and Valentinian II had both been killed by western usurpers.[100] It was true that Theodosius I, who ultimately ruled both halves of the empire, had proved to be a remarkably successful ruler. Under his son, Honorius, however, the west had undergone numerous barbarian invasions, culminating in Alaric's sack of Rome in 410; yet Honorius had been a pious Catholic.

Augustine's examination of historical events since the accession of Constantine I led him to argue that there was no realistic hope for secular progress. The only true prospect for man's improvement was to be found in the progress towards a heavenly reward.[101] Augustine asserts that temporal bounties had been given to all sorts of men: "And therefore earthly kingdoms are given by Him to both good men and bad men, lest his worshippers still under the direction of a small mind, should desire these gifts from Him as something important."[102]

[97] *Ibid.*, 4. 1. 1 (140 Bidez-Hansen), for the death of Constantine. On the death of Constantine II: *ibid.*, 3. 2. 10 (103-104 Bidez-Hansen).

[98] On Jovian: O. Seeck, "Iovianus," *RE*, 9 (1916) 2,006-2,011.

[99] On the barbarian invasions of Britain, northern Gaul, the Rhine frontier and Pannonia: Stein, *Hist.*, I 181-183.

[100] Sozom., *Hist. Eccl.*, 7. 13. 9-10 (317-318 Bidez-Hansen), for the death of Gratian. For the murder of Valentinian II: *ibid.*, 7. 22. 1-2 (334-335 Bidez-Hansen).

[101] Augustine, *De civ. D.*, 4. 33, 5. 24 (207, 260-261, Hoffmann). Cf. T. E. Mommsen, "St. Augustine and the Christian Idea of Progress," *Medieval and Renaissance Studies* 281-287; and C.N. Cochrane, *Christianity and Classical Culture*, 2nd edn. (London, New York 1957) 488-496, 510-516.

[102] Augustine, *De civ. D.*, 4. 33 (207 Hoffmann).

The ultimate reaction of Saint Augustine to the fall of Rome was that man's trust should not be placed in worldly empires but rather in the City of God. In the east, however, some early fifth-century historians, after pondering events, decided that an emperor through diligent performance of good works and recourse to prayer might successfully intercede with God for divine favor and protection against all enemies, internal and external. The contrasting fortunes of east and west during the first half of the fifth century reinforced the confidence of eastern Christians in their emperor and their empire.

VI

Priscus Panites records important eastern reflections on the weaknesses and strengths of the Roman Empire.[103] He composed a description of his embassy (449) to the court of Attila at approximately the same time as Socrates, Sozomen, and Theodoret were writing their histories.[104] He appears to have been an Orthodox Christian layman, but one cannot be absolutely certain.[105] He reports that while on the embassy to Attila in 449 he met a former Roman who had been captured by the Huns, at Viminacium on the Danube.

[103] On Priscus: Moravcsik, *Byzantinoturcica*, I 479-488; E.A. Thompson, *A History of Attila and the Huns* (Oxford 1948), 184-197; W. Christ, W. Schmid, and O. Stählin, *Geschichte der griechischen litteratur*, 6th edn. (Munich 1924) II Pt. 2 1,036.

[104] The embassy: Priscus, frgs. 7-8 (L. Dindorf, ed., *Historici Graeci minores* [Leipzig 1870] I 286-322); Thompson, *Attila and the Huns*, 102-120; the date: *ibid.*, 102; and Bury, *Later Roman Empire*, 2nd edn., I 279-288.

[105] In one fragment, Priscus describes Bleda, Marcian's ambassador to Geiseric in these terms: ἦν δὲ τῆς τοῦ Γεζερίχου αἱρέσεως ἐπίσκοπος. It would appear unlikely that he would have used the word αἱρέσεως unless he himself were an Orthodox Christian. The text: Priscus, frg. 24 (I 335 Dindorf). One cannot arrive at an unequivocal conclusion on this question. Bury, *Later Roman Empire*, 2nd edn., II 418, thinks it probable that Priscus was a pagan, but admits in n. 2: "This is not so clear in the case of Priscus . . ." (in a discussion of fifth-century paganism).

This Roman later received his freedom, but voluntarily chose to remain among the Huns. Priscus presents to his readers the critical comments of the former captive, criticisms which are a pessimistic commentary on the condition of the Roman Empire at mid-fifth century. They offer a striking contrast to the confident optimism of Sozomen, Socrates, and Theodoret about the situation of the eastern Roman Empire:

He believed that his present life sharing the table with Onegesius was better than his previous life. For those living among the Scythians continue in inactivity after wars, each man enjoying his present property not at all or little burdened. Those living among the Romans, however are easily captured in war, and place their hopes in others for security, as none of them can use arms because of the tyrants. More perilous is the cowardice of the commanders of those bearing arms because they do not accept war at all. But more painful conditions exist in peacetime than the evils of war, namely, the most burdensome exactions of taxes and the injuries of worthless men. The laws do not apply to everyone. If the violator of the law is rich, it is impossible to punish him for his injustice. But if he is poor, and does not understand how to arrange matters, he bears the penalty—if he does not die before the judgment is given, since the cases drag out for a long time and are very costly. What is most grievous of all is that one obtains one's rights for money. For one will not be allowed in court if he does not pay money to the judge and to his assistants.[106]

Priscus declares that he himself defended the government of the Roman Empire:

[106] Priscus, frg. 8 (I 306-307 Dindorf); on Onegesius: W. Ensslin, "Onegesius," *RE*, 18. 1 (1939) 437-438.

I said that the inventors of the Roman constitution were wise and good men. In order that business not proceed at random, they established some men as guardians of the laws and some who took care of arms and who were to practice military exercises. Their only role was to be ready for battle and, as in their exercises, to go to war in confidence having used up their fear during training. The inventors of the Roman constitution assigned others to deal with farming and to care for the land in order to feed themselves and, through their contributions to the military grain supply, also feed those who fight on their behalf. They assigned others to care for those who were wronged and justices to protect those who because of innate weakness were not able to claim their rights, and judges to guard what the law wishes. They did this so that these men would not be deprived of care nor representation by the judges, and would be given consideration. In this way the judge would reach the correct judgment and the guilty party would not pay more than what the law desired. For if these judges did not consider these matters, there might be grounds for another trial. Or the person who had won might follow it up more harshly, or the worst party might win and remain in an unjust disposition. Money is assigned to the judges for those contending at law just as it is assigned to soldiers from farmers. Is it not permissible to support one's ally in exchange for his goodwill? Just as it is good for the shepherd to care for the cattle, and for the hunter to care for the dogs, so men protect and give help to others. Let those who pay money in court and lose it attribute their loss to their unjust case, not to another person. But as for the slowness of legal proceedings—if it happens—that is due to care for justice, so that judges may not by acting hastily miss the exact truth. It is better for judges reflecting late ultimately to decide for justice, rather than by hurrying not only to injure a man but also to sin against God, the Creator of justice.

The laws apply to everyone, so that even the emperor obeys them. It is not possible, as was charged, that the wealthy man may without risk do violence to the poor, except that someone who escaped detection might avoid the penalty. This situation one might discover not only among the rich but also among the poor. For those at fault would not be in doubt that when examined they would pay the penalty. This is true for everyone and it is not merely the case for Romans.

. . . And he [the former Roman] wept and said that the laws were noble and the constitution of the Romans was good, but the rulers, not being as wise as the ancients, were ruining the state.[107]

Priscus, then, shows awareness of some contemporary criticisms of the empire, but he himself firmly maintains that the positive features of the Roman state in the mid-fifth century outweighed any liabilities. He probably is sincerely expressing his own opinions in the above passage—for he himself had once had the opportunity to take asylum among the Huns if he had been totally disenchanted with Roman society.

The passages quoted above are of course well known, but there are several important points which have escaped attention.[108] Priscus' defense of the Roman state should not be considered in isolation, but should be studied in the broader perspective of eastern Christian lay opinions on the condition of the east in the fifth century.

[107] Priscus, 307-309. On the sincerity of Priscus: Thompson, *Attila and the Huns*, 185-187.
[108] On this passage: *ibid.*, 184-187; Bury, *Later Roman Empire*, 2nd edn., I 279-288; T. Hodgkin, *Italy and Her Invaders*, 2nd edn. (Oxford 1892) II 77-80.

Priscus' own views appear to fit into the general pattern of eastern satisfaction with the reign of Theodosius II, as expressed by Sozomen, Socrates, and Theodoret. Priscus himself, having undergone philosophical and rhetorical training (he was described as a *sophist, rhetor*), and having served as secretary and adviser to Maximinus, the emperor's ambassador to Attila, and as an *assessor* (legal adviser) to Euphemius, *magister officiorum* of Marcian, was exposed to the outlook of high eastern officials.[109] Therefore he, like Sozomen, adhered to an ideological viewpoint that was representative of the imperial court. He did not anticipate any collapse of the Roman Empire. His declaration of basic confidence in contemporary Roman institutions was one more example of eastern confidence in the Roman Empire.

VII

The eastern Christian conviction that their empire had been receiving material protection and favor from God as a result of the piety of the emperor and his subjects persisted in the Byzantine Empire long after the fifth century.[110] Priscian, in his panegyric (about 512) to Emperor Anastasius I, declares:

> But the point which surpasses all your other praises is, that as a wise man you choose faithful guardians of the court, by whom Roman power grows, and whomever Old Rome sends, you kindly sustain with all loving respect. You are happy to promote them to distinguished ranks of honors lest they be conscious of the damage to their homeland and be sorrowful. Therefore they owe

---

[109] Cf. Moravcsik, *Byzantinoturcica*, I 479-480, 482.

[110] Cf. Jenkins, *Byzantium and Byzantinism*, 3-6; Baynes, "The Supernatural Defenders of Constantinople," *Byzantine Studies*, 248-260; and C. Baur, "Die Anfänge des byzantinischen Cäsaropapismus," *Archiv für katholisches Kirchenrecht*, 111 (1931) 108-113.

their fortune and safety to you and they undertake vows for you night and day.[111]

He adds a frank remark hoping "that both Romes will obey you alone with the aid of the Father on High who watches all things. . . ."[112] Priscian is encouraging Anastasius not to forget the former western regions of the Roman Empire, and at the same time praising him for reviving the empire.

Cosmas Indicopleustes, about 546-49, offers a favorable opinion on the sound position of the empire under Justinian. He predicts—with sincerity—that the Roman Empire will never decay if the Romans support Christianity:

> Therefore the empire of the Romans shares the dignities of the kingdom of Christ the Lord, surpassing all insofar as is possible in this world, remaining undefeated until the end. For he says, "It will not be destroyed forever." And "forever" applies to Christ the Lord and means endless, as Gabriel said to the Virgin: "And he will reign over the House of Jacob forever and there will be no end to his kingdom." Applied to the Roman Empire, as it has risen together with Christ, this means that within time it will not be destroyed. I declare confidently that although hostile barbarians may rise briefly against the Roman Empire to correct us for our sins, yet through the strength of Him who maintains us the empire will remain undefeated—if no one hinders the expansion of Christianity.[113]

[111] Priscian, *De laude Anastasii imperatoris*, 239-247 (W. Baehrens, ed., *Poetae Latini minores* [Leipzig 1883] 272). On Priscian, R. Helm, "Priscianus," *RE*, 22. 2 (1954), 2,328-2,346. The date: *ibid.*, 2,329. His Christianity: *ibid.*, 2,330.

[112] Priscian, *De laude Anastasii*, 265-266 (273 Baehrens).

[113] Cosmas Indicopleustes, *The Christian Topography* (E.O. Winstedt, ed. [Cambridge, England 1909] 80). Cf. Dan. *ii*.44 and Luke *i*.33. For the date: W. Wolska, *La topographie chrétienne de Cosmas Indicopleustès: théologie et science au VIe siècle* (Paris 1962) 28, 163-164.

Cyril of Scythopolis expresses this view about 557 in his *Vita S. Sabae*. He claims that Saint Sabas in 531 had predicted to Justinian that God would restore the Roman Empire to its former limits if the emperor adhered to an Orthodox religious policy:

> I have faith that God will add to your empire Africa, Rome, and all of the rest of the empire of Honorius which the predecessors of Your Most Pius Serenity lost, if you will eliminate the Arian, Nestorian and Origenist heresies.[114]

Another subject of Justinian, John Lydus, about 559 discusses Roman decline in his *De magistratibus populi romani*. Lydus was an imperial official subordinate to the Pretorian Prefect; therefore his statements may reflect official propaganda. Nevertheless, he does offer a contemporary appraisal of the empire's condition. He notes with satisfaction that Justinian has revived the empire:

> I must still explain the causes of the reduction and such great alteration of affairs, even though it happens that the government is now seen as greater and more famous through the watchfulness of the emperor. There is not a section of the empire that the emperor has not handsomely raised to absolute grandeur and strength by his inspections and attentions, nor has he received any ancestral honors without adding embellishments. But time, being destructive by nature, wholly extinguished or so greatly altered many things beautiful and necessary for faithful order in the empire that the remainder survives only as an indistinct trace of wondrous things. The empire was once powerful but now the order has changed

[114] Cyril of Scythopolis, *Vitae Sabae*, c. 72 (E. Schwartz, ed., *Texte und Untersuchungen*, 49, 2 Bd. [1939] 175-176).

from that, now changed from familiar ease and—if not God and this good emperor had helped with respect to everything—nearly slipped to general dissolution.[115]

Lydus proceeds to describe fourth- and fifth-century events, especially chastising Leo I for wasting so much money on the disastrous Vandal expedition of 468. He finds another fifth-century event had supernatural significance:

> But if someone should wait to receive in a number of books those speculations from predictions which they call oracles, he would find the conclusion once spoken by Fonteius the Roman. For that man says that some lines were given to Romulus once in the paternal language, predicting before the eyes of all that fortune would abandon the Romans when they forgot their ancestral tongue. I placed the said oracle in my work *On the Months.* Indeed such oracles have reached their conclusion. For Cyrus, a certain Egyptian, even now admired for his poetry, held simultaneously the prefecture of the city and the pretorian prefecture and not knowing the verse, dared to transgress the ancient custom and proclaim the edicts in the Greek language, and with the language of the Romans the empire thrust away fortune. For the emperor was persuaded to sign the law taking away all authority from the prefecture. . . . Weeping, I speak so many things concerning the empire.[116]

Lydus perceived a disastrous turn in Roman affairs during the fifth century. He trusted, as did Zosimus, in the ability of ancient oracles to predict the future condition of the empire.

Lydus's entire work on the Roman magistrates is con-

[115] Lydus, *Mag.,* 3. 39 (126-127 Wuensch); Klotz, "Lydos, Ioannes Laurentius," *RE,* 13 (1927) 2,210-2,217.
[116] Lydus, *Mag.,* 3. 42-43 (130-132 Wuensch).

cerned with the Roman past as opposed to the present. Indeed Justinian's reconquests in the west, especially his recovery of old Rome, encouraged, in my opinion, contemporary interest in Roman antiquity. His great contemporary, the historian Procopius of Caesarea, also demonstrates a curiosity for ancient Roman customs, and an interest in the circumstances by which the western Roman Empire succumbed to the barbarians, as well as a dedication to the recording of the actual Justinianic reconquest of those provinces. Procopius's presence in these campaigns increased his own interest in such past developments. His view of western Roman decline is complex, however, and discussion of it could easily become an entire study of his historical work. He stresses, for example, the weakness and foolishness of Honorius during whose reign the barbarians conquered so much:

> They say that in Ravenna some eunuch, apparently a keeper of poultry, announced to the Emperor Honorius that Rome had perished. Crying out, Honorius said: "Yet he had just eaten from my hands," for he possessed a giant cock named "Rome." The eunuch, understanding, said that the city of Rome was destroyed by Alaric, and the emperor, relieved, replied: "But I, O comrade, thought my bird 'Rome' had perished." So much folly, they say, possessed this emperor.[117]

Oral tradition appears to have been Procopius' source for this improbable story. His inclusion of such a tale in his otherwise excellent history indicates the degree to which the events of 410 had become a twisted legend in sixth-century

[117] Quotation: Procop., *Vand.*, 1. 2. 25-26, J. Haury and G. Wirth, eds. (Leipzig 1962), 314-315. On Procopius in general: B. Rubin, "Prokopios von Kaisareia," *RE*, 23. 1 (1957) 273-599; Moravcsik, *Byzantinoturcica*, I 490-500. On Procopius' interest in ancient Roman customs: Procop., *Goth.*, 1. 25. 18-25, J. Haury and G. Wirth, eds. (Leipzig 1963) 126-127.

Byzantium. Procopius proceeds to offer a sketch of Roman difficulties in 410, including the revolt of Britain against Roman rule. He then observes, in a passage very reminiscent of Sozomen's treatment of Honorius, that this emperor had received divine protection despite his own weakness:

> As the Emperor Honorius awaited the results of these things, and was borne on the mighty waves of fortune, what a great and amazing good fortune happened. For God loves to give the utmost assistance to those who are neither shrewd nor able enough from their own resources to manage for themselves, and yet who are not evil, and that is what happened to this emperor. From Libya it was suddenly reported that the commanders of Attalus were destroyed, and that a mass of ships with many soldiers had arrived unexpectedly from Byzantium to offer assistance. And Alaric, having quarreled with Attalus, removed his imperial dress and confined him under guard as a private citizen. After Alaric died of illness, the army of the Visigoths, under the command of Athaulf, went to Gaul, and Constantine, defeated in battle, died with his sons. The Romans, however, never recovered Britain which remained under usurpers.[118]

While Sozomen had argued that divine aid rewarded Honorius for his piety, Procopius, who was not a contemporary of Honorius and had no reason to interpret events for the pleasure of the long-dead Theodosius II, presents an unflattering portrait of Honorius. Divine aid came to the rescue of Honorius because he was too weak and lacked the ability and intelligence to defend himself, and not for any positive piety, but rather for the negative characteristic of lack-

[118] Procop., *Vand.*, 1. 2. 34-37 (I 316-317 Haury-Wirth). Cf. above, n. 32-34, for Sozomen's description of divine favor for Honorius. Athaulf was King of the Visigoths 410-415; Constantine was usurper of the imperial throne in Britain, Gaul, and Spain 407-411.

ing any evil or malicious nature. Procopius, as had Sozomen and Zosimus, emphasizes the importance of Byzantine or eastern Roman military assistance to Honorius in the emergency of 410. In addition, his *History of the Wars* of Justinian (namely *De bello Vandalico* and *De bello Gothico*) describes such necessary background as the Gothic occupation of Pannonia, the Vandal capture of Africa, the overthrow of Romulus Augustulus by Odoacer, and Zeno's invitation to Theodoric to invade and occupy Italy.[119]

Procopius' perception of the relative position of the empire is more complex, of course, than that of Lydus or Cosmas. In *Buildings* he gives a positive picture of the condition of the state:

> In our time the Emperor Justinian has been born, who finding the state harshly disturbed, has made it greater and more renowned, driving from it the barbarians who from ancient times had pressed it hard, as was made clear in detail by me in my books on the wars. Indeed they say that Themistocles son of Neocles once boasted that he did not lack the ability to make a small state large. But this emperor [Justinian] does not lack the intelligence to create other governments. Of course he has already added other states to the Roman Empire which had belonged to others, and created countless cities that previously did not exist.[120]

Yet in the *Anecdota,* or *Secret History*, Procopius appraises the condition of the empire very differently. He

---

[119] Goths occupy Pannonia: Procop., *Vand.*, 1. 2. 39 (317 Haury-Wirth). Vandals overrun Africa: *Vand.*, 1. 3. 1-36 (317-324 Haury-Wirth). The overthrow of Romulus Augustulus: *Goth.*, 1. 1. 2-8 (II 4-5 Haury-Wirth). Zeno invites Theodoric to invade Italy: *Goth.*, 1. 1. 10-25 (5-8 Haury-Wirth).

[120] Procop., *De aedificiis libri vi*, 1. 1. 6-8, J. Haury and G. Wirth, eds. (Leipzig 1964) 6. A balanced assessment of Justinian: J. W. Barker, *Justinian and the Later Roman Empire* (Madison, Wis. 1966) 201-210.

states that Justinian I "became the cause of misfortunes, the
nature and number of which no one anywhere previously
has heard."[121] Again he says of Justinian: "He did not deem
it worthy to preserve established things, but he wished to
innovate in everything, and to summarize, this man was the
greatest destroyer of well-established things."[122] Here Procopius shows himself an adherent of the older order of affairs, perhaps because of his closeness to the senatorial
order, and perhaps also from honest conviction arising from
his appreciation for Roman precedents. He proceeds to af-
firm that "By Justinian the Roman Empire was brought to
its knees"[123] and in a memorable passage: ". . . the whole
Roman Empire from end to end was disturbed as though
an earthquake or inundation fell upon it, or as though every
city had been captured by the enemy. For everything was
thrown into confusion against everything, and nothing remained as it had been. Confusion ensuing, the laws and
order of the constitution reversed themselves."[124] Procopius
then by 550 perceived Roman decline, but largely in the
sense of a departure from established precedents rather than
a diminution of territory. Although he may have been a
secret pagan or pagan sympathizer, his criticisms of Justinian have no apparent connection with the criticisms of
Zosimus, or the other pagan apologetical historians.[125]

VIII

The strongest eastern Christian denial of Roman decline,

---

[121] Procopii Caesariensis, *Opera omnia*, III: *Historia quae dicitur
Arcana*, 6. 19, J. Haury and G. Wirth, eds. (Leipzig 1963) 41.

[122] Procop., *Hist. arc.*, 6. 21 (41-42 Haury Wirth).

[123] *Ibid.*, 7. 1 (43 Haury-Wirth).

[124] *Ibid.*, 7. 6-7 (44 Haury-Wirth).

[125] On the possible adhesion of Procopius to paganism see: G.
Downey, "Paganism and Christianity in Procopius," *Church History*,
18 (1949) 89-102. For arguments that Procopius held a fundamentally
Christian outlook: B. Rubin, "Prokopios von Kaisareia," *RE*, 23.
1 (1957) 329-344.

however, appears at the end of the sixth century. The Orthodox Christian layman, Evagrius Scholasticus, was more than
a mere lawyer, for he held important honors under two emperors. Tiberius II made him *quaestor* and Maurice appointed him *ex praefectis*.[126] Like Sozomen, Evagrius was
close to the imperial court at Constantinople and his views
reflected the outlook of high officials. He believed the survival of the Roman Empire in the east was cause for optimism and a confirmation of the power and readiness of God
to assist the empire. Evagrius wrote an *Ecclesiastical History* in six books covering the years 431 to 593. His work,
written around 593-94, is particularly significant because it
includes the only known, explicit Christian refutation of the
arguments of Zosimus.[127]

Evagrius first endeavors to disprove Zosimus' criticisms of
Constantine. He flatly denies Zosimus' contention that Constantine had established the oppressive *chrysargyrum* tax
and refused to believe (erroneously) that Constantine could
have murdered his own wife and son.[128] He notes that Zosimus was no contemporary of Constantine and therefore observes that his information was of questionable authenticity.[129] Evagrius then devotes considerable space to a rebuttal of Zosimus' general thesis that the Roman Empire had
fallen into decay because the pagan gods were not wor-

[126] On Evagrius' career: Evagrius, *Hist. Eccl.*, 6. 24, J. Bidez and
L. Parmentier, eds. (London 1898) 240-241. See also: Moravcsik,
Byzantinoturcica, I 257-259; C. Vailhé, "Evagre," *DTC*, 5 (1913)
1,612-1,613; "Evagrius," *RE*, 6 (1909) 833. This deserves further
study. See also, G. Downey, "The Perspective of the Early Church
Historians," *Greek-Roman-and-Byzantine Studies* 6 (1965) 66-70.

[127] Evagrius, *Hist. Eccl.*, 3. 40-41 (139-144 Bidez-Parmentier).

[128] On the establishment of the *chrysargyrum* and the murder of
Crispus: *ibid.*, 3. 40 (140-141 Bidez-Parmentier). On the *chrysargyrum*: Seeck, "*Collatio lustralis*," *RE*, 4 (1901) 370-376. On Constantine's execution of Crispus and Fausta: Stein, *Hist.*, I 108.

[129] Evagrius, *Hist. Eccl.*, 3. 41 (140 Bidez-Parmentier). Evagrius
erroneously supposes that Zosimus lived at the time of Arcadius and
Honorius, while actually he lived and wrote his *Historia nova* roughly
100 years later.

shipped in the traditional manner. He resorts to historical arguments in his refutation of Zosimus:

> But you say, O you accursed and abominable person, that the Roman Empire has waned and totally perished since the appearance of Christianity, either because you did not read the older works or because you shrank from the truth. For on the contrary, it appears evident that the Roman Empire has increased together with our faith. See how at the coming of Christ our God among men, most of the Macedonians were reduced by the Romans, and also Albania, Iberia, Colchos, and the Arabs were subjugated by the Romans. Caius Caesar in the 123rd Olympiad subjugated the Gauls, Germans and Britons and added the inhabitants of 500 cities to the Roman Empire as has been written by the historians. . . . And immediately all Judaea and the surrounding districts were added. . . . After the birth of Christ our God, Egypt was added to the Roman Empire. . . . You along with others narrate the extent to which the Persians were reduced by Ventidius Corbulo, general of Nero, and by Severus, Trajan, Carus, Cassius and Odenaethus of Palmyra, and Apollonius, and others, and how often Nisibis changed sides, and Armenia and neighboring provinces were added to the Roman Empire.[130]

Here Evagrius repeats the same arguments Eusebius of Caesarea had made in his *Praeparatio Evangelica* and *Historia ecclesiastica*, namely that Christianity and the expansion of the Roman Empire and the coming of world peace had all coincided.[131]

---

[130] Evagrius, *Hist. Eccl.*, 3. 41 (141-142 Bidez-Parmentier).
[131] Cf. F.E. Cranz, "Kingdom and Polity in Eusebius of Caesarea," *HThR*, 45 (1952) 51-64; and esp. J. Sirinelli, *Les vues historiques d' Eusèbe de Césarée durant la période prénicéenne* (Dakar 1961) 214-246.

Evagrius also perceives that an important change had occurred several centuries after the appearance of Christ. With the conversion of Constantine I a new era had begun in the history of the empire. Bitterly he flings an avalanche of questions at Zosimus:

> Let us examine how the pagan and Christian emperors concluded their reigns. Did not the first monarch Gaius Julius Caesar close his life by assassination? Did not some of the commanders kill Gaius, grandson of Tiberius, with their swords? Was not Nero murdered by one of his house servants? Did not Galba, Otho, and Vitellius suffer similar fates, reigning only sixteen months? Did not Domitian kill his brother the Emperor Titus with poison? Was not Domitian wretchedly killed by Stephanus? But what do you say about Commodus? Did not this person lose his life to Narcissus? Did not Pertinax and Julianus meet similar fates? Did not Antoninus the son of Severus kill his brother Geta and did he himself not suffer similarly at the hands of Martialius? What of Macrinus? Was he not dragged about Byzantium as a captive and murdered by his soldiers? Was not Aurelius Antoninus of Ephesus killed with his mother? Did not his successor Alexander and his mother fall by a similar act? What shall we say of Maximian who was killed by his own army, or Gordian meeting his end due to the plotting of Philip? Tell me whether Philip and his successor Decius were not destroyed by their enemies? Did not Gallus and Volusianus end their lives at the hands of their armies? Did not Valerian become a prisoner carried about by the Persians? After Gallienus was assassinated and Carinus was slain, the empire came to Diocletian and those whom he took to rule with him. Of these Herculius, Maximian, Maxentius his son, and Licinius were totally destroyed.

But from the time when the renowned Constantine took power, built the city bearing his own name, and dedicated it to Christ, come look with me whether any of the emperors in this city, except Julian your hierophant and emperor, either was killed by domestic or foreign foes, or whether a usurper has completely overthrown an emperor, except that Basiliscus expelled Zeno by whom he was overthrown and killed. I agree with what you say about Valens who did so many harmful things to the Christians. But not even you can speak of another example. Let no one believe that these matters are irrelevant in an ecclesiastical history. They are useful and essential because the pagan historians shrink from the truth.[132]

This passage makes clear once more that a Christian Byzantine historian in the late sixth century might feel sufficiently concerned about pagan charges concerning the religious causes of present conditions of the Roman Empire to write an emphatic denial. Evagrius simply denies that there had been any decline. He apparently believes that one could safely omit any reference to the fate of the former western Roman provinces. In his eyes, the Roman Empire really comprises the eastern provinces and their capital at Constantinople. He does not even mention the causes and significance of the sack of Rome by Alaric and by Geiseric, nor does he describe the subsequent subjugation of the entire western half of the Roman Empire to the various Germanic tribes during the fifth century. Evagrius treats Zosimus' charges as though they were unreal. It seemed an obvious fact to him that the Roman Empire continued to endure and was hardly on the verge of disappearing.

One may offer only a conjecture as to why Evagrius chose

[132] Evagrius, *Hist. Eccl.*, 3. 41 (143-144 Bidez-Parmentier).

to include a refutation of Zosimus at such a late date. By 594 most of the territories which Justinian had reconquered had again lapsed into the hands of barbarians. Above all, the Lombards had overrun Italy in 568, and the Slavs and Avars were threatening to engulf the Balkans.[133] This new series of military crises may have stimulated the remaining Byzantine pagans—some were still reported active as late as the reign of Tiberius II (578-82)—to dust off Zosimus' old arguments about the harmful results of neglecting to worship the gods.[134] It is ironical, however, that approximately eight years after Evagrius had written his argument (593 or 594)[135] that God had protected all Orthodox Byzantine emperors from assassinations and usurpations, his words were to be proven false. Evagrius wrote during the reign of Maurice, who was overthrown and slain together with his family in 602 by the usurper Phocas and his partisans.[136] Phocas himself remained emperor for eight more years until he in

[133] For discussions of the Slavic and Avar threats to the Byzantine Empire after the death of Justinian I (565): E. Stein, "Das Reich und die Barbaren vom Tode Justinians bis zum Beginn des Perserkrieges (565-572)," *Studien zur Geschichte des byzantinischen Reiches* (Stuttgart 1919) 1-37, and, "Der Westen und die Hämushalbinsel (572-582)" in the same vol., 103-116. Other chapters in this work extensively discuss the serious Persian threat to the eastern frontier of the Byzantine Empire in this period. For an important and more recent study of the Balkan problem: P. Lemerle, "Invasions et migrations dans les Balkans depuis la fin de l'époque romaine jusqu'au VIIIe siècle," *RH*, 221 (1954) 265-295. A standard work on the Lombard invasions is T. Hodgkin, *Italy and Her Invaders*, Vol. V: *The Lombard Invasion*, 2nd edn. (Oxford 1916). P. Goubert has not yet published his pertinent volume on the Balkans in his series on *Byzance avant l'Islam*.

[134] John of Ephesus, *Hist. Eccl.*, 3. 27-3. 33 (E.W. Brooks, tr., *CSCO* [Louvain 1952] 6 114-123).

[135] Evagrius presumably was composing up to the point at which his history terminates: M. Pellegrino, "Evagrio Scholastico," *Enciclopedia Cattolica*, 1 (1950) 878-879; Moravcsik, *Byzantinoturcica*, I 257.

[136] Theophanes, *Chronographia*, A.M. 6,094, C. De Boor, ed. (Leipzig 1883) I 285-290. On the usurpation by Phocas: I. A. Kulakovskii, *Istoriia Vizantii* (Kiev 1912) II 485-496.

turn was overthrown and slain by Heraclius.[137] Subsequently violent successions to the Byzantine throne were numerous.[138]

Evagrius wrote the last eastern Christian refutation of pagan arguments concerning the religious origin of Roman disintegration. Although his remarks indicate the subject was still controversial in the east during the sixth century, his rebuttal of Zosimus marked the conclusion of pagan-Christian polemics on the decline and fall of the Roman Empire.

[137] On the overthrow of Phocas by Heraclius: Theophanes, *Chronographia*, A.M. 6,102 (I 298-299 De Boor). Cf. A. Pernice, *L'Imperatore Eraclio* (Florence 1905) 27-40; Kulakovskii, *Istor. Viz.*, III 18-27.

[138] For a general survey of the manner in which various Byzantine emperors died: R. Guilland, "La destinée des empereurs de Byzance," *Études byzantines* (Paris 1959) 1-32.

chapter vi

CONCLUSIONS

A fundamental conclusion emerges from this examination of fifth-century Christian and pagan sources: easterners possessed a clear awareness of, interest in, and firm opinions on the disasters which befell the west and led to the ultimate collapse of Roman authority in that region. There were active eastern responses on the official and individual levels to the western crises. References to fifth-century western misfortunes in such later Byzantine sources as Theophanes, Constantine Manasses, Zonaras, and Nicephorus Callistus provide additional evidence for this conclusion.[1] The east

---

[1] Theophanes, composing his *Chronographia* in 810-814, still mentions Alaric's capture of the city: A.M. 5,903 (81 De Boor). For the date of Theophanes' work: Moravcsik, *Byzantinoturcica*, 2nd edn. (Berlin 1958) I 531. Theophanes rapidly surveyed the declining fortunes of western emperors after the death of Valentinian III (455): *Chronographia*, A.M. 5,947 (108-109 De Boor). John Zonaras in his *Epitome historiarum* completed shortly after 1118 (Moravcsik, *Byzantinoturcica* I 344) mentions the sack of Rome by Alaric: 12.21 C, Dindorf, ed. (Leipzig 1870) III 235. Constantine Manasses in his *Compendium chronicum*, lines 2,474-2,547, I. Bekker, ed. (Bonn 1837) 107-110, briefly sketches the sackings of Rome by Alaric and Geiseric and the disposition of Romulus Augustulus. Manasses composed his chronicle during the reign of Manuel II: Moravcsik, *Byzantinoturcica*, I 353-354. Nicephorus Callistus, *Hist. Eccl.*, 13. 35 (*PG*, 146. 1,040-1,045) mentions Alaric's sack of Rome; the Vandal seizure of Libya: *ibid.*, 14. 56 (*PG*, 146. 1,265-1,269); the last western emperors in the fifth century: *ibid.*, 15. 11 (*PG*, 147. 36-37), where he states in an important passage that Romulus Augustulus ". . . became the last emperor of the Romans 1303 years from Romulus the first king. After this man Odoacer gained possession of the Roman Empire, and robbed himself of the title of Autocrat and he was the first to proclaim himself king." It is very unusual for a Byzantine historian to state that the last "Roman emperor" had lived in the fifth century, since the Byzantines considered them-

did not remain impassive to the sufferings of the west; at various times during the fifth century both eastern emperors, such as Theodosius II and Leo I, and individual Christians, for example, Theodoret of Cyrus, attempted to aid the western Roman Empire and her citizens.

The eastern pagans, in a manner similar to pagans in the western provinces, charged that failure to worship the gods in the prescribed traditional manner had caused these political and military catastrophes. Some eastern Christians, such as Theodoret and Saint Nilus, replied to the pagan arguments.[2] Nevertheless, in general it appears that fifth-century eastern pagans more eagerly strived to expose the harm which neglect of the gods had inflicted on the state than were the eastern Christians attracted to the task of refuting this pagan thesis. Certainly the eastern Christians in the fifth century composed no works of historical apologetics comparable to Saint Augustine's *De civitate Dei* or even Paulus Orosius' *Historiae adversum paganos.*[3]

There was, however, no single general reaction in the east to the problem of Roman decline: eastern responses

selves, including their emperors, as "Romans." Nicephorus Callistus was a priest who lived in Constantinople, born probably in 1256 and died c. 1335: M. Jugie, "Nicéphore Calliste Xanthopoulos," *DTC*, 11 446-448; M. Roncaglia, "Niceforo Callisto Xanthopoulos," *Encic. Catt.*, 8 (1952) 1,836-1,837.

[2] Theodoret, *Quaestiones et responsiones ad orthodoxos*, Papadopoulos-Kerameus, ed., *Zapiski, istoriko-filologicheski fakultet, St. Petersburg University*, 36 [1895] 125-127; Saint Nilus, *Ep.*, 1. 75 (*PG* 36. 116).

[3] On the great significance of Augustine's *De civitate Dei*: E. Gilson, *Introduction à l'étude de Saint Augustin* (Paris 1949), 230-231; G. Bardy, *Saint Augustin l'homme et l'oeuvre*, 7th edn. (Paris 1948) 361-362; J. N. Figgis, *The Political Aspects of Saint Augustine's "City of God"* (London 1921) 1-4; G. Ladner, *The Idea of Reform* (Cambridge, Mass., 1959) 239-268; G. Combès, *La doctrine politique de Saint Augustin* (Paris 1927) 414-415; N. H. Baynes, "The Political Ideas of St. Augustine's 'De Civitate Dei,'" *Byzantine Studies and Other Essays* (London 1955) esp. 288.

varied according to different interests and pressures. Some eastern emperors such as Theodosius II and Leo I pursued active policies to reverse western Roman decline. Other eastern emperors, such as Marcian and Zeno, remained passive. Individual easterners also held different opinions. The variation in religious commitments—pagan, orthodox, Arian, Nestorian, and Monophysite—influenced the conflicting individual responses to fifth-century western Roman misfortunes. However different were eastern reactions to Roman decline, they all shared a characteristic "eastern" imprint. The particular religious convictions of these eastern writers who recorded their views on Roman decline could not prevent their environment from affecting their outlook. Despite the mutual hostility of eastern pagans and Christians, local conditions led members of both religions to some similar conclusions which differed very sharply from those held by both pagans and Christians in the western provinces where conditions were quite different.

The fact that Constantinople and the eastern provinces had escaped the west's misfortunes during the early fifth century made a great impression not only on Sozomen, the Christian historian who was so close to Theodosius II,[4] but also on the former pagan official, Zosimus.[5] Both Christians and pagans in the east agreed that Constantinople enjoyed

[4] Sozom., *Hist. Eccl.*, 9. 6. 1 (397 Bidez-Hansen). On some basic similarities of pagan and Christian patterns of thought: M. Simon, "Christianisme antique et pensée païenne: rencontres et conflits," *Bulletin de la faculté des lettres de Strasbourg*, 38 (1959/60) 314 ff. Cf. also on the assimilation of pagan culture by Christians: W. Jaeger, *Early Christianity and Greek Paideia* (Cambridge, Mass. 1961) 28-85; M.L.W. Laistner, *Christianity and Pagan Culture* (Ithaca 1951) 49-73; and esp. G. Downey, "Education in the Christian Roman Empire: Christian and Pagan Theories under Constantine and his Successors," *Speculum*, 32 (1957) 48-61; A. D. Nock, *Conversion: The Old and the New in Religion from Alexander the Great to Augustine of Hippo* (Oxford 1933) 250-253.

[5] Zosim., *Hist. nov.*, 2. 36-37 (92-95 Mendelssohn).

relative prosperity, security, and good fortune in contrast to the sufferings of Rome. Although some easterners such as Theodoret believed western disasters constituted a divine warning to the east for moral reform or else dire consequences might follow,[6] other easterners—even such pessimists as Zosimus—believed the good fortune of Constantinople might continue forever.[7] In this manner a common physical environment significantly influenced the views of men who started with very different religious frames of reference.

Present in the statements of Zosimus about the good fortune of Constantinople and Sozomen's contrasts between the chaotic conditions of the west and the tranquility of the east were (1) the emergence of an eastern consciousness of the distinct characters of the two halves of the Roman Empire, and (2) a conviction that the eastern provinces with their capital at Constantinople might continue to exist and even thrive although old Rome perished. Indeed, this favorable political situation in the east during the fifth century made it much more difficult for eastern pagans to exploit the misfortunes of the western provinces in order to justify a return to worship of the pagan gods. Consequently, the eastern Christians had little reason to reply.

While western Roman disasters caused such influential western Christians as Saint Augustine to turn away from hopes of divine, earthly rewards for political rulers, and instead to expectations of heavenly rewards, some eastern Christians became ever more confident and proud of their emperors whose successes seemed sure evidence of divine favor. Eastern pagan and Christian interest in the problem of Roman decline led the Byzantine half of the former Ro-

[6] Theodoret, *Ep.*, 22, Azéma, ed., *Correspondance*, I 92-93); *Ep.*, 32, 52 (*PG*, 83. 1,210, 1,228).
[7] Zosim., *Hist. nov.*, 5. 24. 8 (247 Mendelssohn).

man Empire to become a more mature and self-reliant political entity confident in her own ability to survive in a self-contained existence, trusting in divine protection. Due to her own good fortune in the very trying crises of the fifth century Byzantium gradually acquired that self-assurance which became such an important characteristic of the empire and its society in the subsequent centuries.[8]

II

This growing belief in the god-protected character of Constantinople and the Byzantine Empire accompanied and stimulated the emergence in the fifth century of an unusually deep historical interest in the record of events in the Roman Empire, particularly in the eastern half. During the reign of Theodosius II (408-50) scholars undertook a remarkable amount of research into the Byzantine past. The Theodosian Code, commissioned in 429 and completed in 438, comprised a collection of imperial legislation from the reign of Constantine I up to the latest novels of Theodosius II. It was published on 25 December 438.[9]

[8] On the characteristic Byzantine reliance on and confidence in divine protection for their empire: C. Diehl, *Byzance grandeur et décadence* (Paris 1919) 26-28; F. Dölger, "Rom in der Gedankenwelt der Byzantiner," *Byzanz und der europäische Staatenwelt* (Ettal 1953) 94-101; O. Treitinger, *Die oströmische Kaiser-und Reichsidee nach ihrer Gestaltung im höfischen Zeremoniell*, 2nd edn. (Darmstadt 1956) esp. 158-163; R. Jenkins, *Byzantium and Byzantinism* (Cincinnati 1963) 3-6; P. J. Alexander, "The Strength of Empire and Capital as Seen through Byzantine Eyes," *Speculum*, 37 (1962) 343-355; R.L. Wolff, "The Three Romes: The Migration of an Ideology and the Making of an Autocrat," *Daedalus*, 88 (1959) esp. 293-295.

[9] *De Theodosiani codicis auctoritate* (Novellae Theodosii 1) [*Theodosiani libri xvi*, T. Mommsen, ed., 2. 3-5]; *Gesta senatus romani de Theodosiano publicando*, 1-7, esp. 7 (1. 2. 3-4 Mommsen). For discussions of the commissioning: Mommsen, *Theodosiani libri xvi*, 1. 1. ix-xiii; Jörs, "Codex Theodosianus," *RE*, 4 (1901) 170-173; P. Krüger, *Geschichte der Quellen und Litteratur des römischen Rechts*, 2nd edn. (Munich, Leipzig 1912) 324-325; H.F. Jolowicz, *Historical Introduction to the Study of Roman Law* (Cambridge, England 1952) 483-484.

Moreover, four ecclesiastical histories covering approximately this same period, from Constantine I through the middle of the reign of Theodosius II, appeared in Greek in the east. The Eunomian Christian Philostorgius covered the years 300-425 in his *Historia ecclesiastica*, published between 425 and 433.[10] The three other ecclesiastical histories adhered to an orthodox position but described approximately the same chronological span. Sozomen, writing between 439 and 450, narrated events which occurred between 324 and 439,[11] dedicating his history to the Emperor Theodosius II.[12] Socrates Scholasticus recounted the years 305 to 439.[13] Theodoret recorded the historical developments of the years 323 to 428, composing his work around 449-50.[14] These authors regarded their works as continuations of Eusebius' *Historia ecclesiastica*.[15]

Philip Sidetes, a presbyter at Constantinople, about 426 wrote around 434-36 a *Christian History* (not extant) in thirty-six books, which covered events from the creation of the world up to the author's own times.[16] Also, Palladius wrote *The Lausiac History*, an account of the development of Christian monasticism up to the end of the fourth

[10] On the *Ecclesiastical History* of Philostorgius: Bardenhewer, *Geschichte der altkirchlichen Literatur* (Freiburg 1924) IV 132-133; Moravcsik, *Byzantinoturcica*, I 473-474.

[11] Bardenhewer, *Gesch. altkirchl. Lit.*, IV 141; Moravcsik, *Byzantinoturcica*, I 510; Quasten, *Patrology*, III 534-535.

[12] Sozom., *Hist. Eccl., prol.* (1-5 Bidez-Hansen).

[13] Bardenhewer, *Gesch. altkirchl. Lit.*, IV 137-138; Moravcsik, *Byzantinoturcica*, I 508-510; Quasten, *Patrology*, III 532-533.

[14] Moravcsik, *Byzantinoturcica*, I 529-531; Quasten, *Patrology*, III 550-551.

[15] These historians acknowledged that they were continuing the *Historia ecclesiastica* of Eusebius: Philostorgius, *Hist. Eccl.*, 1. 2 (6 Bidez); Sozom., *Hist. Eccl.*, 1. 1. 12-13 (8-9 Bidez-Hansen); Socrates Scholasticus, *Hist. Eccl.*, 1. 1 (*PG*, 67. 33); Theodoret, *Hist. Eccl.*, 1. 4 (*Kirchengeschichte*, L. Parmentier and F. Scheidweiler, eds., 2nd edn. (Berlin 1954) 4.

[16] Bardenhewer, *Gesch. altkirchl. Lit.*, IV 136; Quasten, *Patrology*, III 528.

century. He dedicated this work to Lausus, the Chamberlain of Theodosius II in 419-20.[17] In addition to these Christian histories two major pagan histories appeared during the reign of Theodosius II. Eunapius of Sardis completed his history in roughly 414 which covered events from 270 to 404.[18] Olympiodorus of Thebes wrote his history around 425, covering the years 408 to 425. He dedicated this work to Theodosius II.[19]

What significance does this extensive historical activity have for Byzantine history? It is important that so much of this historical writing—all four ecclesiastical histories—began with the reign of Constantine I. The Theodosian Code included laws beginning with this emperor. All this activity took place under Theodosius II. It appears that either the emperor or imperial court circles felt the period extending from Constantine I to their own day did represent a distinct historical period which deserved to be recorded as a single unit. Eastern intellectuals suddenly felt during Theodosius II's reign that the proper moment had arrived to record these events for posterity.

Unquestionably Theodosius II directly encouraged historical research during his reign. Not only did he commission the compilation of the Code but he also helped to create an environment favorable to historical studies. He himself had a deep personal interest in history. Olympiodorus of Thebes and Sozomen dedicated their histories to him. Sozomen in his important dedication to Theodosius specifi-

[17] Palladius, *The Lausiac History*, Dom C. Butler, ed., 2 v. (Cambridge, England 1898) 1904, Texts and Studies, VI 1-2. The dedication: VI. 2. 6-7. On this work: É. Amann, "Palladius," *DTC*, 11 (1931) 1,823-1,830; Bardenhewer, *Gesch. altkirchl. Lit.*, IV 148-152.

[18] Moravcsik, *Byzantinoturcica*, I 259-260.

[19] The dedication to Theodosius II: Photius, *Bibliothèque*, R. Henry, ed., I 167; for the date: E. A. Thompson, "Olympiodorus of Thebes," *CQ*, 38 (1944) 46.

cally mentions the emperor's knowledge of history: "But you, O emperor, fall behind the generosity of none of your predecessors in rewards for letters. I believe that you are following the proper course. For seeking to conquer all by your virtues, you advance your affairs according to your accurate knowledge of the history of those ancient successes of the Greeks and Romans." Such extensive historical research and publication in Greek occurred at no time during the fourth century nor in the second half of the fifth century. Indeed the only other periods during the course of Byzantine history which may compare in historical productivity were the reigns of Justinian I (527-65) and Constantine VII Porphyrogenitus (913-59).[20]

III

The widespread historical activity during the reign of Theodosius II has implications for a vexatious question in the modern study of Byzantine history. When did Byzantine history begin? Stein suggested the reign of Diocletian (284-302).[21] Ostrogorsky has argued for the reign of Constantine I (306-37).[22] One relevant aspect of the problem of Byzantine periodization that has not yet been noted is the viewpoint of the Byzantines themselves: did they see in the past a historical demarcation of particular importance to

[20] The reference to Theodosius II's knowledge of ancient history: Sozom., *Hist. Eccl., prol.*, 7 (2 Bidez-Hansen). On the historiography of Justinian I's reign: E. Stein, *Hist. du Bas-Empire* (Paris 1949) II 702-734, called this the "Golden Age of Byzantine Literature." For a sketch of historical activity during the reign of Constantine VII: A. Rambaud, *L'Empire grec au dixième siècle. Constantine Porphyrogénète* (Paris 1870, reprinted New York 1963) 114-128.

[21] E. Stein, "Untersuchungen zur spätbyzantinischen Verfassungs- und Wirtschaftsgeschichte," *Mitteilungen zur osmanischen Geschichte,* II (1923/25) 2; "Introduction à l'histoire et aux institutions byzantines," *Traditio,* 7 (1949/51) 99.

[22] G. Ostrogorsky, "Die Perioden der byzantinischen Geschichte," *HZ,* 163 (1941) 236-237.

themselves and which they believed was most influential for the development of their society and civilization?

It appears that the first large group of historians of Byzantine society—Philostorgius, Socrates, Sozomen, and Theodoret—believed the reign of Constantine I had marked a new era. From the reign of Constantine these historians commenced their histories and their emperor, Theodosius II, began his compilation of imperial legislation. Eunapius of Sardis, and later even the pagan Zosimus declared that Constantine's reign marked a new turn in Roman history—the true ruin of Roman affairs began with that emperor.[23] Again, the Christian historian Evagrius Scholasticus in the late sixth century in his refutation of Zosimus' charges confined himself to discussing the good fortune of emperors who had resided in Constantinople, beginning, of course, with Constantine I.[24]

For these historians the reign of Diocletian did not mark a decisive new turn in history. One reason for these church historians' selection of Constantine's reign as their *terminus post quem* was the fact that Eusebius of Caesarea had terminated his *Ecclesiastical History* at that point, and they regarded themselves as his continuators. Yet the appearance of four such histories simultaneously under Theodosius II and the selection of the very same period (Constantine I– Theodosius II) for imperial legislation included in the Theodosian Code does demonstrate that by the early fifth century the reign of Constantine was definitely regarded as the most important recent historical watershed.

The appearance of these ecclesiastical histories during the middle years of Theodosius II's reign has implications for the development of Byzantine political ideology. Seeking to follow Eusebius of Caesarea both in form and in values,

[23] Zosim., *Hist. nov.*, 2. 34; cf. 2. 7 (92, 65 Mendelssohn).
[24] Evagrius, *Hist. Eccl.*, 3. 41 (144 Bidez-Parmentier).

these fifth-century eastern Christian historians accepted Eusebius' assumption that God bestowed clear material rewards such as military and political success upon pious orthodox emperors.[25] They found this outlook justified by the course of events during the fourth and fifth centuries. They were especially impressed by the contrasting fortunes of the eastern and western sections of the Roman Empire. They believed that only divine protection preserved the eastern provinces under the young Theodosius II when many external and domestic crises shook the west and even resulted in the downfall of old Rome.[26] In the midst of a chaotic world these chroniclers affirmed their convictions about the God-protected character of their emperor's domains.

The fifth-century eastern pagan and Christian historians recorded their opinions at a critical early point when Byzantine society was still developing what modern scholars consider to have been its characteristic political ideology as the God-protected empire. In the tenth century Constantine VII Porphyrogenitus expressed this view to his son, Romanus, in the *proem* to the *De administrando imperio*. He spoke of the invincible appearance which the emperor must make to barbarian enemies of the empire:

> Thou shalt appear terrible unto them, and at thy face shall trembling take hold upon them. And the Almighty shall cover thee with his shield, and thy Creator shall endue thee with understanding; He shall direct thy steps, and shall establish thee upon a sure foundation. Thy throne shall be as the sun before Him, and His eyes shall

[25] On the views of Eusebius: E. Peterson, *Der Monotheismus als politisches Problem* (Leipzig 1935) 78-79; F. Cranz, "Kingdom and Polity in Eusebius of Caesarea," *HThR*, 45 (1952) 55-56; J. Straub, *Vom Herrscherideal in der Spätantike* (Stuttgart 1939) 113-129.

[26] Esp. Sozom., *Hist. Eccl.*, 9. 3. 3; 9. 6. 1 (395, 397 Bidez-Hansen).

be looking towards thee, and naught of harm shall touch thee, for He hath chosen thee and set thee apart from thy mother's womb, and hath given unto thee His rule as unto one excellent above all men, and hath set thee as a refuge upon a hill and as a statue of gold upon a high place, and as a city upon a mountain hath He raised thee up, that the nations may bring to thee their gifts and thou mayst be adored of them that dwell upon the earth.[27]

The early fifth-century ecclesiastical historians regarded their own contemporary empire as God-protected in accordance with the view of Eusebius of Caesarea, and they recorded these convictions.[28] In the east they did not undergo the humbling experiences of the western Romans early in that century, which led such western Christians as Saint Augustine to conclude that earthly political and military rewards for piety were unlikely to be regular, let alone truly important. The inclusion of assertions about the God-protected character of the empire in such histories constitute an indication of the hold of this ideology upon eastern intellectuals at that time. It was also in itself a factor which contributed to the formation of Byzantine political ideology. In sum, the Byzantine reactions to the question of Roman decline resulted in the reinforcement of the faith and confidence of easterners in the God-protected nature of their state at a crucial early point in the evolution of Byzantine civilization and values.

---

[27] Constantine Porphyrogenitus, *De administrando imperio, proem,* G. Moravcsik, ed. and R.J.H. Jenkins, tr. (Budapest 1949) 47; cf. P. J. Alexander, "The Strength of Empire and Capital as Seen through Byzantine Eyes," *Speculum,* 18 (1962) 345; on transition from the ancient to the Byzantine world: S. Salaville, "De l'hellénisme au byzantinisme. Essai de démarcation," *Échos d'Orient,* 30 (1931) 61.

[28] Socrates, *Hist. Eccl.,* 7. 42 (*PG,* 67. 832); Theodoret, *Hist. Eccl.,* 5. 36. 3-5 (338-339 Parmentier-Scheidweiler); *ibid.,* 5. 37. 4 (340 Parmentier-Scheidweiler); Sozom., *Hist. Eccl.,* 9. 3. 3; 9. 6. 1 (395, 397 Bidez-Hansen).

IV

One would not, however, maintain that the pagan-Christian dispute on the problem of Roman decline was the most important issue for easterners in the fifth century. At no time were the eastern pagans able to focus general public attention upon this topic. The pagans never seriously threatened eastern Christianity with this question. Clearly the Christological Controversy remained the most important intellectual problem for learned and illiterate individuals.[29] The leading eastern intellectuals of the fifth century devoted most of their efforts to an examination of the nature of Christ. As a result, eastern discussion of western Roman decline remained on a low intellectual level. No contemporary eastern author offered an intelligent explanation of the process of Roman decay. No easterner, for example, ever examined the economic and social causes of western Roman disintegration which the Gaul Salvian so strongly stressed. Easterners simply exploited the issue for its polemical value; thus religious passions prevented any calm analysis of the problem.

Nevertheless, discussion of Roman decline did engage, if only briefly, some of the most eminent figures in the east during the fifth century: Theodoret of Cyrus, Saint Nilus of Ancyra, and such prominent pagans as Eunapius of Sardis and Severus of Alexandria. Although the pagans attempted to exploit this issue to procure the restoration of their right to public worship, their efforts were unsuccessful and this controversy over Roman decline apparently had no effect upon the gradual erosion of paganism in the east.

Indeed, the various arguments of Christians and pagans

---

[29] J. B. Bury, *History of the Later Roman Empire*, 2nd edn., I 349-350, 359, 402; A. Fliche and V. Martin, *Histoire de l'église*, IV 196; B. J. Kidd, *A History of the Church to* A.D. *461* (Oxford 1922) III 396-399.

concerning the responsibility for Roman decline probably convinced few members of the opposing religion, nor did the apologists for either position aim primarily to do this. Each author appears actually to have striven to persuade his own fellow believers of the rectitude of his own group's position. No one seriously attempted to understand the position of his religious opponents in order to convert them. In addition, no one couched arguments in gentle terms in order to woo religious opponents. Instead, Christians bluntly denounced paganism for its "impiety," "deceit," "folly," even "wickedness."[30] Pagans were similarly narrowminded. Eunapius charged Christian monks with committing "countless evil and unspeakable acts."[31] Zosimus simply conceived of the attractiveness of Christianity to some people as its promise of "deliverance from every sin and every impiety."[32] A wide gap of misunderstanding existed between the two religious groups; no attempt to bridge this gap and reconcile the groups apparently was ever considered or desired by either religious party.

v

This examination of fifth-century eastern pagan and Christian reactions to the various calamities of the western Roman Empire further illuminates the broader context in which Saint Augustine and Paulus Orosius wrote the *De civitate Dei* and the *Historiae adversum paganos*, respectively. Pagan charges that neglect of the gods had brought disaster upon the Romans spread widely throughout the empire.

[30] Impiety: Theodoret, *Hist. Eccl.*, 5. 39. 24; 3. 6. 4 (347, 181 Parmentier-Scheidweiler); Saint Nilus, *Ep.*, 1. 75 (*PG*, 79. 116). Deceit: Theodoret, *Hist. Eccl.*, 1. 2. 7; 5. 21. 1; 5. 37. 3 (6, 317, 340 Parmentier-Scheidweiler); Wickedness: Theodoret, *Hist. Eccl.*, 5. 21. 4 (318 Parmentier-Scheidweiler). Folly: Saint Nilus, *Ep.*, 1. 75 (*PG*, 79. 116).

[31] Eunap., *VS*, 6. 11. 6 (39 Giangrande).

[32] Zosim., *Hist. nov.*, 4. 59 (216 Mendelssohn).

Augustine and Orosius were not fighting an isolated western pagan offensive. Such pagan contentions were not confined to those western provinces (or nearby areas) which had suffered direct invasions. These Christian apologetical works were necessary, in east and west, to defend Christianity when paganism was again attempting to raise its head.

The study of eastern responses to Roman decline also brings into sharper relief the uniqueness of the political ideas which Saint Augustine expresses in his *De civitate Dei*. Augustine's views clash with those of Eusebius of Caesarea: Augustine denies that there might be a necessary connection between the welfare and fortunes of the Roman Empire and that of the Christian Church. He also rejects the assumption that God would necessarily grant political and military successes to pious emperors, since all states were ephemeral, including Rome.[33] But at least equally important for the illumination of the distinctiveness of Augustine's thought is the comparison of his views on the Roman Empire with those of his own eastern Christian contemporaries. Sozomen and Socrates continued to find in recent history a confirmation of the political principles of Eusebius, while Augustine emphatically rejected the validity of such a Christian-political philosophy.

In addition, this study illuminates the environment in which the east developed its concept of the "Two Romes"

[33] F. Cranz, "Kingdom and Polity in Eusebius of Caesarea," *HThR*, 45 (1952) 64-66; G. Ladner, *The Idea of Reform* (Cambridge, Mass., 1959) 267-269; T. Mommsen, "St. Augustine and the Christian Idea of Progress; The Background of *The City of God*," *Medieval and Renaissance Studies* (Ithaca 1959) 281-298; cf. also: R. Arbesmann, "The Idea of Rome in the Sermons of St. Augustine," *Augustiniana* (Louvain 1954) 98, 100, 104; E. Peterson, *Der Monotheismus als politisches Problem* (Leipzig 1935) 77. There was, however, no rigid opposition to or total contradiction between the political concepts of Saint Augustine and those of "Christian Hellenism": F. Dvornik, *Early Christian and Byzantine Political Philosophy* (Washington, D.C. 1966) II 840-844.

(the complicated history of this political theory is not within the scope of this essay). This study of eastern pagan opinions concerning Roman decay furthermore provides significant evidence on the state of pagan political theory during the fifth century. Roman decline was the last intellectual issue to attract the energies of eastern pagans. It marked the final step in the evolution of pagan political theory. The inability of eastern pagan thinkers to develop a really persuasive set of arguments on this issue of their own choosing suggests how intellectually deficient paganism had become in the east during the fifth century. Moreover, the hostility of Eunapius and Zosimus to the office of the emperor was so conservative and unrealistic in the fifth century as to call into question the ability of its adherents honestly to face contemporary political realities. The failure of the pagans to adjust their religion to contemporary needs contributed to the inability of mordant paganism to retain adherents and thus to survive. Augustine and the various eastern Christians and pagans all agreed that in some way western Roman calamities had occurred because of man's provocation of God, but their views diverged concerning the origins and nature of this divine provocation, and also concerning the reasons for the survival unscathed of the eastern Roman or Byzantine Empire.

Fifth-century eastern responses to western Roman decline were an important element in the background of Justinian's interventionist policy in the western Mediterranean during the sixth century. Justinian's active interest in the west represented no radical departure from the policy of some Byzantine emperors during the fifth century. Indeed, his expeditions to recover the western provinces involving the commitment of important resources of his empire, arose rather naturally from (1) a long background of fifth-century eastern military expeditions to aid the west against internal and external threats, and (2) from the extensive interest of both eastern pagan and Christian individuals in western misfortunes and their significance for the eastern half of the empire.

Fifth-century eastern materials do offer additional information concerning the precise pagan arguments which were made about Roman decline. Scholars have become very familiar with those pagan charges which were included in the hostile summaries of Saint Augustine and Orosius. But only eastern pagan apologetical works have survived to provide some primary documentation of pagan opinions. Eastern pagans apparently began charging that neglect of the gods had caused disasters sometime after the capture of Rome by Alaric in 410; it is impossible, given only the present sources, to determine the precise moment at which such polemics were first published. These arguments antedate the fifth century, because such Christian apologists as Tertullian, Cyprian and Arnobius had refuted similar charges in previous centuries. The *New History* of Zosimus provides a detailed presentation of the pagan case. On the other hand, caution is required in using primary eastern materials. Eastern pagan apologetical works definitely reflect their eastern environment and do not necessarily mirror the exact arguments of the western opponents of Saint Augustine.[34]

[34] Olympiodorus of Thebes included evidence that neglect of sacred pagan statues had resulted in misfortunes: Photius, *Bibliothèque*, R. Henry, ed., I, 171; I, 177. He composed his history around 425. The reference to pagan charges about Roman decline refuted by Saint Nilus, *Ep.*, 1. 75 (*PG*, 79. 116) is too general for any precise dating, but it would have been written before Nilus' death which occurred c. 430. Likewise the references in the *Quaestiones et responsiones ad orthodoxos*, Papadopoulos-Kerameus, ed., 125-127, are too vague for precise dating, but the entire work is generally thought to have been written before the mid-fifth century: M. de Brok, "De waarde van de 'Graecarum affectionum curatio' van Theodoretus van Cyrus als apologetisch werk," *Studia Catholica*, 27 (1952) 210; F. A. Funk, "Le Pseudo-Justin et Diodore de Tarse," *Revue d'histoire ecclesias-*

Existing statements of the eastern pagan reactions to Roman decline in the west indicate that paganism was far from dead in the eastern provinces during the fifth century. Despite legal prohibitions, pagans continued to worship their gods and some pagans even managed to hold high public office. Finally, there is evidence that not all pagans were afraid to voice their grievances and criticisms either orally or in writing.

There is no proof of any direct borrowing of arguments by eastern Christians from such western writers as Augustine or Orosius, nor by eastern pagans from the western pagan polemicists whose charges were summarized by Augustine and Orosius. Orosius himself appears to have known little about the eastern half of the empire.[35] Augustine never seems to have been widely read in the east. The degree of his proficiency in Greek is a controversial subject among specialists, but it appears that at best he did not become familiar with the language until very late in life. Certainly, although there were some parallels between some of the arguments of eastern and western writers, there is no positive evidence of borrowing; no eastern Christian or pagan, for example, cited by name any fifth-century western author on the subject of Roman decline.[36] Similarly, there is no

---

tique, 3 (1902) 968. For earlier Christian refutations of the pagan theses: Tertullian, *Apologeticum*, 40. 1-15 (Corpus Christianorum, Series Latina, I [Turnholt 1954] 153-155); Saint Cyprian, *Ad Demetrianum* 2-7; and Arnobius, *Adversus nationes libri vii* 1. 1-20, C. Marchesi, ed., 2nd edn. (Milan and Padua 1944) 1-18; cf. P. Courcelle, "Anti-Christian Arguments and Christian Platonism: from Arnobius to St. Ambrose," *Conflict Between Paganism and Christianity in the Fourth Century*, A. Momigliano, ed. (Oxford 1963) esp. 151-152.

[35] A. Lippold, *Rom und die Barbaren in der Beurteilung des Orosius* (diss. Erlangen 1952) 58-59, 62.

[36] Concerning the slight impression made by Augustine on the east, see: B. Altaner, "Augustinus in der griechischen Kirche bis auf Photius," *HJ*, 71 (1952) 55, 76. On his feeble knowledge of Greek: G. Combès, *Saint Augustin et la culture classique* (Paris 1927) 4-6;

evidence to suggest that Augustine, Orosius, or any western Christians or pagans were familiar with works written in Greek on the topic.

The fifth century was not the last period in which easterners discussed and contemplated the prospect of the fall of their empire. Speculation had taken place within the Roman Empire during previous centuries concerning the date at which the empire would terminate.[37] Such theorizing also occurred sporadically during the later course of Byzantine history. There is an extensive record of oracles, prophecies, and other statements concerning the terminal date and circumstances of the empire.[38] Eastern pagan and Christian discussions of Roman decline in the fifth century are a part of this longer series of speculations which culminated in the various pessimistic predictions associated with the Fourth Crusade and the disintegration of the empire in the fourteenth and fifteenth centuries.[39]

Discussion in the eastern provinces or the Byzantine Empire of the topic of western Roman decline diminished after

---

Saint Augustine, *Contra litt. Petiliani*, 2. 91; P. Courcelle, *Les Lettres grecques en occident de Macrobe à Cassiodore*, 2nd edn. (Paris 1948) 137-194; H.-I. Marrou, *Saint Augustin et la fin de la culture antique*, 4th edn. (Paris 1958) 28-37.

[37] Cf. *supra* Chapter II.

[38] C. Diehl, "De quelques croyances byzantines sur la fin de Constantinople," *BZ*, 30 (1929/30) 192-196; P. J. Alexander, "The Strength of Empire and Capital as Seen through Byzantine Eyes," *Speculum*, 87 (1962) 343-345, 354-357; A. A. Vasiliev, "Medieval Ideas of the End of the World: West and East," *Byzantion*, 16 (1942/43) 464-465, 493-497. See also, for eschatology, P.J. Alexander, "Historiens byzantins et croyances eschatologiques," *Actes du XIIᵉ Congrès International d'Études Byzantines* (Ochride 1961, Belgrade 1964) II 1-8. He will present further evidence in his study, *The Oracle of Baalbek*, to be published in the series of *Dumbarton Oak Texts*.

[39] For the discussion of decline in late Byzantine history: I. Ševčenko, "The Decline of Byzantium Seen through the Eyes of Its Intellectuals," *DO Papers*, 15 (1961) 169-186; H.-G. Beck, *Theodoros Metochites, die Krise des byzantinischen Weltbildes im 14. Jahrhundert* (Munich 1952).

the beginning of the sixth century and disappeared, insofar as literary sources indicate, by the end of that century. Why did the discussion of this problem cease? Several explanations may be offered. In the first place, since pagans became increasingly scarce during the course of the sixth century, there were very few men available who were able to present the pagan position.[40] Furthermore, increasingly harsh anti-pagan legislation and a more zealous imperial enforcement of such laws compelled those pagans who did survive to be very secretive, above all avoiding open expression of their views. Justinian I shattered in 529 the remaining intellectual leadership of eastern paganism by prohibiting pagans from holding university professorships.[41] Paganism therefore ultimately lost its able and intelligent spokesmen who had held influential positions. Moreover, the initially sharp impression made by the loss of the western provinces grew dim with the passage of time. The western Roman provinces were so remote that their problems could not hold eastern attention indefinitely. The subject of western Roman decline was temporarily laid to rest by Justinian's recovery of many provinces. Certainly an extremely important factor in reducing discussion was the obvious fact that the continued existence and relative prosperity of the east weakened the logic of pagan arguments that the empire had declined to nothing. The eastern Christians answered such charges by pointing to the sound condition of the east. They

[40] On the decline of paganism in the sixth century: E. Stein, *Histoire du Bas-Empire*, II 371-373, 799-800; J. Geffcken, *Der Ausgang des griechisch-römischen Heidentums*, 2nd edn. (Heidelberg 1929) 189-197; H. Muller, *Christians and Pagans from Constantine to Augustine* (Pretoria 1946) 141-146.

[41] John Malalas, *Chronographia* (451 Dindorf); Agathias, *Historiae* 2. 30 (231 Dindorf). Justinian objected not to pagan philosophy, but to the teaching of it by pagans, instead of Christians: G. Downey "Julian and Justinian and the Unity of Faith and Culture," *Church History*, 28 (1959) 345-346.

saw no need to construct such elaborate arguments as Saint Augustine had made in *De civitate Dei.*

Insofar as eastern Christians did admit that the empire had suffered reverses, they simply asserted that God was punishing them for their sins.[42] Such an explanation seemed satisfactory to them. Political and military reverses thus stirred them to more zealous devotion to religious responsibilities rather than causing them to become disillusioned with their religion. Finally, it must be remembered that in the east the question of the religious origin of Roman decline remained under discussion at least as long as it did in the western provinces. Salvian of Massilia in his *De gubernatione Dei* (late fifth century) wrote the last known western Christian refutation of pagan charges about Roman decline.[43] In the east, however, Evagrius rebutted Zosimus' charges as late as the last decade of the sixth century.[44]

Despite eastern interest in western developments there is no evidence to suggest that fifth-century eastern pagans or Christians ever attempted to pressure eastern emperors to intervene in the west. Formulation of such policies was a prerogative of the emperor alone. Eastern public opinion did not attempt to impose an active western policy on contemporary emperors. Eastern subjects left the initiative up to their emperors. In the sixth century, however, some east-

---

[42] For eastern Christian statements that contemporary misfortunes were forms of divine punishment: Joshua the Stylite, *Chronicle* 3-6, W. Wright, ed. (Cambridge, England 1882) 3-6; Theodoret, *Ep.*, 22 (92-93 Azéma) *Ep.*, 1,209 (*PG*, 83 1,210).

[43] Salvian, *De gubernatione Dei*, 7. 1. 1-6, M. Petschenig, ed., *CSEL* (Vienna 1891) 8. 155-156. On Salvian: G. Bardy, "Salvien," *DTC*, 14 (1939) 1,056-1,058; Lietzmann, "Salvianus von Massilia," *RE*, 2nd edn., I (1920) 2,017-2,018; G. Madoz, "Salviano di Marsiglia," *Encic. Catt.*, 10 (1953) 1,726-1,727; Bardenhewer, *Geschichte der altkirchlichen Literatur* IV 573-579; R. Thouvenot, "Salvien et la ruine de l'Empire romain," *Mélanges d'archéologie et d'histoire de l'école française de Rome*, 38 (1920) 145-163.

[44] Evagrius, *Hist. Eccl.*, 3. 40-41 (139-144 Bidez-Parmentier).

ern Christians did successfully urge Justinian to liberate Africa from the Vandals.

VI

There are, however, a number of important aspects of the fifth-century eastern response to Roman decline for which the existing sources provide insufficient information. No detailed sources exist, for example, concerning eastern Orthodox Christian opinions on Roman decay during the second half of the fifth century; all of the extant material covers the first half of the century. It is therefore unknown what response was made by contemporary eastern Christians to the news of the deposition of Romulus Augustulus (476) and the final occupation of Gaul, Italy, and Spain by Germanic tribes. Evagrius Scholasticus reports that the early sixth-century, Christian ecclesiastical historian, Eustathius Epiphanius, used the *Historia nova* of Zosimus. Evagrius does not, however, state whether Eustathius endeavored to refute Zosimus' arguments.[45] Indeed, the first and only extant Byzantine reply to Zosimus is the one Evagrius includes in his *Historia ecclesiastica* (last decade of the sixth century).[46]

Numerous problems remain concerning the reactions of dissident, eastern religious groups. Were any Arians, Nestorians, or Monophysites troubled by the continued survival and prosperity of the east, while only the west declined? How successful were these dissident groups in persuading easterners that western disasters were the result of erroneous Christian convictions? There are no known eastern orthodox tracts written in response to such charges. One may surmise, therefore, that such arguments made only a slight impression on the eastern provinces and did not warrant a

[45] *Ibid.*, 5. 24 (219 Bidez-Parmentier).
[46] *Ibid.*, 3. 40-41 (139-144 Bidez-Parmentier).

serious reply. If Orthodox Christians took notice at all, they probably answered these heretics' charges with the same arguments that they gave to pagan criticisms—the obvious security and prosperity of the east refuted any claims that the empire was declining.

More evidence is needed concerning contemporary Monophysite attitudes toward fifth-century Roman decline. One would prefer some evidence earlier than the twelfth-century *Chronicle* of Michael the Syrian, even though he probably echoed older Monophysite opinions. How many Monophysites were interested in western events? Did they, as did some Arians and Nestorians, regard Roman reverses as a divine punishment for the Roman failure to adhere to true— i.e., Monophysite—beliefs and devotional practices?[47] Unquestionably such Monophysite leaders as Cyril of Alexandria and Shanudah participated in anti-pagan campaigns and wrote anti-pagan tracts, but there is nothing to suggest that either they or their fellow Monophysite leaders ever sought to refute pagan charges about the decline of the empire. From what source did the dissident Christian sects take their arguments that contemporary political disasters were divine punishment for erroneous state religious policies? Did they adapt well-known pagan charges to their own purposes? No positive evidence exists on this interesting question, but it is likely that Arian, Nestorian, and Monophysite critics of the imperial government were at least aware of the pagan theses being circulated in the east at that time.

It is impossible to ascertain today how many tracts were written in the fifth century by eastern Christians and pagans on the causes and significance of Roman decline. Ob-

[47] On Monophysitism: M. Jugie, "Eutychès et Eutychianisme," *DTC*, 5 (1939) 1,595-1,609; *id.*, "Monophysisme," *DTC*, 10 (1929) 2,216-2,251; A. Harnack, *Lehrbuch der Dogmengeschichte*, 5th edn. (Tübingen 1931-1932) II 368-424.

viously some fifth-century Christians did write anti-pagan tracts which are no longer extant, but it is uncertain whether these works include discussions of pagan arguments about the disastrous consequences of neglecting to worship the gods properly.[48]

To what extent did the general population of the east, particularly the rural inhabitants, share the concern of some eastern intellectuals for the misfortunes of the western Roman provinces, and to what degree did they develop opinions on Roman decline? The sources provide no definitive answers. The general populace in the east must have been aware of major western events, but except for their weeping at the news of Alaric's capture of Rome, the popular reactions were unreported.[49] It is also unclear just how widely pagan and Christian tracts on Roman decline circulated. The insertion of the pagan thesis and a Christian reply into Theodoret's general manual indicates that pagan arguments were prevalent enough to require a readily available Christian refutation.[50]

The silence of the sources prevent one from knowing whether any eastern pagan or Christian tracts written in Greek on western Roman disasters and on Roman decline ever were circulated in the western part of the Roman Empire. The general western ignorance of Greek, which became especially widespread after the barbarian invasions of the

[48] Philip Sidetes wrote a treatise against Julian: Quasten, *Patrology*, III, 530 and Socrates, *Hist Eccl.*, 7. 27 (*PG*, 67. 800); the tract against pagans by Saint Nilus is lost: Nicephorus Callistus, *Hist. Eccl.* 14. 54 (*PG*, 146 1,256-1,257); Quasten, *Patrology*, III, 502. Also not extant is the treatise *Against the Pagans* of Isidore of Pelusium which he mentioned in his correspondence: *Ep.*, 2. 137, 2. 228 (*PG*, 78, 580, 664-665).

[49] Augustine, *De civ. D*, 1. 33 (56 Hoffmann) on the emotional reaction of eastern peoples to the news of Alaric's capture and sack of Rome.

[50] Theodoret, *Quaestiones et responsiones ad orthodoxos*, 126 (125-127 Papadopoulos-Kerameus).

fifth century, would have placed severe limitations on western familiarity with such eastern works. In particular, Zosimus wrote at such a late date (early in the sixth century) that there would have been extremely few pagans or Christians in Gaul, Spain, and Italy able to read his *Historia nova*.[51]

VII

There are, however, a number of problems raised by this thesis which further research might clarify. Strangely enough, no analysis exists of the actual economic, diplomatic, intellectual, and military consequences for the Byzantine Empire of the disappearance of Roman authority in the former western provinces.[52] While scholars in the twentieth century have, for example, extensively studied the prominence and role of Syrian and other Oriental merchants in western Europe during the early Middle Ages, there has been almost no reflection on this development's consequences for Byzantium. Scholars have debated and continue to dispute the merits of the Pirenne thesis, but have never examined what happened to the wealth which accrued to

[51] On the knowledge of Greek in Italy: P. Courcelle, *Les lettres grecques en occident de Macrobe à Cassiodore*, 2nd edn. (Paris 1948) 134-136; in Africa: 195, 205; in Gaul familiarity with Greek declined, *ibid.*, 221, until c. 470 when there was revival, but knowledge of the language virtually disappeared in the sixth century, *ibid.*, 221-246; cf. P. Riché, *Education et culture dans l'Occident barbare VIe-VIIIe siècles* (Paris 1962) 83-84; also, E. Delaruelle, "La connaissance du grec en occident du Ve au IXe siècle," *Mélanges de la société toulousaine d'études classiques* I (1946) 208-210. The last two references are to knowledge of Greek in Gaul.

[52] Several very competent and fruitful studies of the contrasts between eastern and western conditions have been made: N. H. Baynes, "The Decline of the Roman Power in Western Europe: Some Modern Explanations," *Byzantine Studies and Other Essays* (London 1955) 83-96; E. Demougeot, *De l'unité à la division de l'Empire romain* (Paris 1951); A.H.M. Jones, *The Later Roman Empire* (Oxford 1964) II 1,064-1,068. No detailed examination has yet been given, however, to the various consequences for the Byzantine Empire of the breakdown of the Roman Empire in the west.

these Oriental merchants. Did it all go to Byzantium? Byzantinists have not studied the economic health of Byzantium in the late fifth century with regard to the extensive findings of scholars who were discussing the Pirenne thesis. There is no reason here to offer a mere repetition of the evidence on the existence of Syrian—and often forgotten, Egyptian—merchants in one city or another in Gaul, Italy, and Spain.[53] They served as a medium for communication of information on western conditions to the east, and for transporting refugees from the west to the east, as in the case of Saint Melania the Elder from Rome to Egypt and Palestine, and back from the east to the west, as in the interesting case of Maria, a victim of the Vandal conquest of Africa, which Theodoret has preserved for us in a memorable letter:

> Fit for a tragedy is the story of the most able Maria. For she is, as she and certain others say, the daughter of the most magnificent Eudaimon. But in the catastrophe which has seized Africa, she lost her ancestral freedom and fell into slavery. Some merchants bought her from

[53] On Oriental merchants doing trade with the west: H. Pirenne, *Mahomet et Charlemagne* (Paris 1937) esp. 62-78; L. Bréhier, "Les colonies d'Orientaux en occident au commencement du moyen-âge VIe-VIIIe siècle," *BZ*, 12 (1903) 1-39; P. Scheffer-Boichorst, "Zur Geschichte der Syrer im Abendlande," *Mitteilungen des Instituts für oesterreichische Geschichtsforschung*, 6 (Innsbruck, 1885) 521-550; P. Lambrechts, "Le commerce des Syriens en Gaule du Haut-Empire à l'époque merovingienne," *Ant Clas*, 6 (1937) 35-61. The literature on the Pirenne Theses has been reviewed by A. Riising, "The Fate of Henri Pirenne's Theses on the Consequences of the Islamic Expansion," *ClMed*, 13 (1952) 87-130. P. C. Roberts, "The Pirenne Theses: Economies or Civilizations, Towards Reformulation," *ClMed*, 25 (1964) 297-315 contains no new evidence on Oriental merchants. This is the latest work on the Pirenne Theses, which unconvincingly attempts to restate Pirenne's views. It does discuss the recent bibliography on the Pirenne Theses and therefore there is no reason here to list such titles. But for some confirmation of the positive economic effects of this trade on Syria: M. Rodinson, "De l'archéologie à la sociologie historique, notes méthodologiques sur le dernier ouvrage de G. Tchalenko," *Syria*, 38 (1961) esp. 196-199.

the barbarians and sold her to some persons living near us. Sold with her was a young girl, who formerly was in her service. Thus the servant girl and mistress in common bore the bitter yoke of slavery. But the servant girl did not wish to ignore the difference, not having forgotten the former authority. But she guarded her good will in the misfortune, and after serving their common masters, she also served her supposed fellow slave, washing off her feet, preparing her bed, and attending to her other cares. This became known to those who had bought them. Then in the city people talked about the free status of the one and of the good disposition of the other. Having learned this, the most faithful soldiers stationed with us—for I was absent at that time—gave the price to those who had purchased her and tore her from slavery. And after my return, having learned the facts of her misfortune and the very praiseworthy desire of the soldiers, I prayed blessings upon them and I confided this most noble young girl to one of the most pious deacons, whom I commanded to furnish her sufficient food. Ten months having passed, however, she learned that her father still lived and governed in the west, and she appropriately desired to return to him. And since some said that many merchants from the west are putting into port for the festival now being held among you, she asked to make the journey with a letter from me. I have written this letter on behalf of this matter, asking your piety to take care of this noble girl and to order some one of those ornamented with piety to talk with shipmasters, pilots, and merchants in order to confide her to sure men who can restore her to her father. For they who against all human expectation bring a child to her father will gain all things.[54]

This letter is one of the few Byzantine sources which, in

[54] Theodoret, *Ep.*, 70 (*Correspondance*, Y. Azéma, ed. [Paris 1964] II 152-154).

addition to showing once again eastern solicitude for western Roman sufferings, testify to the extensive commerce between east and west in the fifth century. Clearly slaves were a significant item shipped from the west. The importance of church festivals or fairs in this international commerce is emphasized here. Another evidence of such trade —and the desire to continue it—is Zeno's treaty with Geiseric in 474 which indemnified Carthaginian merchants for the previous seizure by Leo I of their ships and goods which were caught in Byzantine ports, when war commenced. If anything, the decline of the western Roman Empire may have, as Latouche suggests, offered relatively underdeveloped commercial fields for exploitation by enterprising eastern merchants. But Rémondon hypothesizes, to the contrary, —without documentation—that the barbarian invasions ultimately caused, not a drain of gold to the east, but rather disturbed and interrupted the already existing drain of gold from west to east (due to the fact that the invasions impoverished the west).[55] Western decline did not immediately cause economic harm to the eastern provinces. In fact, the transfer of large sums of liquid cash by refugees such as Saint Melania the Elder and her daughter, Saint Melania the Younger, brought additional wealth to the east. Palladius reports of Saint Melania the Younger:

> Entrusting her silver and gold to Paul, a certain priest, a monk of Dalmatia, she sent by sea to the east, to Egypt and the Thebaid 10,000 *nomismata*, to Antioch and its districts 10,000 *nomismata*, to Palestine 15,000 *nomismata*, to the churches in the islands and beyond 10,000 *nomis-*

[55] Malchus, frg. 13 (*FHG*, IV 120-121). See also: R. Latouche, *Les origines de l'économie occidentale* (*IV-IXe siècle*) (Paris 1956), 144-145; R. Rémondon, *La crise de l'Empire romain de Marc-Aurèle à Anastase* ("Nouvelle Clio" L'Histoire et ses problèmes, No. 11, R. Boutruche and P. Lemerle, eds. [Paris 1964] 311-312).

mata. She made similar donations to churches in the west. All this and four times more before God she tore from the mouth of the lion—Alaric—by her faith.[56]

Yet some refugees, such as Maria above, and those others whom Theodoret strove to aid, were penniless charges upon eastern hospitality. Few had the foresight or fortune of the two Saint Melanias to liquefy their western properties and transfer their wealth to the more secure east. If the recent research of the able specialist on Palestine, Avi-Yonah, is correct, Palestine profited economically from pilgrims, refugees, and general boom conditions continued until roughly the reign of Anastasius I. The detailed studies of Tchalenko also indicate that olive cultivation, presumably for shipment (as oil) to the western Mediterranean, increased and brought great prosperity to northern Syria during the fifth century. Further research is needed to determine whether Egypt also enjoyed economic effects from the trade of her merchants with the west, yet such would seem to be the case, if one believes the Latin sources on oriental merchants in Gaul, Italy, and Spain. Yet Byzantine sources are rare. Systematic examination of fifth-century coin hoards may offer additional evidence not only concerning east-west commercial relations, but also material on the broader question of general intercourse between the two regions.[57]

To what extent did the Byzantines themselves understand

[56] On Melania the Younger: Palladius, *Lausiac History* c. 61 (*Texts and Studies*, Dom C. Butler, ed. [Cambridge, England] 1904, VI. 2. 156); Melania the Elder converts her holdings into gold: c. 46 (134-135 Butler); she distributes her wealth at Jerusalem within forty days: c. 54 (147-148 Butler).

[57] M. Avi-Yonah, "The Economics of Byzantine Palestine," *IEJ*, 8 (1958) 39-51; G. Tchalenko, *Villages antiques de la Syrie du Nord. Le massif du Bélus à l'époque romaine*, Institut français d'archéologie de Beyrouth, Bibliothèque archéologique et historique, 50 (Paris 1953) Pt. 1, 422-426; and M. Robinson, "De l'archéologie à la sociologie historique . . ." 196-199.

the implications of the breakdown of the Roman Empire in the west? The entire subject of Christian-pagan conflict after the reign of Constantine I deserves a more comprehensive examination. In particular all available archaeological evidence and other nonliterary sources should be examined; for example, how rapidly did pagan places of worship disappear?

What significance did later Byzantines (i.e., post-sixth century) see in the sack of Rome by Alaric and the disappearance of Roman authority from the former Roman provinces?[58] how interested and well informed before 410 were easterners about developments in the west? to what extent was the Greek-speaking half of the Roman Empire self-contained in its basic outlook and interests before the crises of the fifth century? To answer this last question would require an extensive study of fourth-century Greek literature, but it would offer further evidence for understanding the early cultural basis for what became Byzantine civilization.[59] The military repercussions of western Roman decline for Byzantium—such as increased frontier defense problems in the Balkans and Cyrenaica—also deserve additional study. Fifth-century ecclesiastical relations in the wake of western political dissolution have received considerable scholarly attention, but these developments may call for further study

---

[58] Some important materials on this topic have been collected by F. Dölger in his essay, "Rom in der Gedankenwelt der Byzantiner," *Byzanz und die europäische Staatenwelt* (Ettal 1953) 70-115.

[59] Some works which cover this subject are: L. Hahn, *Rom und Romanismus im griechisch-römischen Osten* (Leipzig 1906); J. Palm, *Rom, Römertum und Imperium in der griechischen Literatur der Kaiserzeit* (Acta Regius Societatis Humaniorum Litterarum Lundensis, 57) (Lund 1959); A.H.M. Jones, "The Greeks under the Roman Empire," *DO Papers*, 16 (1963) 1-19. Another significant study is G.W. Bowersock, *Augustus and the Greek World* (Oxford 1965). On the self-contained outlook of Byzantine hagiography: P. Peeters, *Orient et Byzance: le tréfonds oriental de l'hagiographie byzantine, Subsidia hagiographica*, 26 (Brussels 1950) 71-78.

to ascertain the role of actual western political and military disintegration in determining ecclesiastical affairs in east and west, and the broader impact of these developments on the Byzantine Empire.

VIII

Despite their superficiality the recorded eastern discussions of fifth-century western Roman political and military reverses have important implications for the more general historical problem of the fall of Rome. Fifth-century eastern Christians and pagans found themselves embroiled in semantic disputes over whether the Roman Empire was really in decline. No consensus was reached concerning the soundness of the Roman state. Damascius reported that some pagans considered Rome as having "fallen" already in the 460s.[60] A few decades later Zosimus described the state of the empire in such terms as "gradually became something small, barbarized and ruined," "diminished little by little," "sank to our present misfortune."[61]

Those who agreed that Roman decline had taken place disagreed, however, concerning the date at which this deterioration had begun. The pagans pointed to the reign of Constantine I, the Nestorians to the moment when Nestorius' views were repudiated, while the Monophysites traced decay from the reign of Marcian and the Council of Chalcedon. Likewise, those who spoke of Roman decline differed concerning the causes, and each disaffected religious group argued that the failure of the Roman state to accept or tolerate a particular set of indispensable religious doctrines or practices had brought divine anger and disintegration to the Roman Empire.

[60] Damascius, *Vita Isidori* = Photius, *Bibliotheca* c. 242 (*PG*, 103. 1,265) = Damaskios, *Das Leben des Philosophen Isidoros*, R. Asmus, ed. tr. (Leipzig 1911) 40.

[61] Zosim., *Hist. nov.*, 1. 58. 4; 4. 59. 3; 4. 38. 1; 1. 1. 2 (42, 216, 193-194, 2 Mendelssohn).

On the other hand, there were eastern Christians like Theodoret of Cyrus and Sozomen in the fifth century and Evagrius in the late sixth century who denied that there had been any decline. They pointed instead to current and recent conditions as very prosperous and satisfactory, and indeed as an improvement over the material situation of the empire during the pagan period.[62] For these eastern Christians it was sufficient that the eastern section of the Roman Empire survived; this constituted the Roman Empire for them. In their eyes, what had fallen? Indeed the pagan Zosimus found himself in difficulty when he sought to reconcile his arguments about Roman decline with the prosperity of Constantinople. He had to confess that Constantinople might enjoy divine protection forever.[63]

If fifth-century "contemporaries" of the alleged fall of the Roman Empire could remain so vague, imprecise, and contradictory in their opinions on the condition of their society, it is hardly surprising that modern scholarship has encountered difficulties in attempting to define what, if anything, constituted the decline and fall of the Roman Empire. The nature and causes of the fall of Rome have been controversial issues since the fifth century and doubtless will remain so. The experience of the Byzantines in the fifth and sixth centuries demonstrated how difficult it was to phrase the problem of Roman decline properly for rational consideration. Modern scholarship, in attempting to explain the decline of the Roman Empire, has encountered the same challenge Zosimus did: the difficulty of explaining in one theory both the decay of the western Roman Em-

[62] Evagrius, *Hist. Eccl.*, 3. 41 (141-142 Bidez-Parmentier); Theodoret, *Quaestiones et responsiones ad orthodoxos* (126-127 Papadopoulos-Kerameus); Sozom., *Hist. Eccl.*, 1. 1. 2; 9. 6. 1; 9. 16. 1-4 (390, 397, 406-407 Bidez-Hansen).
[63] Zosim., *Hist. nov.*, 5. 24. 8 (247 Mendelssohn).

pire and the survival of the eastern Roman, or Byzantine, Empire.[64]

[64] Cf. N.H. Baynes, "The Decline of the Roman Power in Western Europe: Some Modern Explanations," *Byzantine Studies and Other Essays* (London 1955, reprinted 1960) 93-96; and J.B. Bury, "Causes of the Survival of the Roman Empire in the East," *Selected Essays* (Cambridge, England 1930) 231-242.

PRIMARY SOURCES

Acta sanctorum quotquot tote orbe coluntur. . . . 66 v. Paris 1863-1940. Basic hagiographical collection.

Aeneas of Gaza and Zacharias of Mitylene. *De immortalitate animae et mundi consummatione.* J.F. Boissonade, ed. Paris 1836.

Aeneas of Gaza. *Teofrasto.* M.E. Colonna, ed. tr. Naples 1958.

Agathias Scholasticus. *Historiae.* L. Dindorf, ed. Historici Graeci minores, II, 132-392. Leipzig 1871.

Anonymus Valesianus. *Excerpta Valesiana.* J. Moreau, ed. Leipzig 1961.

Arnobius. *Adversus nationes libri vii.* C. Marchesi, ed. Milan and Padua 1944.

Auctarium Prosperi Havniensis. T. Mommsen, ed. *MGHa.a.* 9, Chronica Minora I 266-271, 298-339. Berlin 1894.

Sanctus Aurelius Augustinus episcopus. *De civitate Dei.* E. Hoffmann, ed. *CSEL,* 40, Pts. 1-2. Vienna, Prague, Leipzig, 1899-1900. The most important Christian refutation of pagan political charges.

———. *De excidio urbis Romae sermo; A Critical Text and Translation with Introduction and Commentary.* Sister Marie Vianney O'Reilly, ed. Catholic University of America Patristic Studies, 89, Washington 1955. A neglected work.

———. *Epistolae.* J.P. Migne, ed. *Patrologia Latina,* 38. Saint Basil, *Lettres.* Y. Courtonne, ed. tr. 3 v. Paris 1957-1966.

Candidus Isaurus. *Fragmenta.* C. Muller, ed. Fragmenta Historicorum Graecorum IV 135-137. Paris 1868. Important source for late fifth century.

Cassiodorus Senator. *Chronica ad a. DXIX.* T. Mommsen, ed. *MGHa.a.* XI; Chronica Minora, II 109-161. Berlin 1894.

Catalogus codicum astrologorum graecorum. A. Olivieri *et al.,* ed. 12 v. Brussels 1898-1936. Contains Rhetorius.

Chronica gallica a. CCCCLII et DXI. T. Mommsen, ed. *MGHa.a.* IX; Chronica Minora I, 615-666. Berlin 1892.

Chronicon paschale. L. Dindorf, ed. 2 v. Bonn 1832. Includes considerable data on fifth-century events.

Chronicon pseudo-Dionysianum vulgo dictum. J.-B. Chabot, *Corpus Scriptorum Christianorum Orientalium* 121 Scriptores Syri, Ser. 3, Vol. I. Louvain 1927-1949. Contains unique, sometimes confused material.

Claudius Claudianus. *Carmina.* T. Birt, ed. *MGHa.a.* X. Berlin 1892. Important source on Stilicho.

Constantine Porphyrogenitus. *De administrando imperio.* G. Moravcsik, ed. and R.J.H. Jenkins, tr. 2 v. Budapest, London 1949-1962. Manual of Diplomacy.

———. *De cerimoniis aulae byzantinae libri ii.* J.J. Reiske, ed. 2 v. Bonn 1829-1830. Standard source on court ceremonial; contains fifth-century data.

Constantine Manasses. *Breviarium historiae metricum*. I. Bekker, ed. Bonn 1837.

Consularia italica. T. Mommsen, ed. *MGHa.a.* IX; Chronica Minora, I 249-339. Berlin 1892.

Corippus Africanus grammaticus. *Libri qui supersunt*. I. Partsch, ed. *MGHa.a.* III, Pt. 2. Berlin 1879.

Corpus juris civilis. P. Krueger, T. Mommsen, R. Schoell, eds. 3v. 16th, 12th and 6th edn. Berlin 1959. Basic edition.

Cosmas Indicopleustes. *The Christian Topography*. E.O. Winstedt, ed. Cambridge, England 1909. Important for ideology of sixth century.

Sanctus Thascus Caecilius Cyprianus. *Opera omnia*. W. Hartel, ed. *CSEL (Corpus Scriptorum Ecclesiasticorum Latinorum)* III. Pt. 1. Vienna 1868.

Sanctus Cyrillus Alexandriae Archiepiscopus. *Adversus Julianum imperatorem libri decem*. J.-P. Migne, ed. *Patrologia Graeca* 76, 503-1,065. Contains fragments of Julian's *Contra Christianos*.

Cyril of Scythopolis. *Vitae Sabae*. E. Schwartz, ed. *Texte und Untersuchungen* 13, Reihe 4, Bd. 4, 1939.

Damascius. *Das Leben des Philosophen Isidoros*. R. Asmus. ed. tr. Leipzig, 1911. Significant source on fifth-century pagan intellectuals.

Magnus Felix Ennodus. *Opera*. F. Vogel, ed. *MGHa.a.* VII. Berlin 1885.

Sanctus Ephraem Syrus. *Hymni et sermones*. T.J. Lamy, ed. 4 v. Malines 1882-1915.

Eudocia Augusta. *Carminum graecorum reliquiae*. A. Ludwich, ed. Leipzig 1897.

Eunapius Sardianus. *Historia*. C. Muller, ed. *FHG*. 4. 7-56. Paris 1868. Includes all known fragments of this important pagan history.

―――. *Vitae sophistarum*. G. Giangrande, ed. Rome 1956. Bitter anti-Christian sentiments.

Eusebius Caesariensis. *Kirchengeschichte*. E. Schwartz, ed. 3 v. Leipzig 1903-1909. Standard critical edition.

Evagrius Scholasticus. *Ecclesiastical History*. J. Bidez and L. Parmentier, eds. London 1898. Contains last Christian refutation of Zosimus.

Excerpta de insidiis, C. De Boor, ed. Excerpta Historica iussu Imp. Constantini Porphyrogeneti, III. Berlin 1905.

Fragmenta historicorum graecorum. T. Muller and C. Muller, eds. 5 v. Paris 1848-1874.

Fredegarius. *Chronica*. B. Krusch, ed. Monumenta Germaniae Historica, Scriptores rerum Merovingicarum, II. Hannover 1888.

George Cedrenus. *Historiarum compendium*. I. Bekker, ed. 2 v. Bonn 1838-1839.

George Codinus. *Excerpta de antiquitatibus Constantinopolitanis*. I. Bekker, ed. Bonn 1843.

Gerontius (?). *Vie de Sainte Mélanie*. D. Gorce, ed. Paris 1962.

Sanctus Gregorius Nazianzus. *Contra Julianum* I-II. J.-P. Migne, ed. *Patrologia Graeca* 35. 525-720.

Gregorius episcopus Turonensis. *Historia Francorum.* W. Arndt, ed. *MGH.* Scriptores rerum Merovingicarum, I, 1-450. Hannover 1885.

Hydatius Lemicus. *Continuatio chronicorum hieronymianorum ad a. CCCCLXVIII.* T. Mommsen, ed. *MGHa.a.* XI Chronica Minora, II, 1-36. Berlin 1894.

Isaac of Antioch. *Homily on the Royal City,* C. Moss, ed. tr., *Zeitschrift für Semitistik und verwandte Gebiete,* 7 (1929) 295-306; 8 (1932) 61-72.

Sanctus Isaac Antiochenus. *Opera omnia.* G. Bickell, ed. 2 v. Giessen 1873-1877. Standard edition.

Sanctus Isidorus Pelusiotae. *Epistolarum libri v.* J.-P. Migne, ed. *Patrologia Graeca,* 78. Includes anti-pagan arguments.

Saint Jerome. *Commentariorum in Ezechielem prophetam libri quatuordecim.* J.-P. Migne, ed. *Patrologia Latina,* 25 15-512. Important source for his reactions to the sack of Rome.

———. *Lettres.* J. Labourt, ed. tr. 8 v. Paris 1949-1963. Includes material concerning the sack of Rome.

Johannes Antiochenus. *Fragmenta.* C. Muller, ed. Fragmenta Historicorum Graecorum, IV, 535-622. Paris 1868. Significant source for fifth century.

Johannes Ephesinus. *Hist. Eccl. pars tertia.* E. W. Brooks, ed. tr. *Corpus Scriptorum Christianorum Orientalium,* 105-106. Scriptores Syri, Ser. 3, vol. 3, Textus et Versio. 2 v. in 1. Louvain 1935-1936.

———. *Lives of the Eastern Saints.* E.W. Brooks, ed. tr. *Patrologia Orientalis,* Fasc. 1; Fasc. 4; Fasc. 2. Paris 1923-1926. Source on fifth-century paganism.

Johannes Lydus. *De magistratibus populi romani libri tres.* R. Wuensch, ed. Leipzig 1903. Source for fifth-century events and sixth-century ideology.

Johannes Malalas. *Chronographia.* L. Dindorf, ed. Bonn 1831. Important chronicle.

Johannes, episcopus Nikiu. *The Chronicle.* R. H. Charles, tr. London, Oxford 1916.

Johannes Philoponus. *De aeternitate mundi contra Proclum.* H. Rabe, ed. Leipzig 1899.

Jordanes. *Romana et Getica.* T. Mommsen, ed. Monumenta Germaniae Historica, Auctores antiquissimi, V, Pt. 1. Berlin 1882.

Joshua the Stylite. *The Chronicle.* W. Wright, tr. Cambridge, England 1882. Source for late fifth century.

Julianus imperator. *Librorum contra Christianos quae supersunt.* C. I. Neumann, ed. Leipzig 1880. A basic work of pagan apologetics.

Leo Grammaticus. *Chronographia.* I. Bekker, ed. Bonn 1842.

Libanius. *Opera.* R. Förster, ed. 12 v. in 13. Rev. edn. Hildesheim 1963. Important fourth-century pagan.

Macarius Magnes. *Macarii Magnetis quae supersunt.* C. Blondel, ed. Paris 1876. Refutes pagan charges.

———. *Apocriticus.* T.W. Crafer, tr. London 1919.

Malchus Philadelphensis. *Fragmenta.* C. Muller, ed. Fragmenta Historicorum Graecorum, IV, 111-132. Paris 1868. Basic source for fifth century.

Marcellinus V. C. Comes. *Chronicon.* . . . T. Mommsen, ed. Monumenta Germaniae Historica, Auctores antiquissimi, XI; Chronica Minora, II, 37-108. Berlin 1894.

Marcus Diaconus. *Vie de Porphyre, évêque de Gaza.* H. Grégoire and M.-A. Kugener, ed. tr. Paris 1930. Indispensable source for pagan-Christian struggle at Gaza.

Marius episcopus Aventicensis. *Chronica a. CCCCLV-DLXXXI.* T. Mommsen, ed. Monumenta Germaniae Historica, Auctores antiquissimi, XI; Chronica Minora, II, 225-239. Berlin 1894.

Michael the Syrian. *Chronique.* J.-B. Chabot, ed. tr. 3 v. Paris 1899-1905. Includes Monophysite reaction to Roman decline.

Nestorius. *The Bazaar of Heracleides.* G. R. Driver and L. Hodgson, tr. Oxford 1925. Nestorian views on the decline of Rome. Difficult translation.

————. *Le livre d'Héraclide de Damas.* F. Nau, tr. Paris 1910.

————. *Nestoriana: Die Fragmente des Nestorius.* F. Loofs, ed. Halle 1905.

Nicephorus Callistus Xanthopulus. *Ecclesiasticae historiae libri xviii.* J.-P. Migne, ed. *Patrologia Graeca* 145-147.

St. Nilus of Ancyra. *Epistolae.* J.-P. Migne, ed. *Patrologia Graeca* 79. 81-582. Important anti-pagan arguments.

Origen. *Contra Celsum.* H. Chadwick, tr. Cambridge, England 1953.

Origenes. *Die acht Bücher gegen Celsus.* P. Koetschau, ed. 2 v. Leipzig 1899.

Orosius. *Historiarum adversum paganos libri vii.* C. Zangemeister, ed. *Corpus Scriptorum Ecclesiasticorum Latinorum* 5. Vienna 1882. Significant Christian refutation of pagan arguments in the early fifth century.

Palladius. *The Lausiac History Edited with Discussion.* C. Butler, ed. Texts and Studies: Contributions to Biblical and Patristic Literature, J.A. Robinson, ed. 2 v. Cambridge, England 1898-1904 VI, Nos. 1 and 2.

Paulini Pellaei *Eucharisticos.* W. Brandes, ed. *Corpus Scriptorum Ecclesiasticorum* 16. Vienna 1888.

Philostorgius. *Kirchengeschichte.* J. Bidez, ed. Leipzig 1913. Arian views.

Photius. *Opera omnia.* J.-P. Migne, ed. *Patrologia Graeca* 101-104.

————. *Bibliothèque.* R. Henry, ed. tr., Paris 1959- . Critical edition of fragments of Olympiodorus is included.

————. *Homilies.* C. Mango, tr. and comment. Dumbarton Oaks Studies, III. Cambridge, Mass. 1958.

Polybius. *Historiae.* L. Dindorf and T. Buettner-Wobst, eds. Rev. edn. 5 v. Stuttgart 1962-1963.

————. *The Histories.* W. R. Paton, tr. 6 v. Cambridge, Mass. 1960-1964.

Priscian. *De laude Anastasii imperatoris.* W. Baehrens, ed. Poetae Latini minores. Vol. V. Leipzig 1883.

Priscus Panites. *Fragmenta*. L. Dindorf, ed. Historici graeci minores, I, 275-352. Leipzig 1870. Important source on fifth-century.
————. *Fragmenta*. C. Muller, ed. *Fragmenta Historicorum Graecorum* 4. 69-110. Paris 1868.
Procli Diadochi. *Tria opuscula*. Berlin 1960.
Procopius Caesariensis. *Opera omnia*. J. Haury and G. Wirth, eds. 4 v. 2nd edn. Leipzig 1962-1964. Important for fifth-century military events.
Prosper Tironis. *Epit. chron*. T. Mommsen, ed. *MGHa.a.* IX; Chronica Minora, Berlin 1892 I, 341-499.
Cl. Rutilius Namatianus. *Édition critique . . . suivie d'une étude historique et littéraire sur l'oeuvre et l'auteur*. J. Vessereau, ed. Paris 1904. Basic study.
————. *De reditu suo*. R. Helm, ed. Heidelberg 1933.
————. *Sur son retour*. J. Vessereau and F. Préchac, eds., tr. 2nd edn. Paris 1961.
Salvianus presbyter Massiliensis. *De gubernatione Dei libri viii*. C. Halm ed. *MGHa.a.* Berlin 1877 I, Pt. 1. Important views on imperial decay.
Shanudah. *Sinuthii archimandritae vita et opera omnia*. J. Leipoldt and W. Crum, eds. H. Wiesmann, tr. Corpus Scriptorum Christianorum Orientalium, Scriptores Coptici, Louvain 1906-1952 Ser. II, Vols. II, IV, V. Source on Egyptian struggle against paganism in the fifth century.
Gaius Sollius Apollinaris Sidonius. *Epistulae et carmina*. C. Luetjohann, ed. *MGHa.a.* VIII. Berlin 1887.
————. *Poèmes*. A. Loyen, ed. tr. Paris 1960.
Socrates Scholasticus. *Historia Ecclesiastica*. J.-P. Migne, ed. *Patrologia Graeca*, 67. 29-842. Best ecclesiastical history.
Sophronius Monachus. "Narratio miraculorum SS. Cyri et Iohannis," *Spicilegium romanum. . . .* A. Mai, ed. Rome 1840 III, 97-670.
Sozomenus. *Kirchengeschichte*. J. Bidez and G.C. Hansen, eds. Berlin 1960. Useful for fifth-century ideology and history.
Suidas. *Lexicon*. A. Adler, ed. 5 v. Leipzig 1928-1938. Includes useful biographical data on pagans.
Synesius. *Epistolae*. J.-P. Migne, ed. *Patrologia Graeca* 66. 1,321-1,560. Source on early fifth-century Libya.
Synesius Cyrenensis. *Hymni*. N. Terzaghi, ed. Rome 1949.
————. *Opuscula*. N. Terzaghi, ed. Rome 1944.
Tacitus, Cornelius. *Annalium ab excessu Divi Augusti libri*. C. D. Fisher, ed. Oxford 1963.
Tertullian. *Opera*. Corpus Christianorum, Series Latina, I. Turnholt 1954.
Theodore Lector. *Hist. Eccl*. J.-P. Migne, ed. 86. 1. 165-228.
Theodoretus of Cyrus. *Correspondance*. Y. Azéma, ed. 3 v. Paris 1955-1965. Critical edition. His reactions to Vandal conquest of Africa.
————. *De providentia*. J.-P. Migne, ed. 83. 555-774.
————. *Discours sur la Providence*. Y. Azéma, tr. Paris 1954.

Theodoretus of Cyrus. *Kirchengeschichte*. L. Parmentier and F. Scheidweiler, eds. 2nd edn. Berlin 1954. A basic source.

————. *Quaestiones et responsiones ad orthodoxos = Otviety na voprosy obrashchennye k nemu niektorymi egypetskimi episkopami = πρὸς τὰς ἐπενεχθείσας αὐτῷ ἐπερωτήσεις παρὰ τινὸς τῶν ἐξ Αἰγύπτου ἐπισκόπων ἀπόκρισεις ἐκδιδόμεναι κατὰ κώδικα τῆς δεκάτης ἑκατοναετηρίδος.* A. Papadopoulos-Kerameus, ed. *Zapiski, Istoriko-filologicheski fakultet.* St. Petersburg University 36 (1895). One of the most significant eastern refutations of pagan political arguments.

————. *Religiosa historia seu ascetica vivendi ratio*. J.-P. Migne, ed. *Patrologia Graeca* 82. 1,283-1,496.

————. *Thérapeutique des maladies helléniques*. P. Canivet, ed. tr. 2 v. Paris 1958. Refutes pagan philosophical contentions.

Theodosiani libri xvi cum constitutionibus Sirmondianis et leges novellae ad Theodosianum pertinentes. Th. Mommsen and P. Krüger, ed. Rev. edn. 2 v. Berlin 1954. Basic edition of imperial legislation against pagan worship.

The Theodosian Code and Novels and the Sirmondian Constitutions. C. Pharr, ed. Princeton 1952. Good translation, with some notes.

Theophanes. *Chronographia*. C. De Boor, ed. 2 v. Leipzig, 1883-1885. Critical edition of this important source.

Victor Tonnennensis episcopus. *Chronica a. CCCCXLIV-DLXVII*. Th. Mommsen, ed. *MGHa.a.*, Chronica Minora, XI 163-206. Berlin 1894.

Victor Vitensis. *Historia persecutionis Africanae provinciae sub Geiserico et Hunirico regibus Wandalorum*. C. Halm, ed. *MGHa.a.* 3, Pt. 1. Berlin 1879. Appeals for eastern aid to Africa.

Zachariah of Mitylene. *The Chronicle*. F.J. Hamilton and E.W. Brooks, tr. London 1899.

————. *Vie de Sévère*. M.-A. Kugener, ed. tr. Patrologia Orientalis, II, Fasc. 1. Paris 1903. One of the best sources on fifth-century paganism in Egypt and Syria.

Zacharias Rhetor. *De immortalitate animae et mundi consummatione*. J. F. Boissonade, ed. Paris 1836.

————. *Vita Isaiae*. E. W. Brooks, ed. tr. *Corpus Scriptorum Christianorum Orientalium*, Scriptores Syria, Ser. 3, Vol. 25, 2-10. Paris 1907. Source on pagans in Palestine.

Zhitie izhe vo sviatych ottsa nashego Arsenii Velikago. G. Tsereteli, ed. Zapiski, Istoriko-filologicheski fakultet, St. Petersburg University, Vol. 50, Pt. 1. (1899). Includes Arsenius' reactions to the sack of Rome.

Zonaras, Johannes. *Epitome historiarum*. L. Dindorf, ed. 6 v. Leipzig 1868-1875.

Zosimus, comes et exadvocatus fisci. *Historia nova*. L. Mendelssohn, ed. Leipzig 1887; reprinted Hildesheim 1963. The most important work of pagan historical apologetics.

SECONDARY SOURCES

Abramowski, L. *Untersuchungen zum Liber Heraclidis des Nestorius.*

Corpus Scriptorum Christianorum Orientalium, Subsidia, 22. Louvain 1963.

Alexander, P.J. "Historiens byzantins et croyances eschatologiques," *Actes du XIIe Congrès International d'Études byzantines* [Ohride 1961] (Belgrade 1964) II 1-8.

————. "The Strength of Empire and Capital as Seen Through Byzantine Eyes," *Speculum* 37 (1962) 339-357. Introduces new material.

Alföldi, A. *A Conflict of Ideas in the Late Roman Empire: The Clash Between the Senate and Valentinian I.* H. Mattingly, tr. Oxford 1952. Important study of fourth-century political views.

————. *The Conversion of Constantine and Pagan Rome.* H. Mattingly, tr. Oxford 1948. Uses numismatic data.

————. "Insignien und Tracht der römischen Kaiser," *Mitteilungen des deutschen archaeologischen Instituts, römische Abteilung*, 50 (1935) 1-171. The basic work.

————. *Die Kontorniaten: Ein verkanntes Propagandamittel der stadtrömischen heidnischen Aristokratie in ihrem Kampfe gegen das christliche Kaisertum.* 2 v. Budapest 1942-1943.

————. *Der Untergang der Römerherrschaft in Pannonien.* Ungarische Bibliothek, I. Reihe, X, XII. 2 v. Berlin and Leipzig 1924-1926. Standard.

Altaner, B. "Augustinus in der griechischen Kirche bis auf Photius," *Historisches Jahrbuch* 71 (1952) 37-76.

————. *Patrology.* H.C. Graef, tr. New York 1960. Useful, especially for the post-Chalcedonian period.

Altheim, F. *Geschichte der Hunnen.* 5 v. Berlin 1959-1962.

————. *Niedergang der alten Welt: Eine Untersuchung der Ursachen.* 2 v. Frankfurt 1952.

Amand, D. *Fatalisme et liberté dans l'antiquité grecque.* Louvain 1945.

Anastos, M. V. *The Mind of Byzantium.* (Unpublished manuscript read through the kindness of the author.)

————. "Nestorius was Orthodox," *Dumbarton Oaks Papers* 16 (1962) 117-140. Significant arguments.

Andreotti, R. *Il regno dell'imperatore Giuliano.* Bologna 1936. Perceptive, often neglected study.

Andresen, C. *Logos und Nomos: Die Polemik des Kelsos wider das Christentum.* Arbeiten zur Kirchengeschichte, 30. Berlin 1955.

Asmus, R. "Pamprepios, ein byzantinischer Gelehrter und Staatsmann des 5. Jahrhunderts," *Byzantinische Zeitschrift*, 22 (1913) 320-347.

Avi-Yonah, M. "The Economics of Byzantine Palestine," *Israel Exploration Journal* 8 (1959) 39-51.

Babelon, E. "Attila dans la numismatique," *Revue numismatique*, Ser. IV, Vol. 18 (1914) 297-328. Must use with caution.

Balogh, E. "Die Datierung der byzantinischen Periode," *Studi in memoria di Aldo Albertoni*, II, 153-189. Padova 1938.

Bardenhewer, O. *Geschichte der altkirchlichen Literatur.* 5 v. Freiburg 1913-1932. Still indispensable.

Bardy, G. "La littérature patristique des '*Quaestiones et responsiones*' sur l'Écriture Sainte," *Revue Biblique*, 41 (1932) 210-236, 341-369, 515-537; 42 (1933) 14-30, 211-229, 328-352. A careful study.

Barker, J. W. *Justinian and the Later Roman Empire.* Madison, Wis., 1966.

Baumstark, A. *Geschichte der syrischen Literatur.* Bonn 1922. Useful in the absence of more recent works.

Baur, C. "Die Anfänge des byzantinischen Cäsaropapismus," *Archiv für katholisches Kirchenrecht*, 111 (1931) 99-113.

Baynes, N. H. *Byzantine Studies and Other Essays.* London 1955; reprinted 1960. Excellent analytical essays.

————. "A Note on Professor Bury's 'History of the Later Roman Empire,'" *Journal of Roman Studies* 12 (1922) 207-228. Doubtful.

————. Review of E. Stein, *Geschichte des spätrömischen Reiches*, I, in *Journal of Roman Studies* 18 (1928) 217-225. Not generally accepted.

Beaujeu, J. *La religion romaine à l'apogée de l'empire*, I: *La politique des Antonins (96-192).* Paris 1955.

Beck, H. G. *Theodoros Metochites, die Krise des byzantinischen Weltbildes im 14. Jahrhundert.* Munich 1952.

Biagi, V. "Eunapio e il Cristianesimo," *Les quarante années de l'activité de Théophile Boreas*, II 179-182. Athens 1940.

Bidez, J. "L'Historien Philostorge," *Mélanges d'histoire offerts à Henri Pirenne*, I 23-30. Brussels 1926. Perceptive, brief.

————. *La vie de l'empereur Julien.* Paris 1930. Standard.

Bloch, H. "A New Document of the Last Pagan Revival in the West, A.D. 393-394," *Harvard Theological Review* 38 (1945) 199-244. Important.

Boak, A.E.R. *Manpower Shortage and the Fall of the Roman Empire in the West.* Ann Arbor 1955. Overstated.

Boissier, G. *La fin du paganisme: étude sur les dernières luttes religieuses en Occident au quatrième siècle.* 7th edn. 2 v. Paris 1922. Old classic.

Bowersock, G.W. *Augustus and the Greek World.* Oxford 1965.

Boyce, A.A. "Eudoxia, Eudocia, Eudoxia: Dated Solidi of the Fifth Century," *Museum Notes* [American Numismatic Society], VI (1954) 131-141.

————. *Festal and Dated Coins of the Roman Empire: Four Papers.* Numismatic Notes and Monographs, No. 153. New York 1965.

Boyd, W.K. *The Ecclesiastical Edicts of the Theodosian Code.* Columbia University Studies in History, Economics and Public Law, Vol. XXIV, No. 2. New York 1905. Uncritical.

Braaten, C.E. "Modern Interpretations of Nestorius," *Church History* 32 (1963) 251-267. Useful summary.

Brambilla, C. *Altre annotazioni numismatiche.* Pavia 1870.

Bratianu, G.I. *Études byzantines d'histoire économique et sociale.* Paris 1938.

Bréhier, L. "La crise de l'Empire romain en 457," *Šišićev Zbornik = Mélanges Šišić*, 85-96. Zagreb 1929. Unfamiliar with all contemporary literature.

Brok, M.F.A. de "De waarde van de 'Graecarum affectionum curatio' van Theodoretus van Cyrus als apologetisch werk," *Studia Catholica*, 27 (1952) 201-212. Questions attribution to Theodoret.

Brooks, E.W. "The Emperor Zenon and the Isaurians," *English Historical Review*, 8 (1893) 209-238.

Bulic, F. "Stridone luogo natale di S. Girolamo," *Miscellanea Geronimiana*, 253-330. Rome 1920. Basic.

Bury, J. B. *History of the Later Roman Empire.* 2nd edn. 2 v. London, 1923; reprinted New York 1958. Important for narrative and chronology.

——. "A Note on the Emperor Olybrius," *English Historical Review*, 1 (1886) 507-509.

——. *Selected Essays.* Cambridge, England 1930.

Cambridge Medieval History. Planned by J. B. Bury; H. M. Gwatkin, 2nd edn. 8 v. Cambridge, England 1924-1958. Obsolete.

Canivet, P. *Histoire d'une entreprise apologétique au Ve siècle.* Paris 1959. Detailed study.

Casini, N. "Le discussioni sull' 'Ara Victoriae' nella curia romana," *Studi Romani*, 5 (1957) 501-517.

Cavallera, F. *Saint Jérôme sa vie et son oeuvre.* Louvain, Paris 1922.

Chabot, J.-B. *Littérature syriaque.* Paris 1935. Brief.

Chalmers, W.R. "Eunapius, Ammianus Marcellinus, and Zosimus on Julian's Persian Expedition," *Classical Quarterly*, N.S., 10 (1960) 152-160.

——. "The Νέα ἔκδοσις of Eunapius' Histories," *Classical Quarterly*, N.S., 3 (1953) 165-170. Important analysis.

Chambers, M., ed. *The Fall of Rome: Can It be Explained?* New York, 1963.

Charlesworth, M. P. "Providentia and Aeternitas," *Harvard Theological Review*, 27 (1936) 107-132.

Chastel, E. *Histoire de la destruction du paganisme dans l'Empire d'Orient.* Paris 1850. Obsolete.

Christ, W. von. *Geschichte der griechischen Litteratur.* W. Schmid and O. Stählin, rev. 6th edn. 2 v. Munich 1912-1924. Still useful.

Cochrane, C.N. *Christianity and Classical Culture: A Study of Thought and Action from Augustus to Augustine.* Rev. edn. London, New York 1957. A basic study.

Cohen, H. *Description historique des monnaies frappées sous l'Empire romain.* 2nd edn. 8 v. Paris 1880-1892. Unfortunately still the only general catalogue for the fifth century.

Coleman, C. B. *Constantine the Great and Christianity. Three Phases: the Historical, the Legendary, and the Spurious.* Columbia University Studies in History, Economics and Public Law, Vol. 60, No. 1. New York 1914.

Colonna, M. E. *Gli storici bizantini dal IV al XV secolo.* Vol. I: *Storici profani.* Naples 1956. Superseded by Moravcsik.

Combès, G. *La doctrine politique de Saint Augustin.* Paris 1927.

——. *Saint Augustin et la culture classique.* Paris 1927.

Condurachi, E. "Les idées politiques de Zosime," *Revista Clasică*, 13-

14 (1941-1942) 115-127. A neglected but basic article, although must be used with caution.

Corsaro, F. "L'Apocritico' di Macario di Magnesia e le Sacre Scritture," *Nuovo Didaskaleion,* 7 (1957) 1-24.

Coster, C. H. "Synesius, A Curialis of the Time of the Emperor Arcadius," *Byzantion* 15 (1940-1941) 10-38.

Courcelle, P. *Histoire littéraire des grandes invasions germaniques.* 3rd edn. Paris 1964.

————. *Les lettres grecques en occident de Macrobe à Cassiodore.* Rev. edn. Paris 1948. Basic.

————. "Propos antichrétiens rapportés par Saint Augustin," *Recherches Augustiniennes,* I (1958) 149-186.

Courtois, C. *Les Vandales et l'Afrique.* Paris 1955. Excellent scholarship.

————. *Victor de Vita et son oeuvre. Étude critique.* Algiers 1954.

Cramer, F. *Astrology in Roman Law and Politics.* Memoirs of the American Philosophical Society, 37. Philadelphia 1954.

Cranz, F. E. "*De civitate Dei,* XV, 2, and Augustine's Idea of the Christian Society," *Speculum* 25 (1950) 215-225.

————. "The Development of Augustine's Ideas on Society Before the Donatist Controversy," *Harvard Theological Review,* 47 (1954) 255-316.

————. "Kingdom and Polity in Eusebius of Caesarea," *Harvard Theological Review,* 45 (1952) 47-66. Careful analysis.

Croiset, A. and M. *Histoire de la littérature grecque.* 5 v. Paris 1896-1899.

Deane, H. A. *The Political and Social Ideas of St. Augustine.* New York, London 1963. Useful survey.

Deér, J. "Der Globus des spätrömischen und des byzantinischen Kaisers. Symbol oder Insigne?" *Byzantinische Zeitschrift,* 54 (1961) 53-85, 291-318.

Degenhart, F. *Der Heilige Nilus Sinaita. Sein Leben und seine Lehre vom Mönchtum.* Beiträge zur Geschichte des alten Mönchtums und des Benediktinerordens. I. Herwegen, ed. H. 6. Münster 1915. Unreliable.

Degrassi, A. *I fasti consolari dell' Impero romano dal 30 avanti Cristo al 613 dopo Cristo.* Rome 1952.

Delaruelle, E. "La connaissance du grec en occident du Ve au IXe siècle," *Mélanges de la société toulousaine d'études classiques,* I (1946) 207-226.

De Lepper, J.L.M. *De rebus gestis Bonifacii comitis Africae et magistri militum.* Tilburg-Breda 1941.

Demougeot, É. *De l'unité à la division de l'Empire romain 395-410. Essai sur le gouvernement impérial.* Paris 1951. Careful scholarship but conclusions somewhat overstated.

————. "La théorie du pouvoir impérial au début du Ve siècle,"

Mélanges de la société toulousaine d'études classiques, I (1946) 191-206.

Diakonov, A. *Ioann' Efesskii i ego Tserkovno-istoricheskie trudy.* St. Petersburg 1908.

Dictionnaire d'histoire et de géographie ecclésiastiques. Mgr. A. Baudrillart *et al.,* ed. I- . Paris 1912- .

Dictionnaire de théologie catholique. A. Vacant, E. Mangenot, E. Amann, eds. 15 v. Paris 1909-1950. Necessary reference work.

Diehl, C. *Byzance, grandeur et décadence.* Paris 1919.

――――. "De quelques croyances byzantines sur la fin de Constantinople," *Byzantinische Zeitschrift,* 30 (1929-1930) 192-196. Interesting general survey.

――――. *Figures byzantines,* Série I and II. Rev. edn. 2 v. Paris 1938-1939.

Diesner, H.-J. "Orosius und Augustinus," *Acta Antiqua,* 9 (1963) 89-102.

Dölger, F. "Rom in der Gedankenwelt der Byzantiner," *Byzanz und die europäische Staatenwelt,* 70-115. Ettal 1953. Important.

――――. "Vom Altertum zum Mittelalter," *PARASPORA,* 54-72. Ettal 1961.

Dörries, H. *Das Selbstzeugnis Kaiser Konstantins.* Abhandlungen der Akademie der Wissenschaften in Göttingen, Philologisch-historische Klasse, 3. Folge, Nr. 34. (1954). Critical examination of sources.

Downey, G. "Education in the Christian Roman Empire; Christian and Pagan Theories under Constantine and his Successors," *Speculum,* 32 (1957) 48-61. Important.

――――. *A History of Antioch in Syria from Seleucus to the Arab Conquest.* Princeton 1961. Basic general work.

――――. "Julian and Justinian and the Unity of Faith and Culture," *Church History,* 28 (1959) 339-349.

――――. "The Pagan Virtue of *Megalopsychia* in Byzantine Syria," *Transactions of the American Philological Association,* 76 (1945) 279-286.

――――. "Paganism and Christianity in Procopius," *Church History,* 18 (1949) 89-102. Exhaustive study of subject.

――――. "The Perspective of the Early Church Historians," *Greek-Roman-and Byzantine Studies,* 6 (1965) 57-70.

――――. "Philanthropia in Religion and Statecraft in the Fourth Century After Christ," *Historia,* 4 (1955) 199-208.

――――. "Review Article: Byzantium and the Classical Tradition," *The Phoenix,* 12 (1958) 125-129.

Du Cange, C. *Glossarium ad scriptores mediae et infimae Graecitatis* 2 v. Lugduni 1688; reprinted Paris 1945. Still useful.

Duchesne, L. *Histoire ancienne de l'église.* 3 v. Paris 1910-1929.

Dvornik, F. *Early Christian and Byzantine Political Philosophy* 2 v. Washington, D.C. 1966. Many insights and new interpretations.

――――. "The Emperor Julian's 'Reactionary' Ideas on Kingship," *Late Classical and Mediaeval Studies in Honor of Albert Mathias Friend, Jr.,* 71-81. Princeton 1955. Significant.

Dvornik, F. "Emperors, Popes and General Councils," *Dumbarton Oaks Papers*, 6 (1951) 1-23.

Enciclopedia Cattolica. 12 v. Vatican City 1949-1954.

Ensslin, W. *Die Religionspolitik des Kaisers Theodosius d. Gr.* Sitzungsberichte der bayerischen Akademie der Wissenschaften, Philosophisch-historische Klasse, Heft II. Munich 1953. Basic.

————. *Theoderich der Grosse,* 2nd edn. Munich 1959.

Festugière, A. J. *Antioche païenne et chrétienne: Libanius, Chrysostome, et les moines de Syrie.* Paris 1959. Primarily covers fourth and fifth centuries.

Figgis, J. N. *The Political Aspects of Saint Augustine's 'City of God.'* London 1921.

Fliche, A. and V. Martin. *Histoire de l'église depuis les origines jusqu'à nos jours.* I-   Paris 1935-   . Standard.

Florovsky, G. *Vizantiiskie ottsy V-VIII.* Paris 1933.

Frantz, A. "From Paganism to Christianity in the Temples of Athens," *Dumbarton Oaks Papers*, 19 (1965) 185-205.

Friedländer, J. *Die Münzen der Vandalen.* Leipzig 1849.

Fritz, K. von. *The Theory of the Mixed Constitution in Antiquity: A Critical Analysis of Polybius' Political Ideas.* New York 1954. Excellent study.

Frolow, A. "La dédicace de Constantinople dans la tradition byzantine," *Revue de l'Histoire des Religions*, 127 (1944) 61-127.

Fuchs, H. *Der geistige Widerstand gegen Rom in der antiken Welt.* Berlin 1938.

Funk, F. X. "Le Pseudo-Justin et Diodore de Tarse," *Revue d'Histoire Ecclésiastique*, 3 Pt. 2 (1902) 947-971. Refutes Harnack.

————. "Pseudo-Justin und Diodor von Tarse," *Kirchengeschichtliche Abhandlungen und Untersuchungen*, III (Paderborn 1907) 323-350.

Gabba, E. "Storici greci dell'impero romano da Augusto ai Severi," *Rivista Storica Italiana*, 71 (1959) 361-381.

Galavaris, G. P. "The Symbolism of the Imperial Costume as Displayed on Byzantine Coins," *Museum Notes* [American Numismatic Society], 8 (1958) 99-117.

Geffcken, J. *Der Ausgang des griechisch-römischen Heidentums.* 2nd edn. Heidelberg 1929. The best general work, with extensive references.

————. *Kaiser Julianus.* Das Erbe der Alten, 8. Leipzig 1914.

Giangrande, G. "Vermutungen und Bermerkungen zum Text der Vitae Sophistarum des Eunapios," *Rheinisches Museum für Philologie*, N.F., 99 (1956) 133-153.

Gibbon, E. *The History of the Decline and Fall of the Roman Empire.* J. B. Bury, ed. 7 v. London 1897-1902. Judicious use of literary sources.

Gigli, G. *La crisi dell'impero romano.* Palermo 1947.

Gilson, E. *Introduction à l'étude de Saint Augustin.* Paris 1949.

Gitti, A. *Ricerche sui rapporti tra i Vandali e l'impero romano.* Bari, 1953.

Giunta, F. *Genserico e la Sicilia*. Palermo 1958.

Glubokovskii, N. *Blazhennyi Feodorit*. 2 v. Moscow 1890.

————. *Istoricheskoe polozhenie i znachenie lichnosti Feodorita, episkopa Kirrskago*. St. Petersburg 1911.

Golubtsova, N. I. "Sobytia 410 goda v Rime v otsenke sovremennikov," *Doklady i soobshcheniia*, Istoricheski Fakultet, Moscow University, 10, 51-55. Moscow 1950. Superficial.

Goodacre, H. *A Handbook of the Coinage of the Byzantine Empire*. 3 v. London 1928-1933; reprinted London 1957.

Gordon, C. D. *The Age of Attila*. Ann Arbor 1960.

Gothofredus, J. *Codex Theodosianus cum perpetuis commentariis*. . . . 6 v. Leipzig 1737.

Graebner, F. "Eine Zosimosquelle," *Byzantinische Zeitschrift* 14 (1905) 87-159.

Grégoire, H., and P. Orgels, et al., *Les persécutions dans l'Empire romain*. 2nd edn. Mémoires de l'Académie royale de Belgique, Classe des lettres et des sciences morales et politiques, 56, fasc. 5. Brussels 1964.

Gregorovius, F. *Athenaïs, Geschichte einer byzantinischen Kaiserin*. 2nd edn. Leipzig 1882.

————. "Hat Alarich die Nationalgötter Griechenlands zerstört?" *Kleine Schriften zur Geschichte und Cultur*, I 51-72. Leipzig 1887.

Grierson, P. "The Tombs and Obits of the Byzantine Emperors," *Dumbarton Oaks Papers*, 16 (1962) 1-63.

Grillmeier, A. and H. Bacht, *Das Konzil von Chalkedon. Geschichte und Gegenwart*. 3 v. Würzburg 1951-1954. Basic critical studies.

Grosse, R. *Römische Militärgeschichte von Gallienus bis zum Beginn der byzantinischen Themenverfassung*. Berlin 1920.

Guazzoni Foa, V. "Il concetto di provvidenza nel pensiero classico e in quello pagano," *Giornale di Metafisica*, 14 (1959) 69-95.

Guilland, R. *Études byzantines*. Paris 1959.

Güldenpenning, A. *Geschichte des oströmischen Reiches unter den Kaisern Arcadius und Theodosius II*. Halle 1885.

Gwatkin, H.M. *Studies of Arianism*. 2nd edn. Cambridge, England 1900.

Hahn, L. *Rom und Romanismus im griechisch-römischen Osten*. Leipzig 1906.

Hammer, W. "The Concept of the New or Second Rome in the Middle Ages," *Speculum*, 19 (1944) 50-62.

Hammond, M. *The Antonine Monarchy*. Papers and Monographs of the American Academy in Rome, 19. Rome 1959.

Harnack, A. *Diodor von Tarse. Vier pseudojustinische Schriften als Eigentum Diodors*. Texte und Untersuchungen, N. F., Vol. 6, No. 4. Leipzig 1901. His attribution not accepted today.

————. *Lehrbuch der Dogmengeschichte*, 5th edn. 3 v. Tübingen 1931-1932.

Hefele, K.J. von and H. Leclercq. *Histoire des conciles d'après les documents originaux*. 11 v. Paris 1907-1952. Standard survey.

Heussi, K. *Das Nilusproblem. Randglossen zu Friedrich Degenharts Neuen Beiträgen zur Nilusforschung.* Leipzig 1921.
———. *Untersuchungen zu Nilus dem Asketen.* Texte und Untersuchungen, III. Reihe, Vol. XII, Heft 2. Leipzig 1917. Criticizes Degenhart.
Hodgkin, T. *Italy and Her Invaders.* 2nd edn. 8 v. in 9. London 1931. Basic.
Höfler, C. "Kritische Bemerkungen über den Zosimos und den Grad seiner Glaubwürdigkeit." *Sitzungsberichte der Kaiserlichen Akademie der Wissenschaften, Philosophisch-historischen Classe,* 95 (Vienna 1880) 521-565. Perceptive but verbose.
Honigmann, E. "Zacharias of Mitylene," *Patristic Studies,* 194-204. Studi e Testi, 173. Vatican City 1953.
Hubaux, J. "La crise de la trois cent soixante cinquième année," *Antiquité Classique,* 17 (1948) 343-354.
———. "Saint Augustin et la crise eschatologique de la fin du IVᵉ siècle," *Bulletin de la Classe des Lettres et des Sciences morales et politiques, Académie royale de Belgique,* 40 (1954) 658-673.
Huizinga, J. *The Waning of the Middle Ages,* F. Hopman, tr. New York 1948.
Huttmann, M. A. *The Establishment of Christianity and the Proscription of Paganism.* Columbia University Studies in History, Economics, and Public Law, Vol. 60, No. 2. New York 1914. Not analytical.
Hyde, W. W. *Paganism to Christianity in the Roman Empire.* Philadelphia 1946.
Impellizzeri S. *La letteratura bizantina da Costantino agli Iconoclasti.* Bari 1965.
Ivanká, E. von. "Zur Selbstdeutung des römischen Imperiums," *Saeculum,* 8 (1957) 17-31.
Jaeger, W. *Early Christianity and Greek Paideia.* Cambridge, Mass. 1961. Good introduction.
Jenkins, R. *Byzantium and Byzantinism.* Cincinnati 1963.
Jolowicz, H. F. *Historical Introduction to the Study of Roman Law.* 2nd edn. Cambridge, England 1952.
Jones, A.H.M. "The Decline and Fall of the Roman Empire," *History,* N.S. 40 (1955) 209-226.
———. *The Decline of the Ancient World.* New York 1966.
———. "The Greeks under the Roman Empire," *Dumbarton Oaks Papers,* 17 (1963) 1-20. Important.
———. *The Later Roman Empire (284-602): A Social, Economic, and Administrative Survey.* 3 v. Oxford 1964. Indispensable.
Jugie, M. *Nestorius et la controverse nestorienne.* Paris 1912.
Kaegi, W. E. "The Emperor Julian's Assessment of the Significance and Function of History," *Proceedings of the American Philosophical Society,* 108 (1964) 29-38.
———. "The Fifth-Century Twilight of Byzantine Paganism," *Classica et Mediaevalia,* 27 (1968).
Kagan, D. *Decline and Fall of the Roman Empire. Why Did It Collapse?* Boston 1962.

Karayannopulos, J. *Das Finanzwesen des frühbyzantinischen Staates.* Munich 1958.

Katz, S. *The Decline of Rome and the Rise of Mediaeval Europe.* Ithaca 1955.

Kelly, J. N. D. *Early Christian Doctrines.* London 1958. Good manual.

Kennedy, G. *The Art of Persuasion in Greece.* Princeton 1963. Standard.

Kent, J. P. C. 'Auream Monetam. . . . Cum Signo Crucis,' *Numismatic Chronicle,* Ser. VI, Vol. 20 (1960) 129-132. A good critical examination of the coinage of Theodosius II.

Keydell, R. "Palladas und das Christentum," *Byzantinische Zeitschrift,* 50 (1957) 1-3.

King, N. Q. *The Emperor Theodosius and the Establishment of Christianity.* London 1961. Latest work on Theodosius.

————. "The Theodosian Code as a Source for the Religious Policies of the First Byzantine Emperors," *Nottingham Mediaeval Studies,* 6 (1962) 12-17. Questionable conclusions.

Koch, C. "Roma aeterna," *Religio: Studien zu Kult und Glauben der Römer,* O. Seel, ed. Nürnberg 1960, 142-175.

Koch, H. *Pronoia und Paideusis.* Berlin, Leipzig 1932. Important.

Koch, W. "Comment l'Empereur Julien tâcha de fonder une église païenne," *Revue belge de philologie et d'histoire,* 6 (1927), 123-146; 7 (1928), 49-82; 511-550; 1363-1385.

Kraft, H. *Kaiser Konstantins religiöse Entwicklung.* Tübingen 1955.

Krüger, P. *Geschichte der Quellen und Litteratur des römischen Rechts.* 2nd edn. Munich, Leipzig 1912.

Kulakovskii, I. A. *Istoriia Vizantii.* 3 v. Kiev 1910-1915. Very useful for Middle Byzantine Period.

Kurbatov, G.L. "Vosstaniye Prokopiia (365-366 gg.)," *Vizantiiskii Vremennik,* N.S. 14 (1958) 3-26. Important Marxist study.

Labriolle, P. de. *La réaction païenne: étude sur la polémique antichrétienne du Ier au VIe siècle.* 9th edn. Paris 1950. Useful but unsympathetic survey.

Lacombrade, C. *Synésios de Cyrène: hellène et chrétien.* Paris 1951. Standard biography.

Ladner, G. B. *The Idea of Reform: Its Impact on Christian Thought and Action in the Age of the Fathers.* Cambridge, Mass. 1959. Valuable analysis.

Laffranchi, L. "Appunti di critica numismatica," *Numismatica,* 8 (1942) 41-45.

Laistner, M.L.W. *Christianity and Pagan Culture in the Later Roman Empire.* Ithaca 1951.

————. *The Greater Roman Historians.* Berkeley 1947.

Lambrechts, P. "Le commerce des Syriens en Gaule du Haut-Empire à l'époque merovingienne," *Antiquité Classique,* 6 (1937) 35-61.

Latouche, R. *Les origines de l'économie occidentale (IV-IXe siècle).* Paris 1956.

Latte, K. *Römische Religionsgeschichte.* Munich 1960.

Lechner, K. *Hellenen und Barbaren im Weltbild der Byzantiner*. Munich 1954. Useful philological research.

Leidig, J. *Quaestiones Zosimae*. Ansbach 1900.

Leipoldt, J. *Scheneute von Atripe und die Entstehung des national ägyptischen Christentums*. Texte und Untersuchungen zur Geschichte der altchristlichen Literatur, N.F. 10. Leipzig 1903. Standard.

Lemerle, P. "Invasions et migrations dans les Balkans depuis la fin de l'époque romaine jusqu'au VIIIe siècle," *Revue Historique* 211 (1954) 265-308. Excellent survey.

————. "La notion de décadence à propos de l'empire byzantin," *Classicisme et déclin culturel dans l'histoire de l'Islam*, 263-277. Paris 1957.

Le Nain de Tillemont, L. S. *Histoire des empereurs et des autres princes qui ont regné durant les six premiers siècles de l'église*. . . . 6 v. Brussels 1693-1739. Remains a valuable reference work for examination of literary sources.

Lexikon für Theologie und Kirche. J. Höfer and K. Rahner, ed. 10 v. 2nd edn. Freiburg, 1957-1965. Recent reference work.

Lippold, A. *Rom und die Barbaren in der Beurteilung des Orosius*. Erlangen 1952.

Lot, F. *La fin du monde antique et le début du moyen âge*. Rev. edn. Paris 1951. Good general work.

————. *Nouvelles recherches sur l'impôt foncier et la capitation personnelle sous le Bas-Empire*. Paris 1955.

Loyen, A. *Recherches historiques sur les panégyriques de Sidoine Apollinaire*. Bibliothèque de l'école des hautes études, sciences historiques, et philologiques, 285. Paris 1942.

MacMullen, R. *Enemies of the Roman Order*. Cambridge, Mass. 1966.

————. *Soldier and Civilian in the Later Roman Empire*. Cambridge, Mass. 1963. Important recent study, with emphasis on non-Greek materials.

Mango, C. A. "Antique Statuary and the Byzantine Beholder," Dumbarton Oaks *Papers*, 17 (1963) 53-76. Important conclusions.

Markus, R. A. "The Roman Empire in Early Christian Historiography," *The Downside Review*, 81 (1963) 340-354.

Marrou, H.-I. *Saint Augustin et la fin de la culture antique*. 4th edn. Paris 1958. Basic.

Maspéro, J. "Horapollon et la fin du paganisme égyptien," *Bulletin de l'Institut français d'archéologie orientale*, 11 (1913) 163-195. Introduces additional material.

Mattingly, H. *Christianity in the Roman Empire. Six Lectures*. Dunedin, N.Z. 1955.

————. "The Imperial 'Vota' I-II," *Proceedings of the British Academy*, 36 (1950) 155-195; 37 (1951) 219-268. Important general study.

Mazzarino, S. *Aspetti sociali del quarto secolo: Ricerche di storia tardo-romana*. Rome 1951.

————. *La fine del mondo antico*. Milan 1959.

————. "La propaganda senatoriale nel tardo impero," *Doxa*, 4 (1951) 121-148.

————. *Stilicone: La crisi imperiale dopo Teodosio*. Rome 1942. The best study of Stilicho.

Merone, E. *Rutilius Claudius Namatianus. De reditu suo. Commento filologico-semantico*. Naples 1955.

Mohrmann, C. "Encore une fois: Paganus," *Vigiliae Christianae*, 6 (1952) 109-121.

Momigliano, A., ed. *The Conflict Between Paganism and Christianity in the Fourth Century*. Oxford 1963. Recent important collection of essays.

Mommsen, T. "Zosimus," *Byzantinische Zeitschrift*, 12 (1903) 533.

Mommsen, T. E. *Medieval and Renaissance Studies*. E. F. Rice, Jr., ed. Ithaca 1959. Perceptive.

Montesquieu, Charles Louis de Secondat. *Oeuvres complètes*. R. Caillois, ed. 2 v. Paris 1958.

Moravcsik, G. *Byzantinoturcica*. 2nd edn. 2 v. Berlin 1958. The best introduction to Byzantine historical works.

Morrison, K. F. "Rome and the City of God: An Essay on the Constitutional Relationships of Empire and Church in the Fourth Century," *Transactions of the American Philosophical Society*, Vol. 54, No. 1. Philadelphia 1964.

Muller, H. *Christians and Pagans from Constantine to Augustine*. Pretoria 1946.

Murphy, F. X., ed. *A Monument to St. Jerome, Essays on Some Aspects of His Life, Works, and Influence*. New York 1952.

Mylonas, G. E. *Eleusis and the Eleusinian Mysteries*. Princeton 1961.

Naville et Cⁱᵉ. *Catalogue des monnaies romaines antiques en or. argent et bronze. . . .* VIII: Collection Saint Bement. Geneva 1924.

————. *Catalogue des monnaies antiques grecques romaines et byzantines*, 15: Woodward Collection. Geneva 1930.

Neugebauer, O. and H. B. Van Hoesen. *Greek Horoscopes* (Memoirs of the American Philosophical Society, 48) [Philadelphia 1959].

Nicolosi, S. *Il 'De Providentia' di Sinesto di Cirene*. Padova 1959.

Nigg, W. *Die Kirchengeschichtsschreibung: Grundzüge ihrer historischen Entwicklung*. Munich 1934. General.

Nissen, T. "Eine christliche Polemik gegen Julians Rede auf den König Helios," *Byzantinische Zeitschrift*, 40 (1940) 15-22.

Nock, A. D. *Conversion: the Old and the New in Religion from Alexander the Great to Augustine of Hippo*. Oxford 1933. Many insights.

Noë, A. R. *Die Proklosbiographie des Marinos*. Heidelberg 1938.

Norman, A. F. "Magnus in Ammianus, Eunapius, and Zosimus: New Evidence," *Classical Quarterly*, N.S. 7 (1957) 129-133.

Ohnsorge, W. *Abendland und Byzanz: Gesammelte Aufsätze zur Geschichte der byzantinisch-abendländlischen Beziehungen und des Kaisertums*. Darmstadt 1958.

————. *Das Zweikaiserproblem im früheren Mittelalter*. Hildesheim 1947.

O'Leary, D. L. "The Destruction of Temples in Egypt," *Bulletin de la société d'archéologie copte,* 4 (1938) 51-57.

Ortiz de Urbina, I. *Patrologia Syriaca.* 2nd edn. Rome 1965.

Ostrogorsky, G. *Geschichte des byzantinischen Staates.* 3rd edn. Munich 1963.

———. "Die Perioden der byzantinischen Geschichte," *Historische Zeitschrift* 163 (1941) 229-254. The best article on the topic.

Palanque, J.-R. "Collégialité et partages dans l'empire romain aux IVe et Ve siècles," *Revue des Études Anciennes,* 46 (1944) 47-64, 280-298.

———. *Saint Ambroise et l'empire romain.* Paris 1933. Standard.

Palm, J. *Rom, Römertum und Imperium in der griechischen Literatur der Kaiserzeit.* Acta reg. societatis humaniorum litterarum Lundensis, 57. Lund 1959. Valuable collection of sources.

Paribeni, R. *Storia di Roma,* VIII: *Da Diocleziano alla caduta dell' impero d'occidente.* Bologna 1941.

Pauly, A. F. von and G. Wissowa. *Paulys Real-encyclopädie der classischen Altertumswissenschaft.* Rev. edn. I- . Stuttgart, 1893- . Basic reference work for classical studies.

Pedech, P. *La méthode historique de Polybe.* Paris 1964.

Peeters, P. *Orient et Byzance: le tréfonds oriental de l'hagiographie byzantine.* Subsidia hagiographica, 26. Brussels 1950.

Pellegrino, M. *Salviano di Marsiglia: studio critico.* Rome 1943.

Penna, A. S. *Gerolamo.* Turin, Rome 1949.

Pernice, A. *L'Imperatore Eraclio.* Florence 1905. Old but basic.

Peterson, E. *Der Monotheismus als politisches Problem: Ein Beitrag zur Geschichte der politischen Ideologie im Imperium Romanum.* Leipzig 1935. Important insights.

Petit, P. *Les étudiants de Libanius.* Paris 1957.

———. *Précis d'histoire ancienne.* 2nd edn. Paris 1965.

Petre, Z. "La pensée historique de Zosime," *Studii clasice,* 7 (1965) 263-272.

Pfister, K. *Der Untergang der antiken Welt.* Leipzig 1943.

Piganiol, A. *L'Empire chrétien (325-395).* Paris 1947. Best general study of the fourth century.

———. "L'État actuel de la question constantinienne 1930/49," *Historia* 1 (1950) 82-96.

———. *Le sac de Rome, vue d'ensemble.* Paris 1964.

Quasten, J. *Patrology,* III: *The Golden Age of Greek Patristic Literature.* Utrecht, Antwerp 1960. Excellent biographical guide.

Rambaud, A. *L'Empire grec au dixième siècle. Constantin Porphyrogénète.* Paris 1870; reprinted, New York 1963.

Rand, E. K. *The Building of Eternal Rome.* Cambridge, Mass. 1943.

Ranke, L. von. *Weltgeschichte.* 9 v. Leipzig 1888-1902.

Reallexikon für Antike und Christentum. I, Stuttgart 1950- .

Regazzoni, P. "Il *Contra Galilaeos* dell' Imperatore Giuliano e il *Contra Julianum* di S. Cirillo Alessandrino," *Didaskaleion* N.S. 6 (1928) 1-114. Important in the absence of other studies.

Rehm, W. *Der Untergang Roms in abendländischen Denken.* Leipzig 1930.

Die Religion in Geschichte und Gegenwart. III. Auflage. 6 v. Tübingen 1957-1962.

Rémondon, R. *La crise de l'Empire romain de Marc-Aurèle à Anastase* ("Nouvelle Clio." L'Histoire et ses problèmes, No. 11, R. Boutrouche, P. Lemerle, eds. Paris 1964).

Reta, J. O. "Imperium sine fine dedi: Christianismo y paganismo ante la caida del imperio," *Nuovo Didaskaleion,* 13 (1963) 83-95.

Reynolds, R. L. and R. S. Lopez. "Odoacer: German or Hun?" *American Historical Review,* 50 (1946) 36-53.

Richard, M. "Les citations de Théodoret conservées dans la chaîne de Nicétas sur l'Évangile selon Saint Luc," *Revue Biblique* 43 (1934) 88-96.

Riché, P. *Education et culture dans l'occident barbare, VIe-VIIIe siècles.* Paris 1962.

Riising, A. "The Fate of Henri Pirenne's Theses on the Consequences of the Islamic Expansion," *Classica et Mediaevalia* 13 (1952) 87-130.

Roberts, P. C. "The Pirenne Thesis: Economies or Civilizations," *Classica et Mediaevalia,* 25 (1964) 297-315.

Robinson, D.N. "An Analysis of the Pagan Revival of the late Fourth Century," *Transactions of the American Philological Association,* 46 (1915) 87-101.

Robinson, J. H. *The Fall of Rome: Some Current Misapprehensions in Regard to the Process of Dissolution of the Roman Empire.* Boston 1907.

Rodinson, M. "De l'archéologie à la sociologie historique. Notes méthodologiques sur le dernier ouvrage de G. Tchalenko," *Syria,* 38 (1961) 170-200.

Rosan, L. J. *The Philosophy of Proclus: The Final Phase of Ancient Thought.* New York 1949.

Roveri, A. *Studi su Polibio.* Studi pubblicati dall' Istituto di Filologia Classica, Università degli studi di Bologna, facoltà di lettere e filosofia, 17. Bologna 1964.

Rozental, N. N. "Religiozno-politicheskaia ideologiia Zosima," *Drevnii mir: Sbornik statei* (N. V. Pigulevskaia, ed., Akademiia nauk SSSR, Ist. narodov Azii, Moscow 1962) 611-617.

Rubin, B. *Das Zeitalter Iustinians,* I. Berlin 1960.

Rühl, F. "Wann Schrieb Zosimus?" *Rheinisches Museum,* 46 (1891) 146-147.

Sabatier, J. *Description générale des monnaies byzantines.* 2 v. Paris, London 1862. Still must be consulted.

Salaville, S. "De l'hellénisme au byzantinisme: essai de démarcation," *Échos d'Orient,* 30 (1931) 28-64.

Sanford, E. M. "Contrasting Views of the Roman Empire," *American Journal of Philology,* 58 (1937) 437-456.

Saunders, J. J. "The Debate on the Fall of Rome," *History,* 48 (1963) 1-17.

Schaefer, A. *Römer und Germanen bei Salvian.* Breslau 1930.

Schanz, M. and C. Hosius. *Geschichte der römischen Literatur*, Rev. edn. 4 v. Munich 1959.

Scheffer-Boichorst, P. "Zur Geschichte der Syrer im Abendlande," *Mitteilungen des Instituts für oesterreichische Geschichtsforschung*, 6 (1885) 521-550.

Scheidweiler, F. "Die Kirchengeschichte des Gelasios von Kaisareia," *Byzantinische Zeitschrift*, 46 (1953) 277-301.

Schenkl, H. "Ein spätrömischer Dichter und sein Glaubensbekenntnis," *Rheinisches Museum*, N.F. 66 (1911) 393-416.

Schlachter, A. *Der Globus: Seine Entstehung und Verwendung in der Antike nach den literarischen Quellen und den Darstellungen in der Kunst*. F. Gisinger, ed. Leipzig, Berlin 1927. Standard.

Schramm, P. E. *Sphaira-Globus-Reichsapfel: Wanderung und Wandlung eines Herrschaftszeichens von Caesar bis zu Elisabeth II*. Stuttgart 1958.

Schulte, J. *Theodoret von Cyrus als Apologet: ein Beitrag zur Geschichte der Apologetik*. Theologische Studien der Leo-Gesellschaft, X. Vienna 1904.

Schultze, M. V. *Geschichte des Untergangs des griechisch-römischen Heidentums*. 2 v. Jena 1887.

Scipioni, L. I. *Ricerche sulla cristologia del 'Libro di Eraclide' di Nestorio: la formulazione teologica e il suo contesto filosofico*. Freiburg 1956.

Seeck, O. *Geschichte des Untergangs der antiken Welt*. 6 v. in 12. Stuttgart 1921-1923. Remains indispensable.

————. *Regesten der Kaiser und Päpste für die Jahre 311 bis 476 N. Chr.* Stuttgart 1919. Standard manual for chronology.

Sellers, R. V. *The Council of Chalcedon: A Historical and Doctrinal Survey*. London 1953. Compact.

Seston, W. "L'Opinion païenne et la conversion de Constantin," *Revue d'histoire et de philosophie religieuses*, 16 (1936) 250-264.

Setton, K. M. *The Christian Attitude towards the Emperor in the Fourth Century*. Columbia University Studies in History, Economics, and Public Law, No. 482. New York 1941. Important.

Ševčenko, I. "The Decline of Byzantium Seen through the Eyes of Its Intellectuals," *Dumbarton Oaks Papers*, 15 (1961) 167-186. Includes unpublished materials.

Seznec, J. *The Survival of the Pagan Gods*. B. F. Sessions, tr. Bollingen Series, XXXVIII. New York 1953.

Sheridan, J. J. "The Altar of Victory—Paganism's Last Battle," *L'Antiquité Classique*, 35 (1966) 186-206.

Sihler, E. G. *From Augustus to Augustine: Essays and Studies Dealing with the Contact and Conflict of Classic Paganism and Christianity*. Cambridge, England 1923.

Simon, M. "Christianisme antique et pensée païenne: rencontres et conflits," *Bulletin de la faculté des lettres de Strasbourg*, 38 (1960) 309-323.

Sirago, V. A. *Galla Placidia e la trasformazione politica dell' occidente*. Louvain 1961. Basic modern study.

Sirinelli, J. *Les vues historiques d'Eusèbe de Césarée durant la période prénicéenne.* Dakar 1961. Exhaustive.

Solari, A. *La crisi dell' impero romano.* 4 v. Milan, Naples 1933-1937. Occasionally of use.

———. *Il rinnovamento dell' impero romano.* 2 v. Milan, Naples 1938-1943. Sometimes helpful, should be consulted.

———. "La rivolta procopiana a Constantinopoli," *Byzantion,* 7 (1932) 143-148.

———. "Tolleranza verso il paganesimo nella prima metà del sec. v," *Philologus,* N.F. 45 (1936) 357-360.

Sophocles, E. A., *Greek Lexicon of the Roman and Byzantine Periods.* New York 1900; reprinted 1957.

Stein, E. *Histoire du Bas-Empire,* J.-R. Palanque, ed. Rev. edn. 2 v. Paris 1949-1959. Brings Seeck up to date. A masterful study of the material. Recent bibliography.

———. "Introduction à l'histoire et aux institutions byzantines," *Traditio,* 7 (1949-1951) 95-168.

———. *Studien zur Geschichte des byzantinischen Reiches, vornehmlich unter den Kaisern Justinus II und Tiberius Constantinus.* Stuttgart 1919. Still useful.

———. "Untersuchungen zur spätbyzantinischen Verfassungs- und Wirtschaftsgeschichte," *Mitteilungen zur osmanischen Geschichte,* II, 1, Heft 2. (1924) 1-62.

Steinmann, J. *Saint Jérôme.* Paris 1928.

Stevens, C. E. "Marcus, Gratian, Constantine," *Athenaeum,* 35 (1957) 316-347.

Straub, J. "Christliche Geschichtsapologetik in der Krisis des römischen Reiches," *Historia* I (1950) 52-81.

———. *Heidnische Geschichtsapologetik in der christlichen Spätantike: Untersuchungen über Zeit und Tendenz der Historia Augusta,* Antiquitas, Reihe IV, Bd. I. Bonn 1963.

———. *Vom Herrscherideal in der Spätantike.* Stuttgart 1939.

Stroheker, K. F. "Um die Grenze zwischen Antike und abendländischem Mittelalter," *Saeculum,* 1 (1950) 433-465.

Syme, R. *Tacitus.* 2 v. Oxford 1958. Important recent classic.

Tchalenko, G. *Villages antiques de la Syrie du Nord. Le massif du Bélus à l'époque romaine.* Institut français d'archéologie de Beyrouth, Bibliothèque archéologique et historique, Tome 50. Paris 1953.

Teall, J. L. "The Grain Supply of the Byzantine Empire, 330-1025," *Dumbarton Oaks Papers* 13 (1959) 87-139.

Thompson, E. A. "The Foreign Policies of Theodosius II and Marcian," *Hermathena* 76 (1950) 58-75.

———. *A History of Attila and the Huns.* Oxford 1948. Excellent analytical work.

———. "Olympiodorus of Thebes," *Classical Quarterly,* 38 (1944) 43-52. The only study.

Thouvenot, R. "Salvien et la ruine de l'empire romain," *Mélanges d'archéologie et d'histoire de l'école française de Rome*, 38 (1920) 145-163.

Tolstoi, I. I. *Monnaies byzantines*. 4 v. St. Petersburg 1912-1914. Important collection.

Toynbee, A. J. *A Study of History*. 12 v. London 1934-1961.

Treitinger, O. *Die oströmische Kaiser- und Reichsidee nach ihrer Gestaltung im höfischen Zeremoniell*. 2nd edn. Darmstadt 1956.

Ulrich-Bansa, O. *Moneta Mediolanensis (352-498)*. Venice 1949. Important, but must be used with care.

Valdenberg, V. "La philosophie byzantine aux IVe-Ve siècles," *Byzantion*, 4 (1927-1928) 237-268.

Van Loy, R. "Le 'Pro Templis' de Libanius," *Byzantion*, 8 (1933) 7-39.

Van Rooijen, J.W. *De Theodosii II moribus ac rebus politicis*. Diss. Leiden 1912.

Vasiliev, A. A. "Medieval Ideas of the End of the World: West and East," *Byzantion*, 16 (1942-1943) 462-502.

Vassili, L. "Nota cronologica intorno all' elezione di Maggioriano," *Rivista di filologia e d'istruzione classica*, N.S. 14 (1936) 163-169.

Veh, O. *Zur Geschichtsschreibung und Weltauffassung des Prokop von Caesarea*. 3 Pts. Bayreuth 1950-1953.

Vittinghoff, F. "Zum geschichtlichen Selbstverständnis der Spätantike," *Historische Zeitschrift* 198 (1964) 529-574.

Vogt, J. *Der Niedergang Roms: Metamorphose der antiken Kultur* (Zurich 1965).

Voirol, A. "Münzdokumente der Galla Placidia und ihres Sohnes Valentinian und Versuch einer Chronologie der Münzprägung unter Theodosius II. (408-450)," *Verhandlungen der Naturforschenden Gesellschaft in Basel*, 56 No. 2 (1945) 431-445. Helpful.

Vööbus, A. *History of Asceticism in the Syrian Orient. A Contribution to the History of Culture in the Near East. Corpus Scriptorum Christianorum Orientalium*, 184, 197, *Subsidia*, 14, 17. 2 v. Louvain 1958-1960.

Wagner, M. M. "A Chapter in Byzantine Epistolography: The Letters of Theodoret of Cyrus," *Dumbarton Oaks Papers*, 4 (1948) 119-181.

Walbank, F. W. *The Decline of the Roman Empire in the West*. London 1946.

———. *A Historical Commentary on Polybius*, I. Oxford 1957. Exemplary scholarship.

Werner, H. *Der Untergang Roms: Studien zum Dekadenzproblem in der antiken Geistesgeschichte*. Forschungen zur Kirchen- und Geistesgeschichte, 17. Stuttgart 1939.

White, L. Jr. *The Transformation of the Roman World: Gibbon's Problem after Two Centuries* (Contributions of the UCLA Center for Medieval and Renaissance Studies, III). Berkeley and Los Angeles 1966.

Wiegand, T. et al., eds. *Baalbek: Ergebnisse der Ausgrabungen und Untersuchungen in den Jahren 1898 bis 1905*. 3 v. Berlin, Leipzig 1921-1925. Basic report.

Wissowa, G. *Religion und Kultus der Römer*. 2nd edn. Munich 1912.

Wolff, R. L. "The Three Romes: The Migration of an Ideology and the Making of an Autocrat," *Daedalus*, 88 (1959) 291-311. Important.

Wolska, W. *La topographie chrétienne de Cosmas Indicopleustès: théologie et science au VIᵉ siècle*. Paris 1962.

Wright, F. A. *A History of Later Greek Literature from the Death of Alexander in 323 B.C. to the Death of Justinian in 565 A.D.* London 1932.

Wright, W. *A Short History of Syriac Literature*. London 1894.

Wroth, W. W. *Catalogue of the Imperial Byzantine Coins in the British Museum*. 2 v. London 1908.

Wytzes, J. *Der Streit um den Altar der Viktoria*. Amsterdam 1936. Important study.

Zeiller, J. *L'Empire romain et l'église*. Paris 1928.

————. *Paganus: étude de terminologie historique*. Collectanea Friburgensia, N.S. fasc. 17, Freiburg, Switzerland, and Paris 1917. Still the fundamental work.

————. "*Paganus*: sur l'origine de l'acception religieuse du mot," *Académie des inscriptions et belles-lettres, Comptes rendus* (1940) 526-543.

Two relevant books appeared after this book went to press:

M. A. Wes, *Das Ende des Kaisertums im Westen des römischen Reiches*. The Hague 1967.

Zosimus, *Historia Nova. The Decline of Rome*. J. J. Buchanan and H. T. Davis, tr. San Antonio 1967.

A rapid examination of these works, however, leads me to alter none of my basic conclusions.